PEACE HEROES

in Twentieth-Century America

PEACE HEROES

HEROES

in Twentieth-Century America

Edited and with an Introduction by

Charles DeBenedetti

Indiana University Press

BLOOMINGTON

Manufactured in the United States of America

Library of Congress Cataloging-in-Publication Data
Main entry under title:

Peace heroes in twentieth-century America.

  Includes index.
  Contents: Jane Addams / Michael A. Lutzker—
Eugene V. Debs / Lawrence S. Wittner—Norman Thomas /
Charles Chatfield—[etc.]
  1. Peace—History. 2. Pacifists—United States—
History. I. DeBenedetti, Charles.
JX1952.P336 1986   327.1'72'0922   85-45031
ISBN 0-253-34307-0
  2 3 4 5 90 89 88 87

For Bernice Nichols

Contents

PEACE HEROES

In Twentieth-Century America

Introduction

> For without belittling the courage with
> which men have died, we should not for-
> get those acts of courage with which men
> . . . have *lived.*
>
> John F. Kennedy, *Profiles in Courage*

In 1955, Senator John F. Kennedy set out to study a group of United States senators that he felt had shown extraordinary "moral heroism" in standing by their principles in the face of ferocious public passions. He called his book *Profiles in Courage,* and it became a Pulitzer Prize-winning history, a runaway bestseller, and the moral *coda* for a generation of American leaders. Models of reason and calm grace, Kennedy's heroes were men of character who bravely acted out of a personal commitment to principled public conduct and in light of the lodestar "national interest." They disdained the dreams of idealists, and deflected the demands of more impatient reformers. These were men of "a different kind," wrote one admiring reader. They were leaders of conscience who lived with "the courage of intelligent, farsighted, reasonable men anxious to hold the ship of state to its true course."[1]

This book considers some other people of courage and principle who lived out their commitments in conscience to humankind's higher good. Unlike Kennedy's heroes, these people did not locate the highest good in the "national interest" or in stabilizing "the ship of state." On the contrary, they were avatars of change, who tried to move other Americans into seeing that their national interest was merely part of a greater human interest in global security, peace, and justice. Social activists prominent in a range of reform causes, they were individuals who became peace leaders as they recognized how chances for improving the human condition turned upon the need for lasting peace and as they strove consequently to lend form, direction, and inspiration to America's twentieth-century citizens' peace movement. Like Kennedy's heroes, these figures knew victory and defeat, public acclaim and vilification. Like his heroes, too, they knew fear and isolation, which they fought to overcome through personal struggles and abiding courage. Now they stand precariously on the margins of public memory, slipping toward a world of historical amnesia at the very time when they need most to be remembered. The purpose of this book is to rescue these people from any premature erasure from our public memory. It aims to recall the lives and work of these people through a series of original essays recalling their peace leadership and showing, in the process, how they gave lasting shape and purpose to the modern American tradition of citizen peace activism.

I

The twentieth-century American peace movement has gained and maintained its existence through a shifting combination of individuals and groups committed to the notion that war is an intolerable but resolvable problem that governing authorities have refused to challenge. Citizen peace activists have been people who chose, themselves, to take on that challenge. In large measure, the driving force behind the U.S. peace movement is pride in the success of American nationhood. More specifically, the movement derives its strength from the fundamental national myth that Americans are a peace-loving people with a peculiar missionary responsibility to extend their redeeming way of peace through law, order, and national self-determination throughout the world. Every society lives in light of certain core or *"sustaining myths"* that provide coherent meaning and purpose to the group.[2] Every society also lives, however, with the rank discrepancies that inevitably arise between the governing myths and the actual group practices. Most citizens live unperturbed in the face of these discrepancies. Others can not. American peace activists are citizens who have refused to accept the discrepancy between the myth of America's peace-loving global mission and the country's actual failure to extend working peace practices throughout world politics.

Instead, citizen peace-seekers have organized themselves to attack war as a soluble social and political problem, and to goad governing authorities into joining them in the attack. Like participants in other reform movements, they have remained small in number (approximately 2 percent of the whole population) but impressive in their resolve, resilience, and success in drawing attention to their criticisms and proposed alternatives. In the American peace movement, they have painstakingly assembled a coalition of policy critics, creative thinkers, cranks, and plain folks that has expanded and contracted over time in response to various external and internal pressures and opportunities. Alternately, these citizen peace-seekers have collaborated and quarreled among themselves over matters of strategy, tactics, and direction. Persistently, however, they made a movement based on two main premises: that war is a human institution as vulnerable to control and destruction as past institutions like human slavery; and that the task of responsible citizens is to assist in war's displacement in favor of other means of resolving disputes while enhancing related values of security, freedom, and justice.[3]

The struggle of ordinary citizens to establish peace in place of war is one of the more impressive if underrated aspects of American history. At first it was a matter of religious conscience. In seventeenth-century colonial America, Quakers and other religious sectarians lived their pacifism (i.e., opposition in principle to individual involvement in war) as a matter of faith. During the eighteenth century, some religious pacifists like the Quaker John Woolman tried to extend their peace principles into related areas like women's rights and the abolition of slavery. Then, early in the nineteenth century, reform-minded Christians from a fuller range of denominations invented the first American peace movement through a number of voluntary peace societies, established on the humanitarian assumption that war was a sinful anachronism that needed to be eliminated through prayer, petitions, and alternative international mechanisms for the resolution of disputes. With the formation in 1828 of the American Peace Society, citizen peace-seekers established the peace reform near the center of a constellation of reform endeavours, including women's rights and abolitionism, that would dominate the national consciousness for years after.[4]

Early in the twentieth century, the American peace movement gained such respectability and breadth that it became the "protean" reform of the Progressive years.[5] It served as the touchstone reform for otherwise conservative people. Lawyers and jurists like Secretary of State Elihu Root argued for an international court of justice that would function in the fashion of the U.S. Supreme Court. Philanthropic businessmen like the steel magnate Andrew Carnegie and the textbook publisher Edward Ginn gave millions of dollars to the support of peace education enterprises like the Carnegie Endowment for International Peace and the World Peace Foundation. School-teachers like Fannie Fern Andrews organized to promulgate peace principles through the classroom, while social workers like Jane Addams condemned war for its destruction of family life and proper community values. Reaching across a broad spectrum of American life, a vigorous new peace movement brought together diverse people behind the contention that modern great-power war was a threat to Western civilization that demanded America's most serious attention. Peace became the archetypical Progressive reform. Rational, scientific, and conservative, the Progressive peace reform magnetized the support of people who wanted to purify modern industrial society of egregious social sinfulness (whether war or prostitution) at the same time as they made it more efficient and less wasteful for the sake of greater material productivity.

Then the Great War of 1914–18 tore across Europe, demolished the Progressive peace reform, and opened the way for the formation of the modern American peace movement. With the outbreak of war, conservative peace advocates like Root rallied to support the Allies; and, after the U.S. intervention of 1917, backed the American war effort on the premise that military victory would save the world for democracy. A minority of skeptics professed their doubts; and out of their critical comments, behavior, and commitments emerged the modern American peace movement. These peacemakers were inspired by a variety of motives. Some like Jane Addams were liberal social planners and uplifters. Some like Eugene V. Debs were democratic socialists. Some like Norman Thomas were Christian moralists. All of them, however, saw war as subversive of their vision of the good society; and, out of their determination to end war and build a right social order, they worked to create the modern American peace movement, accomplishing in the process four essential tasks. First, they identified the major problems facing such a movement. Second, they chose to address these problems through a critical mode of rational analysis that, combined with their view of peace as a process of change toward justice, cast the movement into an enterprise of the political and cultural Left. Third, they struggled to resolve the tensions inherent in reform coalition politics and in the contradictions intrinsic to a reform that includes different value commitments. And, finally, they set down and began to move along the three main lines of action in modern American peace-seeking: liberal religious pacifism, internationalism, and war resistance.[6]

First of all, wartime peace activists like Jane Addams and Norman Thomas identified the three great issues confronting citizen peaceseekers: the phenomenon of modern total war waged by science, industry, and mass mobilized societies; the rise of revolutionary socialism in the developed world and antiimperialist revolutionary wars of national self-determination in the colonial world; and the strength of an international right-wing element composed of corporate industrialists, landed oligarchs, conservative politicians, and military forces that favored war as a means of social stability and national unity. Between 1914 and 1920, with these three great problems enveloping them, the makers of the modern American peace movement concluded that organized peace-seeking entailed a twofold challenge. One was to isolate the system of war from the processes of science, industry, and nationalism—the formative forces in making the modern world. The other was to convince their fellow Americans, who had historically profited from war, to take the lead in advancing the international peace reform through a combined attack on war and on domestic social injustices. The inventors of the modern American peace movement believed that, for peace to advance in the world, reform must advance at home through the nonviolent extension of justice under order. They believed that peace was not merely a protean but a *symbiotic* reform. It literally thrived on the success of other reform endeavors, like racial justice and women's rights, that aimed to grant each person his or her due.

Once they identified the challenge, peace activists during the Great War recast the American peace movement into an enterprise of the political left as they argued and acted to fashion a new conception of peace as a political exercise in the nonviolent pursuit of change on behalf of justice. These were not simple-minded sentimentalists who craved some ideal state of peace. They were critical thinkers and actors who worked to analyze, sustain and advance peace as a process in human social relations. Some like Thomas and A. J. Muste were formally trained in scientific methods of social analysis. Others, like Addams and Debs, were absorbed in struggles for social justice and thus familiar with the power realities of class conflict and predisposed toward socialist sentiments. Yet, whatever their background, these people approached social issues with a critical intelligence that led them to see war not so much as a sin or an atavism but as a dynamic social system characterized by authoritarianism, militarism, and coercion. Conversely, they viewed peace as a process of change toward greater justice. Peace, in their minds, involved systemic change through domestic, transnational, and international forms of institutional reformation and cooperation. It was an enterprise in social progress that coincided with the purposes of the democratic Left.

The convergence of the modern peace movement and the political Left was reinforced by the peace-seekers' opposition both to imperialism and the new international Right. Convinced that great-power imperialism was a root cause of the World War, peace workers opposed great-power interventionism in places like Mexico and China, where mass peasant uprisings were taking place against entrenched foreign-supported oligarchies. Their antiimperialism became even more pronounced after 1917, when revolutionary Bolsheviks seized power in St. Petersburg, pulled Russia out of the war, and ignited a domestic and international counterrevolution. American peace activists expressed various reactions toward the new Soviet government, with some offering enthusiastic support and others professing a skeptical neutralism. Uniformly, however, they opposed great-power attempts to invade and destroy the Russian Revolution, on the grounds that the Russian people had the right to determine their own future without outside interference. According to the makers of the modern American peace movement, antiimperialism was an essential component of peace because imperialism was a basic source of hatred and war.

The modern American peace movement furthermore collided head-on with the new American right, made up of corporate industrialists, conservative politicians, and military officers who had succeeded so impressively during the war in massing state power behind their preferred commitments to social order, tribal nationalism, well-armed military preparedness, and counterrevolutionary activism at home and abroad. With the resurgence of the Ku Klux Klan and the formation of conservative veterans groups like the American Legion, a powerful new right came forward in America after 1917, dedicated to America's international preeminence through superior armaments and independent interventionism and decidedly suspicious of most things foreign. Seizing upon the flag as a symbol of true Americanism, the rising new right resisted demands for international collaboration in peace-keeping efforts, and attacked domestic reformers and internationally minded peaceseekers as subverters of American freedoms and independence. Significantly, these rightist views not only won sympathetic support among responsible policymakers, they also made a deep imprint upon orthodox political perceptions. After 1917, most U.S. government officials and popular opinion-shapers saw citizen peace activists as more of a problem than the war system. With their demands for domestic change and international reform, citizen peaceseekers appeared to public officials as more threatening to the national good than war preparations and military interventionism.

In the third place, the American peace movement took on its modern form between 1914 and 1920, as it became the common ground for a shifting coalition of reform causes and the testing ground for competing value commitments. Most peace-seekers during World War I were involved in a number of reform efforts. Consequently, their approach toward the peace reform varied according to their expectation of how the war might enhance or diminish other reform prospects. The women's peace leader Carrie Chapman Catt, for example, shifted from early wartime peace-seeking into support for the U.S. war effort, as part of her successful drive for women's suffrage. Similarly, the philosopher John Dewey and other liberal internationalists changed from initial suspicion to support of the U.S. war effort, on the grounds that the war would strengthen the domestic machinery for democratic central planning and build a new League of Nations into the central mechanism for a more liberal world order.

On the other side, different activists in the country's reform coalition concluded that the means of war invariably destroyed prospects for progressive social change. Norman Thomas, for instance, decided that America's absorption in the European war would undercut chances to convert the American economic order and bring relief to the country's squalid industrial cities through the power of the Christian Social Gospel. He resolved to stand by peace and urban reform, and became an early leader in the pacifist Fellowship of Reconciliation. The St. Louis reformer Roger Baldwin likewise saw that wartime conformity contradicted fundamental civil liberties that the state ostensibly existed to protect. He chose to stand by peace and

First Amendment free-speech rights, and proceeded in the process to help create the American Civil Liberties Union.

In large measure, the fractures that World War I precipitated within the Progressive American reform coalition reflected the larger value-tensions that afflicted various peace activists and that came to distinguish the modern tradition of citizen peace activism. During the Great War, peace activists agonized over the conflict between their commitment to peace and their wish for the kind of liberal national self-determination that would best be realized through a successful Allied war effort. As Western reformers dedicated to the principle of national self-determination, prominent peace-seekers like Jane Addams longed for the destruction of the autocratic empires of East-Central Europe and the liberation there of subject nationalities. But how was this longing to be realized except by force of arms at the expense of their peace principles? Stark and frustrating, this clash in core values typified the persisting value-tensions and sometimes contradictions—between peace and justice, peace and security, peace and freedom—that came to characterize the modern American peace tradition. Twentieth-century peace-seekers have not stood only and always for peace. But they have tried harder than most to adjust their other values to its pursuit.

Finally, citizen reformers of 1914–20 laid down the three main lines of new organizational action that have come to distinguish the modern American peace movement. First, in groups like the Fellowship of Reconciliation (1915) and the American Friends Service Committee (1917), liberal religious pacifists succeeded in fashioning the new-style organizations designed to join faith-based activists in working through a positive love ethic toward transnational harmony and justice. Secondly, feminists, internationalists, and others founded groups like the Women's International League for Peace and Freedom (1919) and the Foreign Policy Association (1920). These groups sought reformed world order that provided for national self-determination of peoples, less great-power interventionism, more mechanisms for juridical and arbitral means of settling disputes, and increased national security through real disarmament. Lastly, a small number of feminists, socialists, and anarchists turned through groups like the War Resisters League (1924) to support war resistance in the belief that peace best lived in the personal commitment to oppose all war and social injustice.

The modern American peace movement that arose during 1914–20 was radically different from its prewar counterparts in its methods of understanding and analysis, its transnational humanism, its left-wing political orientation, and its explicit lines of alternative action. It was also more energetic and resourceful in operation. Functioning as an amorphous coalition of concern, this new movement worked through what proved to be the mainstay constituencies of twentieth-century peace activism: church people, organized women, college students, intellectuals, labor organizers, liberal businessmen, and undifferentiated social reformers. Together, people from such disparate backgrounds joined in efforts that variously succeeded, failed, or persisted through indeterminate struggle. In 1921–22, a coalition of peace activists pressured the U.S. government to call the Washington Naval Disarmament Conference, which effected, in a series of treaties, one of the century's most impressive arms control agreements. Three years later, however, a similar coalition of citizen peace-seekers failed to move the Coolidge administration into joining the World Court; and peace activists tried but failed throughout the decade to bring about Washington's entry into the League of Nations.

In 1928, some peace workers backed President Coolidge in leading the war toward the conclusion of the Pact of Paris, which joined forty-six nations in renouncing war as an instrument of national policy and in pledging to use only pacific means in settling their disputes. At the same time, other peaceseekers joined antiimperialists like the journalist Ernest Gruening and isolationists like Idaho's Republican Senator William E. Borah in opposing administration plans for military intervention in Mexico and Nicaragua, while pacifists protested the War Department's new attempts to propagandize in the country's public schools. With few full-time organizers and little political discipline, organized citizens peace activism functioned in the American 1920s as a kinetic but diffuse reform enterprise. Citizen peace-seekers gained both sympathizers and critics, and flung themselves frequently into related reform enterprises like organizing labor and improving race relations. Except for a hardy few, however, peace remained for reformers merely one concern among many in a world that cried for broad and profound change.

In the 1930s, citizen peace activism became even more complex because of the domestic stresses generated by the Great Depression and because of the aggressive eagerness of Germany, Japan, and Italy to use all available means, including war, to change the international environment in their favor. Within America, peace advocates fought for basic social and economic reforms, while worrying whether working-class Americans could obtain relief and justice without resorting to a cataclysmic class war. Overseas, peace leaders argued for the reform of the existing international distribution of wealth and power in a desperate attempt to avoid both war and appeasement. Many argued for American neutrality in expectation of a new great-power conflict. Progressively, however, it became clear that Nazi aggression was not to be halted except by armed counter-force; and the great bulk of American peace-seekers swung after 1939 behind the Allied war effort, in hopes of crushing Hitlerism and building a more just post-war order through reformed internationalism. Hard-core pacifists held out against the peace-seekers' shift toward war. But, after the Japanese attack at Pearl Harbor threw the U.S. into war on two fronts, they devoted their resources to the support of young men who refused for reasons of conscience to join in the national war effort.[7]

Tellingly, modern American peaceseekers won their country's most powerful expression of approval during World War II, when they led the domestic fight for U.S. leadership in a new United Nations designed to keep the postwar peace.[8] With the encouragement of the Roosevelt administration, citizens gathered in organizations like the American Assocation for the United Nations for the purpose of rallying popular enthusiasm for the new UN idea. Triumphantly, internationalists realized their highest hopes in July 1945, when the UN was formally launched in San Francisco. Three weeks later, however, the atomic destruction of Hiroshima and Nagasaki ended World War II with a shock that opened an altogether new era in global politics and a whole new challenge to the infant UN. Under the shadow of an ominous Atomic Age, Soviet-American differences in Europe became more intractable; the spread of anticolonial revolutionary wars from Asia to North Africa became more unmanageable; and international attempts to control nuclear weaponry became more frustrating. A new United Nations peace-keeping structure rose up on specially designated international territory in mid-town New York. But it was the Cold War that spread around the world, gripping people everywhere in ever-tightening antagonisms.

With the worsening of the Cold War between 1945 and 1955, citizen peace activists tried in different ways to moderate Soviet-

American differences and lessen global tensions. Internationalists like Norman Cousins expressed dissatisfaction with the limited powers of the UN, and formed groups like the United World Federalists (1947) in order to build a true world government along the pattern of the American constitutional experience. Disarmament advocates and atomic scientists like Albert Einstein struggled to move the U.S. into internationalizing control of atomic energy in order to prevent the eruption of a runaway nuclear arms race. Various liberals and leftists backed former Vice President Henry Wallace in an electoral attempt to modify President Harry Truman's hard-line policy of military containment of the Soviet Union in favor of greater support of the UN. And, finally, cadres of war resisters like A. J. Muste expressed their opposition to the U.S. Cold War policies and domestic racial injustice by publicly burning their draft cards and committing nonviolent civil disobedience in support of the burgeoning black civil rights movement.

At the same time, leading peace activists argued over the interrelated issues of the Soviet role in world affairs and the Communist role in domestic peace activism. With the growing polarization of world politics in the late 1940s, the Soviets undertook a major "peace offensive," designed to attract an international coalition of leftists to their side of the global struggle. Most American peace activists steered clear of Soviet-sponsored peace initiatives, and condemned Stalinist repression in East-Central Europe. Yet they rejected Washington's claims that Moscow was bent on world domination: and they criticized American leaders for aggravating Russian fears and hostility with belligerent rhetoric and thinly disguised threats. Similarly, U.S. peace leaders were leery of collaborating with domestic Communists in various peace endeavours, especially in light of the Communists' manipulation of popular peace sentiment on behalf of Soviet foreign policy purposes in the late 1930s. Yet, out of a concern for civil liberties, peaceseekers declined to join in the spreading domestic attack upon Communists. Instead, leading peace activists tried at once to walk two fine lines—condemning Soviet totalitarianism while encouraging great-power conciliation, and defending Communist political activism while avoiding collaboration in all-inclusive left-wing political coalitions—that proved extremely difficult in practice. Their attempt to approach the Soviet Union with critical understanding and domestic Communists from a sympathetic distance not only provoked angry debates within the American left, it also stirred growing popular suspicions that citizen peace-seeking was nothing more than a front for Soviet subversion.

The popular tendency to see peaceseeking as subversive mushroomed after 1949, when spiraling Soviet-American tensions in Europe, the Communist success in China, the development of a Russian atomic bomb, and the outbreak of war in Korea fueled within America a right-wing firestorm that demanded anti-Communistic conformity at home and victory abroad. Commonly called McCarthyism, the right-wing attack shoved peace dissidents hard to the defensive. Some groups nearly disintegrated. The world federalist movement shrank so precipitously that it never regained the popular appeal that it had exerted in the immediate postwar years. The scientists' struggle for international nuclear arms control broke down under governmental loyalty investigations and Washington's quest for new ways to build bigger bombs. Liberals and leftists sympathetic to the internationalist ideals of Henry Wallace were attacked as disloyal if not subversive, while the ideal of war resistance suffered badly in a world that seemed split between Western capitalist democracy and Stalinist totalitarianism. With war raging in Korea, the moral choices at the heart of war/peace questions appeared as stark as they had been in 1941, only this time Stalinism stood in place of Hitlerism. Seemingly, America could achieve security in the name of freedom through gargantuan military preparations; or it could risk defeat in the name of peace while hoping for Soviet self-restraint. But there seemed to be no way to advance jointly the work of peace, freedom, and security that American peace activists valued most highly.

Pressed by conservative nationalists from without and demoralized within, organized citizens' peace activism collapsed in the early 1950s into a hard core of the faithful. Yet, even in decline, there appeared signs of new life. In 1955, a tiny band of pacifist Catholic Workers in New York City publicly defied state laws mandating citizen participation in air-raid drills and gave new momentum to active war resistance. They refused to lend their bodies to preparations for thermonuclear genocide. Emboldened by the Workers, related bands of war resisters organized themselves shortly after in the Committee for Non-Violent Action and launched a five-year-long campaign of nonviolent trespassing into U.S. nuclear weapons in order to communicate their personal rejection of the war system.

Simultaneously, an unexpected mass movement toward the nonviolent realization of black civil rights began in Montgomery, Alabama, and spread across the segregated South through the strength of Southern black Christians and some white supporters. The civil rights movement exhibited little direct concern for larger Cold War issues; but it demonstrated more vividly than any other development in recent American history the political possibilities of active pacifism and loving nonviolence.

It gave others heart. Inspired by the civil rights movement and frightened by the advancing arms race, a combination of internationalists, religious pacifists, and atomic scientists organized themselves during 1957 in the Committee for a Sane Nuclear Policy. They resolved to bring saving sanity to an international system that seemed to be hurtling madly through unchecked nuclear arms competition toward mass disaster. Arguing first for an international treaty against atomic testing in the atmosphere, these nuclear disarmament advocates contended that atmospheric testing was immediately harmful to human health and reproduction. At the same time, they believed that a test-ban treaty would prove the first step toward greater disarmament successes and reawaken popular support for an active UN. With associated activists and war resisters, these antinuclear activists were at first few in number and modest in influence. Yet they managed to regenerate the peace movement into the only body of organized Americans who called for a reduction in Cold War tensions and the reversal of the nuclear arms race. They thought that America's greatest victory would come in ending the Cold War, and not in trying to win it.[9]

The Cold War peace movement came into its own early in the 1960s, when the Cold War vaulted from crises in Cuba and Berlin onto new levels of tension, the pace of demands for domestic racial justice quickened, and the country's two major political parties failed to respond to these crises except by proposing "toughness" abroad and equivocation at home. The Republican Party passed during these years under the influence of a radical right wing that demanded victory over Communism abroad and constraints upon domestic racial change. The Democratic Party largely followed President John F. Kennedy in his confrontational approach toward the Soviets and revolutionary Third World movements; and it split over the race question. With both parties committed to the dream of effecting global peace through

America's superior military strength, the Cold War peace movement took on recognizable form early in the 1960s among traditional peace activists as well as new-fashioned groupings like the impatient housewives gathered in Women Strike for Peace (1961), dissident intellectuals like the Committees of Correspondence (1960), discontented youth like the Students for a Democratic Society (1960), and Roman Catholics like those in the Catholic Peace Fellowship (1964). This assemblage of Cold War dissidents was too inchoate to function as a party. But they made up an identifiable phenomenon that stood as the only domestic opposition to the ongoing international arms race, great power interventionism in Third World countries, Washington's preference for confrontation abroad over change at home, and America's larger failure to lead the world beyond the Cold War and toward détente, disarmament, and fuller global order. Divided but determined, the Cold War peace movement came together from many directions upon one matter of faith: that America could do better at home as well as abroad in advancing the work of social justice and international security through fewer bombs and more negotiations.[10]

Trying to rally their country behind ways of leading the world beyond the Cold War, peace activists proselytized, organized, and protested in favor of a great power détente, anti-interventionism, and disarmament early in the 1960s. They felt politically helpless—even impotent—during the October 1962 Cuban missile crisis. Yet they rebounded by the following summer to support the Kennedy administration in concluding the 1963 Partial Nuclear Test Ban Treaty, which prohibits atmospheric nuclear testing, in one of the most impressive arms control achievements of the Cold War years. Then the United States advanced deeper into Vietnam, and forced the movement to focus its attention upon the necessity and morality of the American intervention.

While Washington pumped money and military power after 1963 to maintain an anti-Communist South Vietnam, a domestic opposition centered in the Cold War peace movement first crystallized, and then galvanized itself into action. Internationalists like Norman Cousins called upon Washington to halt the bombing of North Vietnam and submit the dispute to the UN. Liberals and democratic socialists like Norman Thomas called for direct peace talks. War resisters like A. J. Muste demanded an immediate American withdrawal. Expressing their protest with everything from individual letter-writing to mass marches, Vietnam War critics reached out to include large numbers of people ordinarily uninterested in war/peace issues. But at their center were those activists who had already animated the Cold War peace movement—and who already shared differences over the ways toward advancing peace, justice, and security.[11]

As an *ad hoc* phenomenon distinguished only by its common opposition to U.S. war policies, the anti-Vietnam War movement roiled with internal tensions. Some involved tactical differences over matters like defining the right relationship between antiwar activism and the civil rights movement. Some involved strategic quarrels over the need for a negotiated settlement as opposed to America's immediate military withdrawal. Some involved critical value conflicts over the relative priority of peace and liberation. In general, peace liberals called for a military ceasefire and a quickly negotiated peace, while more radical antiwar critics seized upon the liberationist theme of black nationalism and pressed for the success of anticolonial Vietnamese Communist revolutionaries with the same enthusiasm that they lent to domestic demands for student power and women's liberation. The vast majority of antiwar activists were liberals, leftists, and pacifists who argued for the earliest possible cessation of fighting and a negotiated settlement on the assumption that peace was the preferred way of resolving the political problems of Indochina. But a small minority of social radicals and war resisters believed that liberation was at least as important as peace, and that the two values could not be vindicated in Indochina until the U.S. withdrew and the revolutionaries triumphed.[12]

Despite intramural divisions, the antiwar movement expanded and intensified between 1965 and 1970 as it combined with the demands of dissatisfied blacks, disaffected women, and the dissident young to produce an unprecedented cultural rebellion and shattering political changes. Moving with other forces of discontent, antiwar activists swirled among storms that swept the country in bitter quarrels over matters of race, age, sex, private conscience, true patriotism, and the proper conduct of moral politics. With civil rights leaders like Martin Luther King, Jr., shifting into antiwar activism, the peace commitment again took on the character of a protean reform. It manifested itself in many forms; and it produced predictably mixed results. On the one hand, the antiwar opposition effectively converted popular dislike for another limited war on mainland Asia into a process of citizen empowerment that schooled countless people in ways of dealing democratically with vital international issues. Even more, the opposition rallied popular strength sufficient to thwart the White House's more desperate plans for the drastic expansion and intensification of the war, especially during the critical years of 1968–69. On the other hand, the antiwar movement mixed with other outbursts of racial and cultural rebellion to incite a conservative countermovement that not only put Richard Nixon twice in the White House but also sanctioned Nixon's attempts to win the war through U.S.-subsidized "Vietnamization" and to kill off the Great Society attempts at domestic reform. The antiwar opposition constrained Washington's waging of the war. But it could neither stop the violence in Vietnam, nor overcome the mystique that Vietnam was vital to American security and basic to Nixon's promised "generation of peace."[13]

Inevitably, the tensions and distractions inherent in the work of sustaining a polyglot mass protest against the Vietnam War diverted precious time, resources, and energies from the peace movement in its larger struggle to move the U.S. and the world beyond the Cold War and toward some more secure global order. Inevitably, too, anti-Vietnam activism proved once more the symbiotic nature of organized peaceseeking among a range of related reforms. Women involved in the antiwar protest derived from the experience new interest in the struggle for equal rights for women.[14] The environmental movement gained fresh force as different citizens reacted to the use of napalm and toxic herbicides with sharpened concern over matters of ecological balance, corporate accountability, remote bureaucratic decisionmaking, and immediate injury to innocent people. In a related way, a many-sided movement against nuclear power plants emerged from a mixture of ecological concern, efficacious citizen activism, and suspicion of prevailing authority that ran through the anti-Vietnam War movement. By the mid-1970s, at the same time as the U.S. position in Vietnam finally disintegrated, antinuclear power activists opened campaigns against the construction and certification of plants across the country. Employing both electoral pressure and massive nonviolent civil disobedience, these dissidents disrupted plant construction and operations throughout the latter 1970s, until a combination of skyrocketing production costs, safety problems, financial difficulties, and a near-catastrophe at Pennsylvania's Three Mile Island power plant site cumulatively undercut the burgeoning nuclear power industry.

Otherwise, the Cold War peace movement fell back early in the 1970s, weakened by intramural differences, the utter unpopularity of the war in Vietnam, and by government attacks that soon redounded during the Watergate scandals to reveal the deeper corruption of the Nixon administration. Within a few years, however, the opposition reinvigorated itself with fresh force and visibility. In 1978, a broad-spectrum coalition of left-liberals assembled an umbrella operation called the Mobilization for Survival, in order to link the popular movements against nuclear power plant construction and the nuclear arms race. Shortly after, religious peace workers in the country's Quakers, Brethren, and Mennonite communities issued their first joint call for citizen peace action, while other religious peaceseekers (especially Roman Catholics) organized against the arms race and against militarized injustice in Latin America.

In the early 1980s, the American peace movement concentrated its attentions once again upon the interrelated threats of the nuclear arms race and great-power interventionism in the developing world. With the Reagan administration embarked upon a major new arms buildup and opposed to any thought of arms control, let alone disarmament, the arms race swept through a gigantic new loop in the ongoing spiral of escalation; and peace activists came forward in open opposition. Nearly one million people flooded mid-town Manhattan in June 1982 in order to communicate their demand for real disarmament action at the second meeting of the Special UN Session on Disarmament. Over four thousand people were arrested in the same year in different nonviolent actions at U.S. nuclear weapons installations and bases. And, most of all, grassroots Americans rallied to the idea of a bilateral, verifiable Soviet-American freeze on the testing, production, and deployment of nuclear weapons.

Rapidly, the nuclear freeze campaign galvanized the most popular and polyglot peace offensive since the early 1960s. In a series of local and state referenda held on the issue during fall 1982, roughly 60 percent of the voting public approved of the idea; and public opinion pollsters found that support of the freeze proposal ranged as high as 76–21 percent.[15] The freeze idea furthermore inspired the formation of hundreds of new organized peace efforts, until nearly 1,350 peace groups were in operation at all levels of national life by 1984.[16] Like earlier citizen peace efforts, the freeze campaign advanced for a number of reasons. It had the support of elite figures like Massachusetts Senator Edward Kennedy and atomic scientists like Hans Bethe. It claimed the backing of popular celebrities like actors Paul Newman and Ed Asner. It possessed a natural target in the arms-hungry Reagan administration. It boasted identifiable national spokespeople like the physician Helen Caldicott and the defense analyst Randall Forsberg. It had adequate financial resources, plentiful literature, networks of local volunteer activists. And finally, it seemed both reasonable and realizable. Like nothing else, the freeze idea provided a glimmer of hope to people tired of pounding further along a generation-long treadmill that was designed to develop more costly and devastating weapons in the name of a national security that the weapons only made more tenuous.

Like earlier citizens peace efforts, the nuclear freeze campaign was attacked by leading forces on the political right—including President Reagan—as an instrument of Soviet subversion. The campaign also suffered because of the internal problems familiar to coalition building. There were quarrels over the campaign's scope and definition. Some freeze advocates insisted that the campaign concentrate solely upon the danger of the escalating nuclear arms race; others believed that the genuine concern for peace that began with the freeze must extend into opposition to Washington's growing military involvement in Central America. There were arguments over the tactics of electoral action and popular education as against the wish for direct action through nonviolent civil disobedience. There were differences over strategy. Some freeze supporters viewed the idea as a novel means of advancing arms control; others expressed contempt toward arms control processes that only managed the arms race, and argued instead that the freeze provided the first step toward the true reduction of international tensions and real disarmament.

The differences within the nuclear freeze campaign only reflected the larger difficulty that American peaceseekers have confronted since 1945, when the opening of the Atomic Age framed the central question before the modern era of peace through deterrence: how were America and other nations to survive in peace and security when the weapons that traditionally provided the means of maintaining those processes now promised to produce unparalleled catastrophe? Plainly, the official American answer to this question has been to build more numerous and more destructive weapons, to engage intermittently in local wars in order to demonstrate political credibility, and to subsidize friendly (if often odious and tyrannical) regimes in defense of the country's global position. Members of the peace movement believe that the country should consider and pursue other answers. Some talk of the need for alternative global security systems. Others argue for "transarmament" from the deterrent threat of nuclear weapons to civilian nonviolent national defense. Some talk of "minimal deterrence," in which nuclear knowledge is preserved while the weapons are destroyed.[17]

Fundamentally, however, citizen peaceseekers have thus far been unable to define and promote a new vision of security within the processes of peace and disarmament that might win popular support sufficient to challenge the war system as a preferred means of pursuing the values of community, freedom, and justice. American peace activism has advanced impressively in this century in its numbers, ideas, visibility, and vigor. Now it needs to establish a cohering, compelling vision of a realizable global order in which different peoples would preserve their various traditional values without relying upon a war system that requires well-armed preparedness, threats, and ultimately mass violence. In America, citizen peace activists need to displace the prevailing myth of peace through superior armed strength with some practical understanding of security in disarmament and in the nonviolent multilateral resolution of disputes. They need to show how people can realize strength through peace. In the world, American and other citizen peaceseekers must hammer home the reality that a century of peace activism in the United States has verified: that people must take risks for peace with the same tenacity and sacrifice that they invest unquestioningly in war and war preparations. The risks of peaceseeking are great indeed. But the risks of persisting in the prevailing ways of arms and war are even greater—for individual freedom, for political order, and for humankind's essential security in survival.

II

At first glance, the American peace movement has been an apparently "leaderless" movement, with people at the grassroots providing the impetus for action and direction. In reality, twentieth-century American peace activists have looked at different times to a small number of leading figures to provide them with a coherent commitment and purpose. Considered one way, these various figures emerged as peace leaders in response to unique constellations of time, place, and personality. They became peace leaders as they seized upon immediate opportunities to integrate their different talents, insights, and powers with the needs of followers, in light of peculiar historical circumstances and political conditions. Seen another way, however, these different figures did manifest one common attribute that seems essential to leadership in the twentieth-century American peace tradition. They have been the teachers, preachers, and actors who best provided America's more peace-concerned citizens with a truly *"conscious choice among real alternatives"* that prevailing authorities failed to extend.[18] They symbolized alternative ways toward a peaceful world, and they drew others to follow them in those ways.

With other citizen peaceseekers, American peace leaders have shared a deep concern over the contradiction between America's core peace myth and its lacklustre record in extending organized peace. More than others, however, peace leaders have distinguished themselves by their success in employing symbols that draw attention to this contradiction, in rallying popular support behind their concern, and in proposing and pursuing alternative ways of realizing a global peace vision. The practice of using symbols toward the end of lending new meaning to reality and inspiring new hope in other possibilities is essential to peace leaders and has found various forms of expression at the hands of different people. At times, the ability to act as a peace leader through the management of symbols has shown itself through a person's capability of carrying his or her public *persona* into explicit peace activism. For example, Jane Addams built her personal and public identity as Progressive American reformer upon her determination to serve and nurture the weak and powerless in a maternal spirit suggestive of an archetypal earth-mother. With the outbreak of World War I, she undertook peace activism as the direct extension of this elementary commitment to improve the human condition through bread and love. In the same way, Albert Einstein used his public identity as the paragon of the rational scientific expertise that had opened the Atomic Age as a means of arguing for the control and abolition of nuclear weaponry. The Roman Catholic brother-priests

Daniel and Philip Berrigan employed their priestly status as the ministers of ritual sacrifice when they cast such starkly sacrificial symbols as fire and blood upon draft board records and nuclear missiles in attempts to force others into confronting the sinfulness of the war in Vietnam and the nuclear arms race.

At other times, different people have acted as peace leaders by using more ordinary forms of communication to project into public consciousness those feelings that otherwise remained inchoate or unconscious among the citizenry at large. Norman Cousins was a writer and editorialist who moved significant numbers of literate Americans through the force and logic of the written word into considering the wisdom of extending world order through global institutions and international law. Norman Thomas was a minister whose writings and speeches possessed a gentle but insistent power that proved effective in moving his audiences to support the possibilities of advancing peace through Christian humanitarianism and democratic socialism.

Other leading peace figures used their power to manipulate symbols with a force that literally resonated with feelings already deeply embedded in their followers. Eugene V. Debs was an electrifying orator who understood that some symbolic actions—such as speaking out against World War I and suffering imprisonment for his trouble—were essential to communicating to others the cost that war levied upon fundamental civil liberties let alone demands for radical social change. Like Debs, A. J. Muste believed in leadership through symbolic deeds which, in his day, meant trespassing upon missile installations and bomber bases in attempts to compel others to *feel* the war system around them and thus consider their complicity in its workings. Martin Luther King, Jr., spoke and acted in the tradition of Southern black Christianity that he leavened with Gandhian nonviolence. Like Muste, he believed in moving people through the self-sacrificing example of the nonviolent deed; and, like Debs, he possessed extraordinary oratorical skills that rattled the very bones of his listeners. "'Funny things happen when he talks,'" said one of King's listeners. "'He put into words what I feel and think. He's good! Never heard a man who sounds like I feel.'"[19]

At the same time, these people proved themselves to be peace leaders as they were among the preeminent practitioners of twentieth-century reform coalition politics. Seekers after a better world, these peace leaders were active in several reform enterprises, ranging from women's suffrage to civil rights, that involved them in recurrent quarrels over the ways and means of sustaining ongoing citizen reform efforts in American and international life. They were veritable "reform-mongers" whose various commitments necessarily induced them to adapt their peace ideals to changing opportunities and for other related reforms.[20] In the process, these people not only made the choices that gave direction and purpose to the modern American peace movement. They also shaped in large measure the contours and content of modern American reform coalitionism.

In a related way, the peaceseekers' involvement in various reforms entailed multiple value commitments that required them on some occasions to make painful choices in defense of one value at the expense of others. Jane Addams wanted to make the government into a democratic servant for succoring the weak and dependent. Yet, because of her peace commitment, she opposed America's rush toward war in 1917, even as other Progressive reformers supported the war effort as a means of transforming the government into a rational and humane social service agency of the kind that Addams sought. Eugene Debs devoted his life to helping the working class to achieve a more economically democratic America. Yet he declined to call for a violent class war toward that end. Albert Einstein was a man of peace who wanted to destroy Hitlerism. Yet he could not do both without lending his talents to an enormous war effort that resulted in the creation of incredibly destructive new weaponry.

These figures furthermore distinguished themselves as peace leaders in that they proved willing to take risks in advancing their principles. They used their reputations and sometimes their bodies to stake out advanced and dangerous positions, and called upon others to join them. Accepting the consequences of their commitment, every one of them suffered the ostracism, obloquy, or outright attack frequently visited on those who have argued for peace in a society that has gained so much from war. All felt the friction of Americans who go against the grain. Addams knew the inner pain of loneliness when one-time friends and allies rejected her and her decision to stand for peace. Debs knew government harassment and prison steel, while King faced the mob and the perpetual threat of sudden death. Muste and the Berrigans expected attack in the manner of Old Testament prophets, confident in their message and anticipating popular anger because of their condemnations. Yet none of them practiced the politics of martyrdom, or invited personal destruction in hopes of making some larger point. What they wanted to do was to advance the possibilities for peace; and they were willing to make sacrifices and take risks in order to do so. Others knew this, and accordingly looked to them for leadership.

Finally, these nine stand as the principal leaders of twentieth-century American peace activism in that each personified a major strain in the modern American peace tradition. Jane Addams was a Progressive social worker who both acted out and symbolized the vital role that women have played in the changing American peace movement. Eugene V. Debs was a labor leader and socialist who lived out the common assumption that the advent of peace waited upon the rise of genuine political and economic democracy that expressed the voice of ordinary people. Norman Thomas was a minister and urban reformer who interjected the spirit of Social Gospel Christianity into organized peaceseeking with a force that reverberated through subsequent generations of reformers. A. J. Muste was a labor organizer and religious mystic who contended that the absolute integrity of every person required a personal commitment to war resistance and organized opposition to imperial conquest. Albert Einstein was a scientist who understood that the progressive application of science, technology, and industry to war-making was creating a monstrous menace that required a massive popular demand for international disarmament and true world government. Norman Cousins was a writer and intellectual who lived in the belief that the craving for national security which fed upon the accumulation of ever more destructive weaponry was a danger that required the creation of a responsible world order with authority over such vital matters as war-making and armaments. Martin Luther King, Jr., was a black Christian minister who inspired in America a mass nonviolent crusade to liberate an oppressed people, establishing in the process a model for other nonviolent struggles for justice. Daniel and Philip Berrigan were Roman Catholic priests who developed a tradition of disruptive nonviolent resistance to express their distrust of centralized power and their Christian anarchist faith in the essential goodness of humanity, once freed from fear and tribal hatreds.

Extending from proponents of world government to religious anarchists, from leaders of organized womanhood to champions of the working class, these nine people represent the principal connecting rods within twentieth-century American peace activism. Certainly other people, including the Catholic Worker leader Dorothy

Day or the internationalist Grenville Clark, warrant inclusion in the front ranks of twentieth-century American peace leadership; and they have been excluded from this volume only for reasons of space and duplicative subject-matter. On the other hand, well-known governmental figures like Woodrow Wilson and Henry Kissinger, who presided over the massive deployment of national military power in the name of peace, cannot honestly be considered citizen peace leaders, mostly because they proved far more dedicated to waging interventionist wars than to extending multilateral peace at the risk of Washington's hegemonic interests. Indeed, it is largely because of the failings of duly constituted authorities like Wilson and Kissinger that concerned citizens from Jane Addams to the Berrigans have come forward to lead serious peace activism. Modern America's major peace leaders have not supported U.S. governing authorities in their repeated attempts to expand Washington's unilateral power in the world. Rather, peace leaders have been critics of governmental power and have assembled and sustained a citizens' peace movement on behalf of the human more than the national interest. The movement that they assembled has exhibited many facets. But it has abided in one common vision: that the war system threatens the progress of the human species and that ordinary but organized citizens must move governments to displace that system for the good of all.

Looking back upon them, the remarkable thing about these peace leaders is how much their words and actions, which for so long were either ignored or forgotten, call today for reexamination, reflection, and perhaps even pursuit. When John F. Kennedy compiled his version of *Profiles in Courage*, he gathered together a gallery of politicians whose moral heroism was defined by their commitment in conscience to various principles that Kennedy deemed vital to the national interest. Kennedy idealized his heroes as realists and tough-minded pragmatists, who dismissed as cranks and fanatics those who claimed other ideals. The global system, however, has turned a full revolution since Kennedy conceived of his heroes. In a world of hair-trigger intercontinental ballistic missiles and multipolar power centers, talk of "realism" and "the national interest" represents an important but incomplete approach to the need to assemble a new world order that must accommodate the proliferating technology of increased destruction and the festering insecurity of nation-states that "arm to parley" over issues for which they have no solutions.

The first need of this time, as Einstein said repeatedly, is for new ways of thinking about organizing power in ways appropriate to the control of new weapons of unprecedented destructiveness. In part, this imperative implies a need for a new ethic, a global consciousness of shared survival that integrates concern for the national interest within a greater concern for the dangers that threaten all. In practice, this suggests the need for what the political scientist Robert C. Tucker has called a " 'party of humanity.' "[21] According to Tucker, the reality of modern world politics requires a transnational body of leaders who aspire not to power but to purpose. Specifically, leaders of this " 'party of humanity' " would purpose to depict and communicate accurately the nature and gravity of the global crisis, propose possible solutions, promulgate an inclusive sense of human solidarity, and, most of all, inspire a sense of hope that humankind might yet prevail.

The people profiled in the following pages have been the twentieth-century American progenitors of this " 'party of humanity.' " With their counterparts in other countries, they have been the people of hope who maintained a global consciousness that assumed the fundamental value of peace as the means toward human well-being. They were neither saints nor lunatics, geniuses nor fools. They were simply people of conscience and purpose who decided to act at the risk of being wrong for what they believed was the greater good in living peace. And their experiences make up those "profiles in courage" most fitting to our own times.

The authors would like to thank the members of the American Historical Association's Conference on Peace Research in History, who have worked for nearly a generation to document the story of peace activism in the human experience. This book is dedicated to Bernice Nichols, former director of the Swarthmore College Peace Collection. Her professional efforts paved the way toward the historical reclamation of the American peace tradition; her life typified the peace heroism of everyday people everywhere.

NOTES

1. John F. Kennedy, *Profiles in Courage* (New York: Harper and Brothers, 1955), p. 238; Allan Nevins, foreword, ibid., pp. xi, xiii.

2. Robert C. Tucker, *Politics As Leadership* (Columbia: University of Missouri Press, 1981), p. 99; emphasis in the original.

3. Looking to the work of the historical sociologist Charles Tilly, this essay assumes that the twentieth-century American peace movement represents a changing but real social movement insofar as it is "a political product" that subsists in "sustained *interaction* in which mobilized people, acting in the name of a defined interest make repeated broad demands on powerful others via means which go beyond the current prescriptions of the authorities." Charles Tilly, "Social Movements and National Politics," in *Statemaking and Social Movements: Essays in History and Theory,* ed. Charles Bright and Susan Harding (Ann Arbor: University of Michigan Press, 1984), p. 313; emphasis in the original.

For other thoughts on the relationship between peace advocacy and the peace movement, see Charles Chatfield, "More Than Dovish: Movements and Ideals of Peace in the United States," in *American Thinking About Peace and War,* ed. Ken Booth and Moorhead Wright (New York: Barnes and Noble, 1978), pp. 111–35; and Chatfield, "Concepts of Peace in History," paper presented at the December, 1984, meeting of the American Historical Association.

4. For histories of the American peace movement to 1900, see Peter Brock, *Pacifism in The United States: From The Colonial Era To The First World War* (Princeton: Princeton University Press, 1968); Merle Curti, *The American Peace Crusade, 1815–1860* (Durham, N.C.: Duke University Press, 1929); Curti, *Peace or War: The American Struggle, 1636–1936* (New York: W.W. Norton & Company, 1936); Charles DeBenedetti, *The Peace Reform in American History* (Bloomington: Indiana University Press, 1980); and Warren F. Kuehl, *Seeking World Order: The United States And International Organization To 1920* (Nashville: Vanderbilt University Press, 1969).

For reviews of literature relating to American peace history, see Charles DeBenedetti, "Peace History, in the American Manner," *The History Teacher* 18 (November 1984): 75–110; and Charles F. Howlett and Glenn Zeitzer, *The American Peace Movement: History and Historiography* (Washington: American Historical Association, 1985).

5. C. Roland Marchand, *The American Peace Movement and Social Reform 1898–1918* (Princeton: Princeton University Press, 1972), p. 387. Also, Sondra R. Herman, *Eleven Against War: Studies in American Internationalist Thought, 1898–1921* (Stanford: Hoover Institution Press, 1969); and David S. Patterson, *Toward A Warless World: The Travail Of The American Peace Movement, 1887–1914.* (Bloomington: Indiana University Press, 1976).

6. Marchand, chaps. 5–10; Charles Chatfield, *For Peace and Justice Pacifism In America, 1914–1941* (Knoxville: University of Tennessee Press, 1971), part 1; and Charles DeBenedetti, *Origins Of The Modern American Peace Movement, 1915–1929* (Millwood, NY: KTO Press, 1978), chaps. 1–3.

7. Ernest Bolt, *Ballots Before Bullets: The War Referendum Approach to Peace in America, 1914–1941* (Charlottesville: University of Virginia Press, 1977); Chatfield, parts 2–4; Chatfield, "Alternative Antiwar Strategies of the Thirties," in *Peace Movements in America,* ed. Chatfield (New York: Schocken Books, 1973), pp. 68–80; and Lawrence S. Wittner, *Rebels Against War: The American Peace Movement, 1933–1983* (Philadelphia: Temple University Press, 1984), chap. 1.

8. Robert A. Divine, *Second Chance: The Triumph Of Internationalism in America During World War II* (New York: Atheneum, 1967); and Wittner, chaps. 2–5.

9. Milton S. Katz and Neil H. Katz, "Pragmatists and Visionaries in the Post-World War II American Peace Movement: *SANE and CNVA,*" in *Doves and*

Diplomats: Foreign Offices And Peace Movements in Europe and America in The Twentieth Century, ed. Soloman Wank (Westport, CT: Greenwood Press, 1978), pp. 265–288; and Milton S. Katz, *SANE and American Foreign Policy* (Westport, CT: Greenwood Press, forthcoming).

10. Charles DeBenedetti, "The Cold War Peace Opposition in America, 1955–1965," presented at the April 1981 meeting of the Organization of American Historians.

11. For a contrary view, see Paul Boyer, "From Activism to Apathy: The American People and the Bomb, 1963–1980," *The Journal of American History* 70 (March 1984): 821–844.

12. Thomas Powers, *The War At Home: Vietnam And The American People, 1964–1968* (New York: Grossman Publishers, 1973); Nancy Zaroulis and Gerald Sullivan, *Who Spoke Up?: American Protest Against The War In Vietnam, 1963–1975* (Garden City, NY: Doubleday and Company, 1984); Charles DeBenedetti, "On the Significance of Citizen Peace Activism: America, 1961–1975," *Peace and Change* 9 (Summer 1983): 6–20.

13. For an early historical consideration of the effectiveness of the anti-Vietnam War protest, see Melvin Small, "The Impact of the Antiwar Movement on Lyndon Johnson, 1965–1968: A Preliminary Report," *Peace and Change* 10 (Spring 1984): 1–22.

14. For the subsequent development of a more specific interest in "feminist peace studies," see *Women's Studies Quarterly* 12 (Summer 1984).

15. Louis Harris, "Public Attitudes Toward the Freeze," in *The Nuclear Weapons Freeze And Arms Control,* ed. Steven B. Miller (Cambridge, MA: Ballinger Publishing Company, 1984), p. 40.

16. Melinda Fine and Peter M. Steven, eds., *American Peace Directory, 1984* (Cambridge, MA: Ballinger Publishing Company, 1984), p. 1.

17. For a useful survey of the most prominent alternatives, see Burns H. Weston ed., *Toward Nuclear Disarmament and Global Security: A Search For Alternatives* (Boulder, CO: Westview Press, 1984).

18. James MacGregor Burns, *Leadership* (New York: Harper and Row, 1978), p. 36; emphasis in the original.

19. Reverend Willie K. Smith, "Dr. Martin Luther King, Jr.: The Politics of Sounds and Feelings," in *Leadership in America: Consensus, Corruption And Charisma,* ed. Peter Dennis Bathory (New York: Longman, Inc., 1978), p. 107.

20. Dankwart A. Rustow, "The Study of Leadership," in *Philosophers And Kings: Studies in Leadership,* ed. Rustow (New York: George Braziller, 1970), p. 6.

21. Tucker, p. 130.

MICHAEL A. LUTZKER

Jane Addams

Peacetime Heroine, Wartime Heretic

In the spring of 1915, during the first year of the Great War, all the armies of Europe were on the move. Millions of British and French troops clashed with Germans along a string of trenches that stretched from the Swiss border to the English channel. In the eastern Mediterranean, Australian troops stormed ashore to assault the Turkish forces in the hills surrounding Gallipoli, even as reports from within Turkey told of the widespread starvation and massacre of Armenians. Further north, the polyglot armies of the Austro-Hungarian Empire and their German allies battled Tsarist Russian troops along an eighteen-hundred-mile front in immense collisions, the human cost of which will never be accurately measured. But one thing was certain: The short, cheap, and glorious war that the generals and diplomats of 1914 had expected was turning into a bloodbath which no one had envisioned. And there was no end in sight.

While the great armies heaved and collided, eleven hundred women gathered at an unprecedented international congress at The Hague in Holland in order to help bring the war to an end. Several came from the warring powers (German and English women, in fact, sat side by side on the platform), even as the armies of their nations clashed in nearby Belgium. Other delegates came from neutral countries. Unanimously, however, they were joined in a common horror over the war and the prospect of its continuation; and they intended to persuade the neutral governments, and especially the American, to mediate an end to the bloodletting. The head of the forty-seven-member American delegation to the meeting was Jane Addams, who also served as presiding officer of the Congress.[1]

The audacity of the women's congress at The Hague was all the more remarkable when one remembers that these women not only did not have the right to vote in their home countries but were the objects of vicious attacks led by prowar nationalists. A large number of newspapers ridiculed them as naive and quixotic, while former President Theodore Roosevelt dismissed them as "hysterical pacifists."[2] But there was nothing hysterical about the deliberations of the Congress. The women carried on discussions in an atmosphere of great seriousness; and, after the delegates agreed upon proposals to end the war through neutral mediation, the audience was profoundly moved to see Belgian and German representatives shake hands on the platform.

With their program in hand, Jane Addams and other leading

members of the Congress spent the next weeks traveling to fourteen warring and neutral countries, crossing and recrossing frontiers and battlelines, in desperate attempts to meet the various heads of governments. They were taken seriously enough to be received by leaders. The ensuing discussions were polite but hardly encouraging. Every belligerent leader insisted that his government sought an honorable peace at the earliest possible moment, but all felt that to make a request for mediation would be taken by the other side as a sign of weakness, which would be intolerable. The implication of these talks with the belligerents was that any hope for a mediated settlement of the eight-month-old war must come from the neutral nations.

Addams's strongest hope lay in persuading President Woodrow Wilson to head a mediation effort by all the neturals. With the help of friends in high places, she met with the president in August at the White House. Wilson listened sympathetically while Addams described her conversations with leading representatives of the belligerent governments and communicated her conviction that it was the responsibility of the neutral governments to take the lead in restoring peace. Wilson, however, made clear his refusal to take any initiative toward neutral mediation. Absorbed in a diplomatic crisis with Germany following the sinking of the liner *Lusitania*, the president advised Addams that conditions were not appropriate for mediation; and, in a private letter to his fiancée, his attitude toward an active neutral role was even more skeptical: "I can't see it. And I am quite aware that they [women peaceseekers] consider me either very dull, very deep, or very callous."[3]

Addams was disappointed but not surprised. She had undertaken the leadership of The Hague Congress with few illusions about its possibilities for success. "I know how wild [the plans] must sound in the U.S.A.," she wrote a friend from Europe. "You can never understand unless you are here, how I could be willing to do anything." There was "just one chance in 10 thousand" for success, she estimated, of the women's private work for neutral mediation. But the horror of the war required that she and the other women risk those odds despite the gloomy prospects.[4]

Looking back on the Women's Congress seventy years later, we may well ask if it was reasonable to expect that they could have had any influence on a conflict which experienced diplomats had been unable to prevent. Would the military leaders have countenanced any peace proposals even if *all* the neutral nations had agreed on them? Surely we would have to say that the women's efforts were unrealistic. Instead, the "realists" of the belligerent countries continued to wage a punishing, yet virtually stalemated war for three more years, while a whole generation was sacrificed in the trenches of Europe. In retrospect, those who tried to mediate the war stand out as voices of reason and indeed realism; for, had their proposals been accepted, Europe might have been spared the worst of what followed in the wake of World War I. The ultimate irony of the 1914–18 conflict is that the victory, sought and won at such monstrous cost, seems only to have kindled the spark of an even larger and more disastrous conflagration.

What induced Jane Addams to make the attempt at a mediated settlement of the violence that engulfed Europe? What moved her to take risks for peace at a time when the vast majority of Europeans were caught up in the frenzy of war? In trying to answer these questions, we need to know something about her early life, the special quality of her career, and the particular lessons she drew from these experiences.

Jane Addams grew up shortly after the Civil War, at a time when young women of her class were likely to live out their lives in one of three ways: they could marry, beget children, and become society matrons; they could teach school; or they could become the maiden aunts to children of their siblings. For a time Addams accepted these boundaries of choice as other women of her generation had done. Her uncertain health (a problem throughout her life) could have encouraged her to claim a series of "woman's ailments" common to the accepted notion of female frailty and allowed her to live the life of a semi-invalid. Instead, she searched for an alternative direction and finally rejected the choices set by society and tradition. In so doing, Jane Addams succeeded in fulfilling her own extraordinary potential and by her achievements broadened the possibilities for other women to strike out along new paths.

Born in the little town of Cedarville, Illinois, in 1860, the youngest of five surviving children, Jane Addams was pampered and protected by her older sisters.[5] Her mother was of German ancestry. Her father, a man of English descent, was a prosperous miller who helped to bring a railroad into the county, raised a military company during the Civil War, and served eight terms in the Illinois state senate. Jane's mother died when she was not yet three. Five years later her father remarried a woman who encouraged in the Addams family an appreciation of the arts that was rare in such an isolated setting. Jane's father lavished a wealth of attention and affection on his daughter, and it was he whose counsel she sought and who most influenced her. He encouraged her to read and even rewarded her with money as she finished each of *Plutarch's Lives*. Despite his offering such an inducement to learning, John Addams was hardly a woman's emancipationist. He simply believed in educating his daughters that they might realize their potential within the limits of the traditional womanly roles.

Jane Addams entered Rockville Female Seminary (later Rockville College) in 1877, a period when the earliest women's colleges were being established. College life took her outside the closely knit family group and enabled her to discover that she could speak effectively in public and write persuasively. From the beginning she was held in high regard by her fellow students. Together they debated Darwin's theories, discussed the role of women, analyzed Shakespeare's plays, and even questioned some of the sacrosanct tenets of religion. Several of Jane's classmates left school to marry. Although she had suitors, she seemed at first to be reaching for a career. But shortly after she was graduated from Rockville Jane Addams became ill and despondent; for, while the challenges of education had awakened her mind, the realities of Victorian life severely limited the paths she could follow.

The sudden death of her father in 1881 was a blow which may have led her to seek escape in medical school, in which she enrolled when her family moved to Philadelphia. She had barely completed her first semester, however, when her health broke down completely. Following a long convalescence she sustained another emotional setback when her brother Weber had to be confined to an institution for mental illness.

In 1883, Jane and her stepmother sought solace in a European trip that lasted nearly two years. They visited museums, attended concerts, and made pilgrimages to the great cathedrals throughout the Continent; yet, in spite of all the cultural pursuits, Addams returned to the United States in a melancholy state. A second European trip in the company of two young college friends, including Ellen Gates Starr, enhanced her sense of independence and put her in touch with a world she had not previously seen: a visit to London's East End revealed to her the desperate poverty that accompanied industrialism. She discovered Toynbee Hall, a settlement house where students from Oxford and Cambridge came to teach groups of workingmen and learn from them as well. She began to read extensively in the literature of social reform.

Upon their return from Europe, Jane Addams and Ellen Gates Starr began to consider the possibility of establishing residence in one of Chicago's many impoverished neighborhoods to serve the needs of the immigrant poor. To their college-educated friends, the plan was as startling as it was intriguing. There were already church "missions to the poor" in some areas of the city, but the idea of young society women choosing to *live* there as part of their commitment provoked a great deal of discussion and skepticism. The two remained resolute. After exploring many different locations, they finally settled in the former mansion of a wealthy businessman, which had become a roominghouse in a predominantly Italian neighborhood in Chicago's congested West Side. They called it Hull House.

What Jane Addams and Ellen Starr did may require some explanation for this, more cynical, age. They desired, it is true, to be helpful to people in less fortunate circumstances, but they were no less anxious to break away from the more traditional roles prescribed for women at that time. As their contemporaries viewed it, they were seeking to free women whose education, talents, and energies found inadequate outlets in domestic life or society functions. The two women could reasonably contemplate living safely in a poor neighborhood because working-class people of the time were more likely than their present-day counterparts to be deferential to women.

Once in their pleasantly furnished apartment, the young women found themselves with plenty to do. They took care of the children of working mothers, arranged proper medical care for the sick, and tried to contend with garbage on the streets and the disease it bred. Through it all, they were appalled by the living conditions, the long hours of work, the child labor, and the money spent on funerals by those who could barely afford shelter and clothing. They also sought to enliven the drabness of day-to-day struggles amidst poverty. They communicated their own enthusiasm for the theater and their love of literature and awakened thereby these interests in their neighbors. In the process they enlisted the talents of college students and other middle-class women.[6]

The founders of Hull House learned as much as they gave. They discovered the value of trade unions for sweat-shop workers. They were astonished by the love of learning, the enthusiasm for music and drama on the part of their immigrant neighbors. They became aware of how the local political boss kept his power by providing patronage jobs, buckets of coal in winter, and a turkey at Thanksgiving.[7]

It may seem surprising that the presence of a number of upper middle-class women "doing good" in a neighborhood of poor immigrants should attract so much attention. Charity work among the poor was, of course, nothing new. But there were two novel aspects of the situation that fascinated journalists and made good copy for both the mass-circulation newspapers and the widely read women's magazines. The first was the idea that charity work could entail becoming a part of the community and sharing poor people's day-to-day experiences. The second and even more anomalous notion was that educated, cultured women could learn as much from the experience as the recipients of their beneficence, a point Jane Addams emphasized continually in her many talks to women's clubs, church groups, and college students. As if these elements were not startling enough, Addams drew from her own experience to suggest that the widespread invalidism of society women could be "cured" by active involvement in the lives of others.

"We need" she said, "the thrust in the side . . . which comes from living next door to poverty." And again, "Nothing so deadens the sympathies and shrivels the powers of enjoyment as the persistent keeping away from the great opportunities for helpfulness," to those in need.

> It is inevitable, that those who feel most keenly this deprivation and partial living, are our young people; our so-called favored, educated young people who have to bear the brunt of being cultivated into unnourished, over-sensitive lives . . . young girls feel it most in the first years after they leave school.

Society, in attempting to provide privileged young women freedom from care, succeeded often in making them miserable. "There is nothing after disease, indigence and guilt so fatal to life itself as the want of a proper outlet for active faculties . . . Our young people hear in every sermon, learn in their lessons, read in their very fiction, of the

great social mal-adjustment, but no way is provided for them to help
. . . They come back from college and Europe, and Wagner operas
and philosophical lectures, and wherever else culture is to be found
. . . many of them dissipate their energies into ill health. . . ."8

In this gently eloquent plea, Jane Addams appealed to her listeners' hunger for self-fulfillment as well as to their altruism. The idea
of helping the poor while becoming more knowledgeable oneself had
undoubted appeal to the Protestant conscience troubled by urban
problems.

The reform impulse gathered strength during the 1890s, and
settlement houses came to be recognized as an important agency of
change. Jane Addams's pioneering efforts had made her one of the
movement's leaders, while her lectures and writings helped her become an important voice for reform. The settlements campaigned for
recreation facilities in crowded cities, better sanitation, protection for
female workers, abolition of child labor, improvement of education,
and women's suffrage.

An idealistic generation of college students, both men and
women, brought their energy and exuberance to campaigns for reform. Many of the settlement houses became laboratories in which
students could learn about the city and its problems. Places like Hull
House attracted the civic-minded who wished to learn more about the
experiment. One visitor described it as a crossroads of humankind:

> Through the Hull House drawing rooms there passes a procession of
> Greek fruit vendors, university professors, mayors, aldermen, club-
> women, factory inspectors, novelists, reporters, policemen, Italian
> washerwomen, socialists looking hungrily for all persons yet uncon-
> verted, big businessmen finding the solution to the industrial problem in
> small parts, English members of Parliament, German scientists, and all
> other sorts of conditions of men from the river wards of the city of
> Chicago and from the far corners of five continents.9

Jane Addams received them all, sitting at the head of a long dinner
table ladling soup and presiding over animated discussions. Her
charm, her tact, her femininity were admired by a widening circle of
notables. She chaired conferences with great skill and diplomacy,
composing differences, moderating disputes, and generally finding a
less abrasive expression for platform resolutions.

Living in an area surrounded by a host of immigrant groups all struggling to eke out a living, Jane Addams was deeply impressed by their shared humanity. Despite profound differences in language and culture, they sought a better life for their children and attended English-language classes following exhausting workdays, all the while trying to protect their neighborhoods from crime and disease. The settlement house acted as a locus, teaching immigrants to assert their rights as tenants, serving as a focal point for neighborhood organizations.

Given the optimism of the reformer, it is not surprising that social workers emphasized the mutual support immigrants gave one another rather than the tensions and occasional violence among different ethnic groups. The spirit of excitement and cooperation that pervaded Hull House encouraged Jane Addams in her belief that a new spirit of community was emerging. Her experience in Chicago, matched by the energy she witnessed as she traveled to settlements in other cities, fostered an optimism about the future. She began to imagine the possibility of a peaceful community on a global scale.[10]

In 1896, on one of her European trips, Jane Addams visited Leo Tolstoy, the great Russian novelist and reformer. She had admired his writings for many years; now she looked forward to meeting him. Tolstoy had rejected the life of a celebrated writer in Moscow and, appalled by the contrast between Russian wealth and poverty, had retreated to a small village to live as the nearby peasants did. He seemed to draw strength from his close contact with them, wearing simple clothes and tilling the land as they did. His writings sought to capture the Christian vision of a better world, and his adoption of the simple life made him a powerful symbol for reformers the world over. Although Tolstoy received Addams cordially, the visit was not a comfortable experience for her. He listened gravely as she described the work of Hull House and the poverty of the immigrants in the surrounding community. Then he touched the sleeves of her blouse, which were very wide in the style of the time. He observed that there was enough material in one sleeve to make an entire dress for a little girl, and questioned whether her clothing might not be a barrier between her and the people.

Many of Tolstoy's guests were likely to feel uncomfortable as they watched him eat the peasant food of porridge and black bread while they were served an elaborate meal. The founder of Hull House was no exception. Nevertheless, the celebrated writer's simple style of life made a deep impression upon her. She sought, on her return, to work with her hands as he did and set aside time to bake bread in the settlement kitchen. Before long, however, Addams concluded that she could accomplish more by her exercise of leadership than by laboring in the kitchen. She continued, nonetheless, to write about the example Tolstoy set, particularly his rejection of material wealth and his ideals of Christian brotherhood and world peace.[11]

In the Spring of 1898 the United States declared war on Spain. Cuba and the Philippines were soon freed from Spanish rule, but America's expansion into the Pacific led to conflict with Filipino insurgents who wanted their islands independent of the United States as well as Spain. President McKinley's decision to annex the Philippines set off a national debate and brought about formation of the Anti-Imperialist League. Mark Twain, Andrew Carnegie, and Carl Schurz were among those who denounced the war against the Philippine independence movement.

Jane Addams had given little thought to U.S. policies abroad before the war. Now she found that the war against Spain had its echo on the streets of Chicago. She noticed an increase in violent street crime. The children were playing war games in the streets, and their shrieks and cries told of slaying Spaniards, not of freeing Cubans. The violence that lay just below the surface of man's nature, she noted, revealed itself overtly in wartime.

Addams joined the Chicago branch of the Anti-Imperialist League. Speaking out at one of their public meetings, she criticized the way patriotism had become equated with saluting the flag and singing "America" rather than with the civic responsibility of serving the community. Why, she asked, could not the courage and self-sacrifice required in wartime be adapted to the nation's urgent peacetime needs for justice? In her own fashion, she was seeking constructive outlets for the nationalism turned loose by war. This theme would later form the basis for philosopher William James's famous essay, "The Moral Equivalent of War."[12]

In the years prior to World War I, Jane Addams spoke in many parts of the country before women's groups, social workers, college students, and philanthropic organizations. Popular magazines published her articles, her books were appreciatively reviewed, and she wrote "The Jane Addams Page" regularly for the *Ladies Home Journal.* Political leaders who wished to ameliorate the conditions of the cities sought her support.

The founder of Hull House served as an example for an impressive variety of women. Those in college appreciated the strength of her intellect, while others who remained tied to the home admired her as one who had gone into the world yet who continued to defend the sanctity of the family. She addressed problems of deep concern: abolition of child labor, protection of women workers, punishment of those who profited from prostitution. For many she became a symbol of saintliness. A friend of Woodrow Wilson, Charles R. Crane, wrote the president urging him to meet with Jane Addams upon her return from Europe in 1915. "Of course she is the best we have and has been received everywhere as a spiritual messenger. . . . Added to her great spiritual power is wonderful wisdom and discretion. Every woman in the land and most men would be cheered by knowing that you and she were in conference."[13]

In sum, her ideas combined encouragement to women to realize their potential and an appeal to their sense of tradition. Women were, after all, those who nurtured the young, the traditional protectors of family and home. To do so effectively, Addams asserted, they should be accorded a larger voice in the society. Those who worked in factories needed the laws to protect their health so that they could bear healthy children. To achieve effective legislation in an industrial society they had to possess the right of full citizenship, that is, the vote.

The response to her carefully reasoned appeals revealed both the strengths as well as the drawbacks of her reformist efforts. The popular press found it easier to praise Jane Addams as an individual than to analyze the social ills about which she spoke. Leaders paid tribute to her selflessness and her sacrifice, rather than examining the substantive issues she raised. In part this attitude was a reflection of the optimism that characterized the Progressive era prior to World War I. Reformers believed that by exposing injustice to public scrutiny the wrongs would somehow be put right. If the political machines were unresponsive, they would be defeated. As the immigrants gained a sense of their rights as Americans, they would successfully resist those who sought to exploit their fear and ignorance.

This sense of optimism was so woven into the fabric of Jane

Addams's writings, so much a part of her speeches, that she reassured her audience even while arousing them. Her widely praised auto-biography, *Twenty Years at Hull House*, while filled with examples of poverty and injustice was, at the same time, a saga of accomplishment—people aiding their neighbors, lessons in the importance of community organizations, instances demonstrating the value of education. Jane Addams's life seemed the very embodiment of a new civic concern. She appealed to the altruism of her listeners. Rather than leveling accusations, she offered practical proposals. This non-threatening style of persuasion led middle-class America to view her as a noble figure and, as she began to age, a maternal figure. This aura of beneficence she had earned by her own efforts and the careful, reasoned expression of ideas.[14] That this role pleased her is evident from the way she was careful to save the letters of praise, however extravagant, as well as the poems written about her. The laudatory press accounts were carefully clipped and preserved.

With the outbreak of World War I Jane Addams turned her energies to encouraging mediation among the belligerents and later to seeking to keep the United States from being drawn into the conflict. The war tapped emotions that had surfaced for a time during the Spanish-American hostilities and the fight against the Philippine insurgency. Now they were exacerbated. Jane Addams still spoke in the accents of reason, but as the nation became increasingly aroused by stories of wartime atrocities, Americans were less receptive to reason. The German U-boat assaults on merchant ships without warning, the loss of passenger lives, seemed as barbaric an image early in this century as the death camps would become to a later generation. In the beginning those who questioned the war were praised; after a time they were doubted; and, once America became involved, they were reviled.

From the beginning of the war in Europe the women's suffrage groups responded in a more direct way than the older, conservative peace organizations. While the World Peace Foundation trustees wondered whether the conflict signified the failure of their efforts, Lillian Wald and Fanny Garrison Villard led a parade of twelve hundred women down New York's Fifth Avenue in late August, 1914, to protest the war.[15] Shortly afterward, Jane Addams chaired a meeting of social reformers who gathered at the Henry Street Settlement

House at the invitation of Paul Kellogg, editor of the *Survey* magazine. Many reformers feared what the conflict would do to the spirit that fostered reform. They saw the war as a brutalizing force affecting men everywhere, and they grew increasingly disturbed, as the months passed, over the rising clamor for U.S. military preparedness. Early in 1915 they organized the American League for the Limitation of Armaments. (In 1916 the group changed its name to the American Union Against Militarism.) Jane Addams supported their work, but mainly her energies were absorbed by the Woman's Peace Party, whose leader she became.[16]

The Woman's Peace Party grew out of a whirlwind tour of the U.S. by two militant pacifists from abroad, Rosika Schwimmer from Hungary, and Emmeline Pethick-Lawrence from England. Both were veteran suffragists, dynamic personalities, and their speaking tour brought extensive press coverage. Their example led Carrie Chapman Catt, leader of the American suffrage movement, to propose that she and Jane Addams jointly issue a call to all women's organizations for a conference in Washington to unite women around the issue of peace. They found a widespread and enthusiastic response. On January 10, 1915, three thousand women gathered, and, with the cooperation of many different leaders and the skillful chairmanship of Jane Addams, the organizations avoided partisan divisions such as existed in the suffrage movement between militants and moderates. This coalition formed the Woman's Peace Party, adopted a ringing call for abolition of war, and insisted that women be given a voice in the decisions that would directly affect their lives and the lives of their families.[17]

It was members of the Woman's Peace Party who responded to the call for an international women's conference in 1915 to promote mediation. In July, 1915, Jane Addams returned to the United States following her discussions with leaders of the belligerent nations. At a large meeting in Carnegie Hall, she described The Hague women's conference and related her conversations with people from both sides of the conflict. She had found a growing disenchantment with the war, particularly among young people.

> Generally speaking, we heard everywhere that this war was an old man's war; that the young men who were dying, the young men who were doing the fighting, were not the men who wanted the war, and were not the men who believed in the war; that somewhere in church and state, somewhere in the high places of society, the elderly people, the middle-

aged people, had established themselves and had convinced themselves that this was a righteous war, that this war must be fought out, and the young men must do the fighting. . . .

She cited instances of soldiers who could not bring themselves to kill their fellow human beings. Though far from suggesting that large numbers of men would refuse to fight (indeed in each country people insisted the war was one of self-defense), she spoke of the soldier's horror of hand-to-hand combat in the trench fighting.

> We heard in all countries similar statements in regard to the necessity for the use of stimulant before men would engage in bayonet charges—that they have a regular formula in Germany, that they give them rum in England and absinthe in France: that they have to give them the 'dope' before the bayonet charge is possible.[18]

In the press accounts of the meeting, Addams's reports of the women's conference, her discussions with the statesmen of Europe, her account of disenchantment with the war were all virtually lost in the controversy provoked by her single statement suggesting that combat troops were doped. One typical headline screamed, "Troops Drink-Crazed, says Miss Addams." Without realizing it, Jane Addams had struck at a cherished belief, that the ordinary soldier risked his life for duty and country. Although she was speaking of European troops, Addams seemed to many Americans who prided themselves on their patriotism to be impugning the bravery of all soldiers who had ever answered their country's call.

A stinging reply came from the famous war correspondent Richard Harding Davis, who spoke of the Allied soldiers who had spent the past winter in the trenches:

> . . . he has endured shells, disease, snow and ice. For months he had been separated from his wife, children, friends—all those he most loved. When the order came to charge it was for them he gave his life . . . Miss Addams denies him the credit of his sacrifice. She strips him of honor and courage. She tells his children, "Your father did not die for France, or for England, or for you; he died because he was drunk" . . . I have seen more of this war and other wars than Miss Addams, and I know all war to be wicked, wasteful and unintelligent, and where Miss Addams can furnish one argument in favor of peace I will furnish a hundred. But against this insult, flung by a complacent and self satisfied woman at men who gave their lives for men, I protest. And I believe that with me are those women and men who respect courage and honor.[19]

Newspapers everywhere in the country took up Davis's letter, and most supported his conclusions. Those people who had lost loved ones in past wars would likely have agreed with Davis. Addams received many angry letters from ordinary people who defended the courage and honor of soldiers. Some opponents of women's suffrage used the issue to argue the dangers of women meddling in political affairs that were beyond their capacities. Americans had admired Jane Addams as the embodiment of the highest ideals of American woman-hood. Now, by challenging the aura that surrounded patriotism, national honor, and the self-sacrifice of the soldier, she had violated the image of the heroine the public had come to expect. She defended her remarks and many supporters rallied to her side, but she had become a figure of controversy, and neither her womanhood, nor her gentle nature would henceforth protect her from harsh criticism.[20]

In the summer of 1915, as the war entered its second year, peace groups in America intensified their efforts to promote mediation. It was now clear to all that there was to be no short war as had been widely predicted. Instead each side faced the grim prospect of a drawn out conflict that would compel governments to demand ever greater sacrifices from their people. The war fed upon itself. It had already drawn in Italy and Japan. Now it engulfed three continents. The original reasons for each nation's involvement were already giving way to a blind hatred of the enemy fed by atrocity stories from abroad and hardships at home. After a time nothing except a crushing military victory would satisfy people who had sacrificed so much.

Jane Addams's travels in the belligerent countries had made her realize that the people on one side were completely unaware of any sentiment for peace on the other. Press censorship made it exceedingly difficult to publicize the existence of any peace proposals. A conference of neutrals offering to mediate would have to break through the curtain of silence with which each warring power had surrounded itself. Concerned that opportunities for mediation were dwindling and that governments would not act, she urged that an international conference of distinguished experts be convened to frame initiatives. These individuals would represent not governments, but humanity. The old diplomacy had failed to prevent the war, Addams contended, now new channels had to be found to influence leaders and their peoples.

The Woman's Peace Party continued to press for mediation efforts by the United States. The president had not, after all, opposed them outright. He simply maintained that the time was not right for a mediated settlement. In late 1915, as another winter of suffering in the trenches loomed with no break in the stalemate, peace advocates—and women in particular—increased their efforts. On November 26, 1915, representatives from an international women's delegation met with Wilson. That same day, by prearrangement, over twelve thousand telegrams calling for mediation arrived at the White House from hundreds of women's groups all over the country. The president expressed sympathy with their goal but refused to take any public initiative.[21] He was doubtless fortified by a letter Colonel House had sent him from Lord Bryce. Speaking for the British government Bryce insisted that there was

> not the slightest change in British sentiment regarding the duty and necessity of prosecuting the war with the utmost vigour and listening to no suggestions for negotiations with the German Government . . .[22]

A major financial contributor to the telegram campaign was the automobile manufacturer Henry Ford, who had denounced the war vociferously. On the request of Rosika Schwimmer, Ford helped to organize an international conference of experts from the neutral nations, and hastily chartered a ship, the *Oscar II,* to take an American delegation to Europe. His announcement took Jane Addams and other peace leaders completely by surprise. Ford was profoundly ignorant of foreign affairs, but, as America's most successful businessman, he commanded unusual public attention. The attention soon turned to ridicule, however, when Ford foolishly announced that he and the other Americans sailing for Europe would have the boys in the trenches home for Christmas. Ford's remarks loosed a torrent of abuse directed at the "Peace Ship" and by implication against the whole idea of mediation.[23] They also confronted committed pacifists with a cruel dilemma. Many people, including well-known figures who favored peace initiatives, were thoroughly dismayed by Ford's assertion and hurriedly dissociated themselves from proposed mediation efforts. Some, like Louis Lochner of the Chicago Peace Society, chose to go in spite of public derision. Jane Addams had also planned to sail, believing that some kind of symbolic act was necessary to dramatize the peace idea, but just before the departure her doctors insisted that she be hospitalized for a serious kidney ailment.

As the ship made its way across the Atlantic to join the delegations of other neutrals, the reporters on board filed stories emphasizing the bizarre: the mysterious documents Rosika Schwimmer carried in a black bag, the personality clashes among the delegates, and a shipboard marriage ceremony. When it became clear that the entire international committee would become discredited by the *Oscar II's* journey, Jane Addams wired the women leaders in Europe to "Keep the International Committee distinct from [the] Ford Enterprize." This led Rosika Schwimmer to resign from the international committee while Ford, whose thoughtless public statements had precipitated much of the criticism, became disillusioned and withdrew from the project upon arriving in Europe.[24]

The Peace Ship debacle continued to bedevil Jane Addams long afterwards, and some press accounts suggested that her illness was imaginary. Months later Ford stated in an interview that the idea had originated with the Hull House leader. Despite her denials, she remained linked in the public mind with the whole quixotic venture. Moreover, in 1916, Addams's health remained poor, and she was forced to curtail her activities. While she was convalescing, the idea of military preparedness gained momentum in response to the loss of American lives to German submarines, and President Wilson endorsed a modified proposal for a U.S. military buildup. Despite her ill health, Addams traveled to Washington and voiced her opposition in testimony before a congressional committee. Her statements to the congressmen were perhaps less than persuasive. She ascribed the desire for a larger army and navy to war hysteria that came primarily from men. Insisting that there was no danger of an actual attack upon the United States, she suggested that such men were more prone to hysteria and emotionalism than women. Her remarks struck some raw nerves among men who identified emotionalism with patriotism. One critic urged that the founder of Hull House return to social service, while another decided that what she needed was

> a strong forceful husband who would lift the burden of care from her shoulders and get her intensely interested in fancy work and other things dear to the heart of women who have homes and plenty of time on their hands.[25]

With the presidential campaign of 1916 looming ahead, the country girded itself for an acrimonious contest. Theodore Roosevelt, the reformers' champion in 1912, cried out for U.S. intervention. He stumped the country attacking Wilson as a coward and urging progressives to support Charles Evans Hughes, the Republican nominee. The enthusiasm that Roosevelt and like-minded reformers felt for intervention provoked enormous strains within the progressive coalition. In 1912, Addams had stood up at the Progressive Party's founding convention and seconded Roosevelt's nomination for the presidency while praising the Party's social justice platform. But a great deal had changed in the intervening four years. The Progressive Party had splintered when important sections of its platform were enacted by the Wilson administration, most notably a federal law prohibiting child labor. Moreover, Wilson became a belated convert to women's suffrage. And, above all, notwithstanding his endorsement of military preparedness, Wilson had steered a difficult course and kept the nation out of war. Americans generally favored the Allies and were repelled by Germany's submarine warfare and her clumsy attempts at spying and sabotage. But most still believed that the country had no business in a conflict three thousand miles away. The Democrats campaigned on slogans of maintaining peace, prosperity, and continued social reform. Their leaders assiduously courted progressives like Addams, who had supported Roosevelt in 1912; and, as the campaign heated up, she issued a strong endorsement of the president that doubtlessly rallied pro-Wilson support among many reformers. Wilson certainly valued her backing. After his cliffhanger re-election victory in November, he sent her a warm note of thanks along with a dinner invitation to the White House.[26]

For a brief time following his reelection, Wilson made a powerful effort to encourage both sides in the war to state their conditions for peace. It seemed the beginning of that mediation effort which peace advocates had been urging upon him for nearly two years.[27] In a speech before Congress on January 22, 1917, the president asserted that he spoke for "the silent mass of mankind everywhere," and, appealing to the people of the warring nations over the heads of their governments, he called for a negotiated peace, that he termed a "peace without victory." He also warned against the false lure of fighting on to a spurious victory.

> Victory would mean a peace forced upon the loser, a victor's terms forced upon the vanquished. It would be accepted in humiliation under

duress, at an intolerable sacrifice, and would leave a sting, a resentment, a bitter memory upon which the terms of peace would rest, not permanently, but only as upon quicksand.[28]

But the appeal, eloquent as it was, came too late. While Wilson prepared his speech, the German leaders made their fateful decision to launch all-out submarine warfare against any ships supplying the Allies. For nearly two years the civilian leaders in Germany had resisted such pressures from the military, recognizing that it would inevitably bring America into the war. Now in early 1917 the admirals promised victory if the submarines were unleashed, and the desperate civilian leaders gave in.

As the U-boats began to attack American ships during February and March, Wilson broke diplomatic relations with Germany. Still he hesitated to call for an outright declaration of war. The country remained poised on the brink of conflict. Despite the dismal outlook, peace groups that had resisted U.S. intervention at every turn refused to give up. The Emergency Peace Foundation called a conference in New York that was attended by 150 delegates representing 22 organizations. On February 28 a small delegation of conference leaders, including Jane Addams, met with the president for more than an hour. Led by Professor William I. Hull of Swarthmore, they cited several instances of American restraint in the face of depredations on U.S. ships during the Napoleonic Wars. They praised Wilson's moderate course with Mexico during the previous year, when Pancho Villa had conducted raids across the U.S.-Mexican border, and urged similar restraint toward Germany. Furthermore, Addams expressed her fear that the splendid social reforms of Wilson's administration would be thrust aside by war.[29]

The delegation promised to respect the president's request for confidentiality. The discussion was quite candid. As Addams recounted Wilson's words years later, however, the president spoke earnestly to them as a fellow partisan of peace who had been trying for a long time to hold back the tide of war. At that moment he felt compelled to confess its inevitability. He confided to them the anger he felt over a secret development the details of which he could not yet divulge. (It turned out to be the Zimmerman Telegram from Germany to Mexico, with its promise of American territory if the Mexicans declared war against the United States.) In recounting the conversation, Jane Addams recalled vividly a phrase Wilson had used, because it was identical to one she had heard earlier from Colonel House. The president told them that as head of a nation participating in the war he would have a seat at the peace table, while as a neutral all he could do would be to "call through a crack in the door." It was clear to the peace advocates that Wilson had put aside "peace without victory" and convinced himself that the U.S. entry into the war could transform the conflict that had raged for nearly three years, and enable him to shape the victorious peace that would follow.[30]

Aware that many Americans had little enthusiasm for a war waged on the other side of the Atlantic, Wilson set out to arouse the nation. His belief that he had done everything possible to mediate lent force to his appeal. New reports of U.S. ships being torpedoed and of German efforts to bring the war closer by making Mexico her ally prepared Americans to regard Germany as a threat. Moreover, the overthrow of the Czar in February 1917, and the substitution of parliamentary government in Russia removed some of the taint of autocracy from the Allied coalition. As Russia moved toward seemingly democratic rule, she became more acceptable as a potential ally.

Once launched on the "Great Crusade," the nation was swept with a surge of enthusiasm. Old stock Americans heeded their country's call, while recent immigrants realized that they could best demonstrate their loyalty by answering the call to arms. Wilson enlisted many erstwhile antimilitarists and social justice progressives in support of the war as he held out a vision of a new world order that promised to eliminate the old diplomacy whose failure had produced the war. Convinced that all the alternatives had been exhausted, and embracing Wilson's Fourteen Points, the overwhelming majority of former peace advocates swallowed their regrets and welcomed the president's promise of war to end all wars.

The war brought a host of changes designed to mobilize the nation's economy. Increased efficiency, government ownership, economic planning, measures advocated for years by reformers and socialists, now came almost as a matter of course. Former peace advocates still thought of the institution of war as something horrible, yet many were gratified by the progress of reform. The railroads were nationalized, a War Labor Policies Board protected working men and women, the Coal Commission distributed fuel more equitably.

Many of Jane Addams's friends were appointed to the new government boards. There were, she observed, some encouraging gains. At the same time she cautioned her colleagues that social advancement depended as much on the processes by which it was achieved as on the results.

> . . . if railroads are nationalized solely in order to secure rapid transit or ammunition and men to points of departure for Europe, [then] when that governmental need no longer exists what more natural than that the railroads should no longer be managed by the government?[31]

In this as in other instances her words were prophetic.

She became part of a small group of men and women who were unable to accept the course on which the nation had embarked. Most remained silent, recognizing the futility of any efforts to swim against the tide of an aroused public opinion, and not wishing to be considered German sympathizers. A tiny handful strove to keep alive some older American ideals that were being threatened by war hysteria. Press censorship, government surveillance of dissenters, persecution of aliens and radicals, threats to the lives of conscientious objectors, all represented the less attractive side of the "Great Crusade."[32]

The founder of Hull House felt deeply the isolation from many of her colleagues who became active participants in the war effort. She had always considered herself a moderate.

> But now I was pushed far towards the left on the subject of the war and I gradually became convinced that in order to make the position of the pacifist clear it was perhaps necessary that at least a small number of us should be forced into an unequivocal position.[33]

She later acknowledged that there were times when she came very close to despair. A profound awareness of her inner feelings enabled her to observe that the pacifist in wartime "finds it possible to travel from the mire of self-pity straight to the barren hills of self-righteousness and to hate himself equally in both places."[34]

She tried to act constructively without openly challenging the war and was part of a delegation that visited Secretary of War Newton Baker, a fellow reformer, to gain humane treatment for conscientious objectors. Their appeals were rejected. She and some fellow pacifists declined to work with the Red Cross because it had become part of the military and used the enthusiasm of the war to raise its funds.[35]

Despite recurring illness Jane Addams searched for a way to define patriotism and the life-affirming role of women in such a way as to keep the ideals of peace alive without seeming to subvert the national effort. Reaching back into memories of a happy childhood, she recalled that her forebears had been millers. Her earliest recollection was "being held up in a pair of dusty hands to see the heavy stone mill wheels go round."

Watching the foaming water my childish mind followed the masses of hard yellow wheat through the processes of grinding and bolting into the piled drifts of white flour . . .[36]

She remembered, too, how she had written an essay in college about women in ancient times who cultivated the grain fields while men hunted. Later during her wartime journey through Europe she was struck by scenes of peasant women struggling to plow the land while soldiers everywhere marched to fight. The earlier memories mingled with the wartime images to reinforce her view that women were once more in their role as providers.

Searching for the historical roots of this phenomenon led her to Sir James Fraser's *Golden Bough*, where she found a rich mythological tradition of the Corn Mother and the Corn Maiden in the old civilizations of Europe. The ancient Greek and Roman gods associated with planting and harvest were characteristically feminine and celebrated from earliest times in poetry and song.

Addams's understanding of these ancient rites served to restore a sense of purpose that transcended the war hysteria swirling about her. The need to conserve food for the hungry posed a challenge that she could energetically embrace. She offered her services to the Department of Food Administration, then directed by Herbert Hoover, and was sent to speak before women's groups and school assemblies. Food conservation was necessary to feed America's allies; afterwards there would be no less a need to compensate in all the war-torn lands for the starvation rations endured by the civilian populations, particularly the children.[37]

When the war at last came to an end, the peace conference of victors assembled at Versailles. At the same time the International Congress of Women, which had had its first wartime meeting at The Hague, redeemed its pledge to reconvene at war's end. Sixteen nations sent delegates. The women had hoped to gather in close proximity to the heads of state, but since representatives of the defeated nations were not admitted to France, they decided to meet in Zurich. The reunion was an emotional one. Those who had endured the hardships of wartime shortages were visibly marked by their suffering, and delegates from the Allied states were shocked by the haggard appearance of the women they had last seen in 1915. Between their toil and lack of food, they seemed to have aged a lifetime in four years. Yet all the women felt themselves joined in a strong spiritual bond that was born of their common antiwar dissent. The socialist Florence Kelley, who had accompanied Jane Addams more out of duty than conviction, was deeply moved: "Next time I would go on my knees," she wrote.[38] As in 1915, women from the warring countries shared the platform in the first step toward healing the wounds of war. Hearing first-hand reports of starvation in central Europe, they passed a resolution calling on the peace conference to raise the Allied blockade, which, despite the armistice, was still in force in order to compel Germany to sign the treaty. President Wilson replied with a telegram in which he concurred in sentiment but pleaded that practical difficulties prevented him from persuading the Allied leaders to lift the blockade.

The women's conference spent considerable time discussing an advance copy of the peace treaty. They were deeply distressed by its harsh provisions, particularly when they compared it to the noble promises that Wilson had made in the famous Fourteen Points peace proposal of January, 1918. The victorious powers had delivered over the fruits of the wartime secret treaties, making a mockery of Wilson's promise of open diplomacy. They forced the defeated nations to pay the entire costs of the war. Thus "a hundred million people of this generation in the heart of Europe are condemned to poverty, disease and despair, which must result in the spread of hatred and anarchy within each nation."[39] The women sounded a theme that was to receive more widespread acceptance later in the 1920s, that the punitive provisions of the treaty carried the seeds of a future war.

The proposed League of Nations did not suffice to offset the women's concerns over the treaty. They called for changes in the League Covenant that would incorporate more of the principles of the Fourteen Points. Recognizing that their work had only begun, the congress formed a permanent organization, The Women's International League for Peace and Freedom, and elected Jane Addams president. The women's congress proved a tonic for her spirit after the troubled wartime years. Her leadership of the international peace movement was appreciated far more in Europe than at home.

After the conference, Addams and her American colleagues made a trip to Germany, where they observed the horrible effects of near starvation. Working with the American Friends Service Committee, they helped to organize the first private shipments of desperately needed food. They came too late for many whose weakened resistance to disease had made them victims of tuberculosis, rickets, and the catastrophic influenza epidemic.[40]

Addams returned to the United States to find the fervor of the war replaced by a postwar panic over the imagined threat of revolution at home. Strikes, inflation, unemployment, and radical rhetoric convinced wartime super-patriots that all immigrants were dangerous whether or not they sympathized with the Bolshevik revolution. The federal government went the nativists one better. Although it was peacetime, there were mass raids by federal agents on the homes of aliens, practices all too familiar in the Old World: the knock on the door in the middle of the night, arrests without warrant, detention without hearings, and for many, deportation.

Once again as in wartime, Jane Addams sought to provide a voice of reason in the midst of hysteria. Following a roundup of hundreds of aliens in Chicago, she defended their loyalty and criticized the Justice Department.

> The cure for the spirit of unrest in this country is conciliation and education—not hysteria. Free speech is the greatest safety valve of our United States. Let us give these people a chance to explain their beliefs and desires. Let us end this suppression and spirit of intolerance which is making America another autocracy.[41]

As a consequence she became the target of attacks by the American Legion, the Daughters of the American Revolution, and other self-appointed guardians of Americanism.[42]

During the 1920s, Addams was often more comfortable traveling abroad than in her own country. In Europe, and on a trip to Asia, she was made welcome by dignitaries and treated with reverence by large and sympathetic audiences. Her supporters sought to nominate her for the Nobel Peace Prize. However, the resentments over her wartime pacifism, and editorial criticism of her libertarian defense of free speech for radicals cost her considerable support in the United States.[43] It was not until 1931 that the enmities bred by the war healed to the point where she was awarded the coveted Peace Prize. Even then, however, the honor to Addams was tempered by her having to share it with President Nicholas Murray Butler of Columbia University. Butler had been a hysterical proponent of the war, had dismissed professors from Columbia for their opposition to it, and had fought for abolition of German language instruction throughout the country. The dual award represented one of those compromises that did little credit to the Nobel Committee.[44]

One writer who recognizes the talents of the Hull House pioneers has observed that they lacked a sense of the comic, that is, they failed to recognize the gulf between the reality of what they had achieved and the breadth of their aspirations to reform American society.[45] This judgment may have merit insofar as it applies to domestic political conditions. Where foreign relations are concerned, however, Jane Addams and her colleagues were well aware of the realities. Women could harbor no illusions about the possibility of influencing the course of the Great War. Few had the vote. They had no diplomatic status. They did not hold high office. Accorded the privilege of a hearing by those in power, they could only appeal to the conscience and reason of statesmen. Having labored in vain to promote mediation, they tried to keep America from becoming embroiled in the war; and when this too proved futile, a handful attempted to resist the worst excesses of the superpatriots.

In the final analysis, their effect on government policies was limited. During the period between 1914 and 1917 they had helped mobilize sentiment against militarization and for keeping America out of the war, but ultimately they could not prevent involvement. Thus many will dismiss them as having failed. However, when we examine the actions of those who held power another perspective emerges. One could say that those who truly failed were the diplomats unable to prevent the outbreak of war, the national leaders who watched the conflict slip out of control while dismissing mediation as a sign of weakness, and the civilian officials who failed to resist the military's demands for recurrent rounds of bloodletting. Captive of their own efforts to arouse hatred of the enemy, these same civilian and military leaders proved in the end incapable of constructing a lasting peace.

Measured against the dismal record of those in power, the actions of Jane Addams and her colleagues are worthy of respect. It is hard to imagine that they could have done worse in fashioning a world different from that which was bequeathed to us in the name of "victory" in World War I.

NOTES

1. Jane Addams, Emily G. Balch, Alice Hamilton, *Women at the Hague: The International Congress of Women and its Results* (1915; reprint edition with a new introduction by Mercedes M. Randall, New York: Garland Publishing, Inc., 1972). It is noteworthy that no French women were present at the conference.

2. Allen F. Davis, *American Heroine: The Life and Legend of Jane Addams* (New York: Oxford University Press, 1973, paperback reprint, 1979), p. 223.

3. Arthur S. Link et al., eds., *The Papers of Woodrow Wilson* (Princeton: Princeton University Press, 1980), pp. 34, 243.

4. Davis, *American Heroine*, pp. 220–21.

5. This account of Addams's early life is based primarily on Davis, *American Heroine*, and John C. Farrell, "Beloved Lady": A History of Jane Addams' Ideas on Reform and Peace," Ph.D. diss., Johns Hopkins University, 1965.

6. Jane Addams, *Twenty Years at Hull House* (1910; New York: The Macmillan Co., 1945), chaps. 5, 7, 8.

7. Farrell, "Beloved Lady," pp. 84–87.

8. Quoted in Davis, *American Heroine*, pp. 64–65.

9. Quoted in ibid., p. 96.

10. Jane Addams, *Newer Ideals of Peace* (New York: Macmillan Co., 1907), chap. 8.

11. Davis, *American Heroine*, pp. 135–39.

12. Ibid., pp. 140–42.

13. Crane to Wilson, July 2, 1915, in Link, *Papers of Woodrow Wilson*, pp. 33, 469.

14. Davis, *American Heroine*, pp. 104–105, chap. 11.

15. C. Roland Marchand, *The American Peace Movement and Social Reform* (Princeton: Princeton University Press, 1972), pp. 182–85.

16. Ibid., pp. 223–29.

17. Farrell, "Beloved Lady," pp. 232–42.

18. Quoted in Davis, *American Heroine*, pp. 224–26.

19. Quoted in ibid., 226–27.

20. Ibid., 228–31.

21. Farrell, "Beloved Lady," pp. 254–60.

22. Bryce to House (private), in Link, *Papers of Woodrow Wilson*, pp. 35, 346–48.

23. Keith Sward, *The Legend of Henry Ford* (1948; reprinted with a new preface by William Greenleaf, New York: Atheneum, 1968), pp. 83–93.

24. Davis, *American Heroine*, pp. 237–40.

25. Ibid., 240.

26. Jane Addams, *Peace and Bread in Time of War* (with an introductory essay by John Dewey, 1945; reprinted with a new introduction by Blanche Wiesen Cook, New York: Garland Publishing Co., 1972), pp. 63–64.

27. Arthur S. Link, *Wilson: Campaigns for Progressivism and Peace, 1916–1917* (Princeton: Princeton University Press, 1965), 5, chap. 5. The fascinating and complex problem of mediation and Wilson's efforts in that direction are also analyzed in David Patterson, "Woodrow Wilson and the Mediation Movement," *Historian* 33 (Aug., 1971): 535–56; and in Blanche Wiesen Cook, "Woodrow Wilson and the Anti-Militarists," (diss., Johns Hopkins University, 1970).

28. Link, *Wilson: Campaigns*, pp. 265–66.

29. Link, *Papers of Woodrow Wilson*, pp. 41, 302–305.

30. Addams, *Peace and Bread*, pp. 63–64.

31. Ibid., pp. 132–33.

32. Donald Johnson, *Challenge to American Freedoms, World War I and the Rise of the American Civil Liberties Union* (Lexington: University of Kentucky Press, 1963).

33. Addams, *Peace and Bread*, p. 133.

34. Ibid., p. 139.

35. Ibid., pp. 120–26.

36. Ibid., pp. 76–80.

37. Ibid.; Davis, *American Heroine*, pp. 248–49.

38. Ibid.; pp. 257–59.

39. Quoted in Farrell, "Beloved Lady," p. 292.

40. Ibid., pp. 292–96.

41. Davis, *American Heroine*, pp. 260–61.

42. Ibid., pp. 260–68; Farrell, "Beloved Lady," pp. 309–12.

43. Davis, *American Heroine*, pp. 270ff.

44. Ibid., p. 286; Carol Gruber, *Mars and Minerva: World War I and the Uses of Higher Learning in America* (Baton Rouge: Louisiana State University Press, 1975).

45. Jill Conway, "Jane Addams: An American Heroine," *Daedalus* 93 (Spring, 1964): 767.

FURTHER READING

There is a substantial literature on the life of Jane Addams and the period covered by this essay. In addition to the works cited in the notes, the reader can consult James Weber Linn, *Jane Addams, A Biography* (New York: D. Appleton Century Co., 1935), written by her nephew. Her later years are recalled in Jane Addams, *The Second Twenty Years at Hull House* (New York: Macmillan, 1930).

A study of her peace ideas as compared to other peace advocates is Sondra Herman, *Eleven Against War, Studies in American Internationalist Thought, 1898–1921* (Stanford: Hoover Institution Press, 1969). A general work on the early years of the settlement house movement is Allen F. Davis, *Spearheads for Reform: The Social Settlements and the Progressive Movement, 1890–1914* (New York: Oxford University Press, 1967).

The peace movement prior to World War I is examined in David S. Patterson, *Toward a Warless World: The Travail of the American Peace Movement, 1887–1914,* (Bloomington: Indiana University Press, 1976); and Michael A. Lutzker, "The Pacifist as Militarist; A Critique of the American Peace Movement, 1898–1914," *Societas, A Review of Social History* 5, no. 2 (Spring, 1975). A study of those who opposed the war is H. C. Peterson and Gilbert C. Fite, *Opponents of War, 1917–1918* (Madison: The University of Wisconsin Press, 1957). Two important works analyzing the peace movement in the wartime and post-World War I eras are Charles Chatfield, *For Peace and Justice: Pacifism in America, 1914–1941* (Boston: Beacon Press, 1971); and Charles DeBenedetti, *Origins of the Modern Peace Movement, 1915–1929* (Millwood, N.Y.: KTO Press, 1978).

LAWRENCE S. WITTNER

Eugene V. Debs

Socialist and War Resister

> As individual wage-slaves you are help-
> less and your condition hopeless. As a
> class, you are the greatest power between
> the earth and the stars.
>
> Eugene V. Debs, 1905[1]

The story of Eugene V. Debs is also the story of millions of Americans whose lives were transformed by the rapid development of industrial capitalism. During the late nineteenth and early twentieth centuries, the rise of giant corporations revolutionized life in the United States. Cycles of economic growth alternated with periods of depression and mass misery. Driven by their lust for higher profits, corporations unscrupulously ground down all who stood in their way. To consumers, they sold shoddy and harmful products. To workers, they behaved like arrogant tyrants—lengthening the work day, slashing wages, exploiting child labor, and condemning millions of Americans to dangerous and brutal working conditions. The owners and managers of these giant business ventures, the new men of wealth, took control of the nation's political parties and governing institutions, turning them into accessories of corporate plunder. Naturally, many Americans keenly resented the growth of economic injustice and plutocracy. Gradually, they organized a powerful counteroffensive—through labor unions, farmers' organizations, reform movements, and radical third parties. No one was more prominent in these efforts than Eugene V. Debs. As a labor leader and, later, as a Socialist, Debs mobilized American working people to demand their rights—on the job and in politics. In place of elite rule, he called for economic and social equality, for the extension of democratic principles to all of American life. Through his uncompromising attack on corporate privilege, Debs became one of the foremost champions of the American working class, building a movement for social justice that has left a deep imprint upon the American political tradition.

Along the way, Debs also emerged as a prominent American peace leader. This role reflected not only his commitment to humanitarian ideals, but his gradual realization that, in the struggle for a just society, violence was self-defeating. In labor-management struggles, it undermined working class morale and participation, just as it created the pretext for ruling class repression. Furthermore, Debs came to the conclusion that international violence—or war—contributed nothing to the welfare of the masses. Quite the contrary, war led logically to their wholesale butchery, to the extension of great power imperialism, and to the destruction of prospects for a just society. Until World War I, Debs focused his energies largely upon securing domestic social change. But the eruption of that world conflict forced him to confront warfare directly. Thereafter, he became one of the most vigorous critics of American intervention. Indeed, through his own courageous opposition to World War I—which led to his dramatic arrest, trial, and imprisonment—Debs became a founder of modern American war resistance.

Eugene V. Debs was the son of Jean Daniel and Marguerite Marie Debs, two French immigrants from Alsace. Settling in Terre Haute, Indiana, during the mid-nineteenth century, when it was little more than a frontier village, they found their first years in the Middle West economically pinched and difficult. Eventually, however, Jean Daniel—whom everyone called Daniel—managed to obtain some measure of economic security by operating a small grocery store. An intelligent and educated man, Daniel was charmed by the works of Eugène Sue and Victor Hugo, two writers whom he believed had charted a course of reason and justice for humanity. Consequently, on November 5, 1855, when Marguerite bore him a son, Daniel named him Eugene Victor Debs.

Raised in a large, generous family in the expanding village of Terre Haute, young Eugene enjoyed a happy childhood. Marguerite was warm and attentive, while Daniel read frequently to the children from the classics of French literature—most notably Voltaire, Alexander Dumas, Sue, and Hugo. In this fashion, Eugene became acquainted with the French Enlightenment and with the republican tradition. Hugo's *Les Misérables,* a story of poverty and injustice, especially moved him, as did the works of Johann Schiller, who applauded the deeds of generous young men in their assault upon ugliness and cruelty.[2]

This rather idyllic childhood came to an abrupt end in May 1870, when Eugene impulsively dropped out of high school to take a job on the nearby railroad. Although both parents urged him to remain in school, Eugene had a romantic view of railroads, and proved irrepressible. Thus, at the age of fourteen, Eugene began his working life far less glamorously than he had imagined: scraping grease from the trucks of freight engines. It was tedious and brutal toil; the potash he used ate into his hands until they were raw and bleeding. When Eugene saved enough money to buy his own scraper, he kept it until the end of his life, a symbol of grinding labor at fifty cents a day. Fortunately, he soon advanced to somewhat less onerous employment—first as a painter of switches and lettering on locomotives and, later, as a locomotive fireman. Railroad employment remained uncertain, however, and in 1874 he was laid off in the midst of a depression. Traveling to East St. Louis, where he found temporary work as a substitute fireman, he came face to face with urban poverty. Shocked, he wrote to his family: "It makes a person's heart ache to go along some of the main sts. . . . and see men, women and children begging for something to eat."[3]

In the following years, his fortunes began to improve. At the urging of his mother, Debs gave up his efforts to regain regular employment as a fireman and, in 1874, at the age of nineteen, returned to Terre Haute. Here he accepted a position as an accounting clerk with a wholesale grocery company. Yet he remained fascinated by railroads. Consequently, in February 1875, when an organizing meeting of the Brotherhood of Locomotive Firemen took place in Terre Haute, Debs enrolled in the organization and became the first secretary of Vigo Lodge. Although a labor union, the Brotherhood was actually a fairly placid organization, which believed in a natural harmony of interests between employer and employee. It opposed strikes and proclaimed as its motto: "Benevolence, Sobriety, and Industry." Debs, however, was not a particularly militant unionist at this time, and this—together with his intelligence, affability, and diligence—led to his rapid advancement within the Brotherhood. By 1880, he had become its secretary-treasurer and editor of the *Locomotive Firemen's Magazine*. Two years later, he was elected city clerk on the Democratic ticket. And in 1884, local voters sent him—again as a Democrat—to the state legislature. Viewed as one of Terre Haute's most eligible bachelors, Debs married Kate Metzel, the daughter of a prosperous local druggist, the following year.[4]

But success was not so easily attained. Taking his seat in the Indiana Assembly, Debs introduced a bill to require railroad corporations to compensate their employees for on-the-job injuries. Thanks to business pressure, the Indiana Senate gutted it. Indeed, so thoroughly was the bill eviscerated in response to corporate demands, that Debs refused to vote for the final version. The Terre Haute legislator happily supported bills to abolish racial distinctions in Indiana laws and to extend suffrage to women, but these were easily defeated by conservative forces. Disgusted by what he had seen, Debs decided not to run for reelection. "I am through with [this] business forever," he told his brother Theodore. Nor was Debs's marriage a happy one. Eager for economic and social advancement, Kate Debs found Eugene shockingly lacking in conventional ambition. Debs spent much of his time traveling from town to town, organizing struggling railway workers and often giving away much of his money. Meanwhile, Kate occupied herself with the management of a rather ostentatious house, built with money from her inheritance. It was a curious marriage, although one that lasted.[5]

As a railway union leader—and in the years to come—Debs enjoyed remarkable personal popularity. This rested less upon spectacular achievements than upon his extraordinary generosity. People noticed that, when traveling with others, Debs carried the heaviest luggage, sat in the aisle seat, and—if confronted by a shortage of food—took the smallest portion. He never seemed to complain about a shabby room or to hurry a waitress. This did not result from any sort of puritan self-denial, for Debs liked nothing better than to stay up late at night drinking, joking, and talking with his friends. Rather, it reflected a basic sympathy for others. Approached constantly on his travels by down-and-out railway workers, Debs invariably emptied his pockets. Once Debs heard that a fireman's promotion was blocked by his lack of a good watch. That was easy enough to remedy, he remarked, and handed the man his own. Indeed, Debs grew so impoverished on his organizing trips that he was sometimes forced to borrow money from his local host to pay his return fare.[6]

A popular union leader, Debs also became a more militant one during the late 1880s, as the ravages of industrial capitalism grew ever more apparent. The corporations "trample upon the divine declaration 'that all men are created equal,'" he wrote in 1888. If "the dollar is to be everything," then the corporation, with its vast capital, "is to rule, and workingmen, with their faces in the dust, are to serve." Only by collective struggle, he reasoned, could workers offset the crushing power of big business. The strike, he concluded, "is the weapon of the oppressed," of people "capable of appreciating justice and having the courage to resist wrong and contend for principle."

Furthermore, Debs increasingly understood that racial, religious, sexual, and ethnic discrimination, by fostering disunity among workers, worked to the advantage of their corporate overlords. Blacks and whites, Catholics, Protestants, Jews, and atheists, men and women, native and foreign born—all workers belonged in unions. Awakened to the realities of class exploitation, Debs sympathized for a time with Samuel Gompers's American Federation of Labor, and then moved beyond it.[7]

Debs was particularly eager to promote labor unity in the railroad industry. Thanks to the division of railway workers into narrow craft Brotherhoods—which, all told, had organized only one-tenth the work force—they were an easy prey for the giant railroad companies. Consequently, Debs labored from 1885 to 1892 to bring the railway Brotherhoods into an industry-wide federation. The top officers of the Brotherhoods, however, anxious to preserve craft autonomy and their own power, sabotaged the effort. Consequently, in September 1892 Debs resigned as secretary-treasurer of the Brotherhood of Locomotive Firemen and announced his intention to establish a new organization—one that would unite all railway workers, regardless of craft. After considerable discussion, Debs and a group of his associates met in Chicago in June 1893 to form the American Railway Union. Here, at last, was the industrial union that Debs and other critics of union conservatism had championed. Would it succeed? In the following months, a headlong rush of firemen, conductors, engineers, and unskilled workers poured into the new organization. Never in American history had a union organizing drive met with such success.[8]

A strike on the Great Northern Railroad, owned by the powerful corporate magnate James J. Hill, provided the first serious test for the ARU. Having convinced the Brotherhoods to accept contracts providing for wage cuts, Hill had every reason to think that he could polish off the industry's isolated upstart. But the ARU strike efforts sparked the immediate solidarity of railroad workers across craft lines. Nor could Debs be intimidated by Hill and his powerful cronies. Called to the office of the governor of Minnesota and browbeaten as an "agitator, foreigner, and anarchist," Debs replied coolly that, unlike the governor, he had never "worn the collar of a plutocrat, nor jumped . . . when he pulled the string." Railway worker unity now sent the Great Northern reeling—first to arbitration and then to an unprecedented defeat. It was a dramatic moment in the history of American labor. Debs recalled that, as his train pulled out of St. Paul, masses of railway workers—their frames "bent with grinding toil"—lined the tracks and lifted their hats in victory. In the weeks after the strike, 2,000 workers joined the ARU every day. By the end of its first year, the new union claimed 150,000 members—far more than all the Brotherhoods combined.[9]

Even as railway workers were developing an unprecedented strength, a new and more dangerous situation was emerging in Pullman, Illinois, a town totally owned and controlled by the Pullman Palace Car Company. Beginning in 1893, George M. Pullman had fired 2,200 of his 5,500 workers and reduced wage rates for the remainder by an average of 33 percent. Rents, water charges, library fees, and grocery bills—all set by Pullman and deducted directly from workers' wages—remained the same, thus reducing worker take-home pay in many instances to no more than a few cents. During the icy winter of 1893–94, as the company increased dividends to stockholders, terrible suffering swept through the company town. Children lacked the shoes and coats to go to school; in some homes, they were kept in bed all day because there was no coal for heat; in others, they were sent to bed early because there was no food for dinner. Although unions were officially banned, by the spring of 1894 most employees had signed up with the ARU. When workers sent a committee to meet with the company vice president and outline their grievances, three members of the committee were summarily fired. On May 11, as word of the firings spread through the Pullman plant, the workers—without exception—put down their tools and walked off the job. The bitter Pullman strike had begun.[10]

Well aware that the ARU was a new, inexperienced union and that the railroad corporations would seize any opportunity to destroy it, Debs performed a delicate balancing act—addressing strike meetings and raising relief funds, while avoiding formal ARU involvement in the strike. But this position simply could not be sustained. When the strike began, Debs rushed to Pullman and was shocked by what he found—not only immense human suffering, but disgraceful working conditions. The company allowed foremen to freely curse and abuse its workers, utilized "speed-up" systems to wring out their last drops of energy, blacklisted employees without compunction, and refused to provide pensions to retired workers, who often ended up in the poorhouse. In June 1894, when the ARU held its first national convention in Chicago, a committee of Pullman strikers arrived to deliver an appeal for assistance. They told the delegates of the situation in Pullman, concluding: "We will make you proud of us, brothers, if you will give us the hand we need. Help us make our country better. . . . Teach arrogant grinders of the faces of the poor that there is still a God of Israel, and if need be a Jehovah—a God of battles."

A showdown soon became inevitable. The sentimental railroaders, deeply moved by stories of human suffering, stampeded toward a boycott of all Pullman cars. Still concerned by the prospect of a bitter and perhaps futile struggle, Debs postponed such action by arranging for an ARU delegation to call on the Pullman company and propose arbitration. On June 16, however, the delegation reported that the company refused to even meet with members of the ARU. Twice more the delegation sought to confer with the company representatives, and twice more it was rebuffed. With no options remaining except surrender, the ARU voted to begin a boycott. According to a plan Debs proposed, railway workers would refuse to switch the sleeping cars. If they were fired for this action, every other ARU worker on the affected trains would immediately walk off the job. On June 26, 1894, the boycott began.[11]

Within days, the Pullman strike erupted into the greatest labor upheaval in American history. The General Managers Association—representing twenty-four railroads with 41,000 miles of track and nearly a billion dollars in capital—stood solidly in Pullman's corner. Anxious to destroy the ARU and eliminate militant unionism in the railroad industry, the Managers moved immediately to fire all strikers and demand federal intervention to smash the ARU. Meanwhile, more than a hundred thousand workers walked off their jobs, shutting down virtually the entire railroad system from Chicago to the West Coast. The corporate press launched a shrill and hysterical attack, charging that Debs was a dictator and personally profiting from the strike, that the ARU was violating countless laws, and that the strikers had become a violent mob. Actually, nothing could be further from the truth. Debs had no use for chaos and destruction, which he realized could only harm labor's cause. At strike headquarters in Chicago, ARU leaders worked around the clock, warning against violence and the obstruction of mail trains, issuing press releases, and sending appeals for aid to unions from New York to San Diego. The hall was packed with determined, excited men—shouting questions, cheering, singing, and spreading the strike to the East Coast. This was no ordinary dispute, Debs announced, but a fundamental struggle "between the producing classes and the money power of the country."12

Corporate leaders and their friends in government understood this as well, and acted accordingly. With the inception of the boycott, the General Managers Association wired U.S. Attorney General Richard Olney, urging him to appoint Edwin Walker as special federal attorney handling the strike. A corporation lawyer for thirty-five years, Olney had been a board member of numerous railroad corporations; indeed, he then sat on the board of one of the companies involved in the Pullman strike. Walker, in turn, was also a corporation lawyer with extensive railroad interests. In fact, he was then serving as the lawyer for the General Managers Association! The attorney general promptly appointed Walker as special federal attorney, instructing him to secure a federal court injunction against the ARU for interfering with the mails and hindering interstate commerce. Accordingly, on July 3 an unprecedented federal court order was issued that—drawing upon the Sherman Antitrust Act as its flimsy pretext—prohibited ARU leaders from communicating with their locals, urging people to join the boycott, and even answering questions. At Olney's insistence, President Grover Cleveland backed this up by dispatching U.S. troops to Chicago. Realizing that compliance with the court order would doom the strike effort, ARU leaders voted to ignore it. Consequently, a week later, federal agents arrested Debs and other ARU leaders, ransacked their offices, and confiscated their records. With the strike tottering toward defeat, Debs offered to end it if the railroads rehired their workers. But the General Managers Association, on the verge of victory, refused. Boxed in by this corporate-government alliance, the strike now collapsed.13

The aftermath was a bitter one. Tried without jury, Debs and the other ARU leaders were found guilty of contempt of court; he received a six month prison term, the others three months. Almost immediately, the government initiated a new trial, this time on the more serious charge of conspiracy. Clarence Darrow, leading the defense efforts, assailed the prosecution, the General Managers Association, Pullman, and corporate-government collusion so effectively that, when the trial was adjourned thanks to a juror's illness, it was never reconvened. The weakness of the government's position was underscored by the report of a commission appointed by President Cleveland to investigate the Pullman strike. The report denounced Pullman's refusal to arbitrate and highlighted the efforts of the railroad corporations to reduce wages and destroy the ARU. The blame for the strike, the commission concluded, "rests with the people themselves and with the government for not adequately controlling monopolies and corporations."

This vindication, however, could provide only meager comfort to Debs and the other ARU leaders, who languished in Woodstock prison, near Chicago, and watched helplessly while the ARU was destroyed. Having surmounted all serious obstacles to their power, the railroad corporations instituted a devastatingly effective blacklist of ARU members and other former strikers. Even many of those who survived the blacklist severed all union connections in a desperate effort to retain their jobs. In the great struggle that Debs had proclaimed, the money power had won.[14]

Imprisoned, during 1895, in Woodstock jail with his fellow union leaders, Debs had the time and motivation to reflect upon labor's defeat. Gradually, it became clear to him that, if corporations controlled the government, the cause of working people was hopeless. But what was the alternative? Only a few years before, Debs had been greatly impressed by Lawrence Gronlund's *The Cooperative Commonwealth* and Edward Bellamy's *Looking Backward*—two books that had made the case for a transition from capitalism to an economy that was democratically managed to serve human needs. Through its pointed critique of corporate power and its demand for democratic control, the Populist Party had also won Debs's sympathies since the early 1890s.

Now, in prison, these thoughts came flooding back, along with some new ones. Victor Berger, the Milwaukee socialist leader, visited Debs in prison and presented him with socialist literature. Keir Hardie, a prominent English trade unionist, also met with Debs for a discussion of socialism. In Europe, the workers were busy forming labor and socialist parties. Why not in America? Still uncertain of his future course, Debs surely realized that it lay in an anticapitalist direction. Released from Woodstock prison on November 22, 1895, he traveled first to Chicago, where he was greeted by a cheering crowd of 100,000 people. American liberty had once meant something, he said, "before corporations knew the price of judges, legislators, and public officials." And it could mean something again, when the people rescued their society from the clutches of "millionaires and corporations."[15]

Committed to cleansing the American government of corporate predators, Debs plunged into the arena of electoral politics. Although he resisted a drive to draft him as the Populist candidate for president in 1896, he did campaign extensively for the Populist–Democratic fusion candidate of that year: William Jennings Bryan. With the Democratic Party's formal repudiation of President Cleveland's "government by injunction" and its support for Bryan's reform campaign, Debs clung to hopes that a political breakthrough might be in the making. However, Bryan's crushing defeat at the hands of the Republicans and their corporate allies convinced Debs that the struggle against plutocracy would be a long and difficult one. For several weeks, Debs pondered the matter. Then, on January 1, 1897, in an open letter to the remaining members of the ARU, he presented his conclusions: "The issue is Socialism versus Capitalism. I am for Socialism because I am for humanity. We have been cursed with the reign of gold long enough. . . . The time has come to regenerate society," to forge an American socialist movement.[16]

In the next few years, Debs worked tirelessly to develop an effective socialist political organization. Five months after his political manifesto to the ARU, Debs called together its last remnants for a convention. They officially dissolved the union and established a new political party: the Social Democracy of America. It supported public ownership of monopolies and utilities, public works projects for the unemployed, a shorter workday, and a curious plan for socialist "colonization" of a Western state. When controversy flared up over the latter idea, Debs broke with the colonizationists and formed the Social Democratic Party of America. Opening a national office in Chicago, the new party was pathetically weak. In the 1898 elections, it drew only 12,000 votes. Gradually, however, it took on national dimensions. Debs brought in his loyalists from the ARU. Victor Berger contributed his expanding social democratic political machine in Milwaukee. In New York, Morris Hillquit, disgusted with the doctrinaire, authoritarian leadership of the small Socialist Labor Party, brought a substantial group of SLP dissidents into an alliance with Debs and Berger. In 1900, they rallied behind Debs's presidential candidacy, garnering 96,000 votes. While small, the socialist movement was gaining momentum. In 1901, meeting in Indianapolis, assorted socialists and radicals were eager to press forward. There were Bellamyites, former Populists, ARU veterans, dissidents from the SLP, Christian socialists, Marxist immigrants, settlement house workers, western miners, and a sprinkling of intellectuals and reformers. Under Debs's leadership, the enthusiastic delegates voted to unite, rose to sing the "Marseillaise," and formed what would become the most important socialist organization in American history: the Socialist Party of America.[17]

Never before or since did an American socialist movement grow the way the Socialist Party did during the following years. In the state and local races of 1902, the Socialists doubled their vote; two years later, when Debs campaigned once more for president, the Socialist vote doubled again, to 402,000. From the start, Socialist Party campaigns were a mixture of "immediate demands"—minimum wages, maximum hours, abolition of child labor, and women's suffrage—and utopian visions. Each reform, the party stressed, led to "the one great end of the cooperative commonwealth." By 1908, when Debs again entered the presidential race, the Socialist Party had become a force to be reckoned with. Hurtling across thirty-three states on a special three-car railway train—dubbed "The Red Special"—Debs spoke from five to twenty times a day for a grueling sixty-five consecutive days. In Billings, Montana, he addressed an open-air crowd of 3,000; in St. Paul, an audience of 6,000; in Chicago, 16,000. Growing rattled, the opposition parties sought to discredit the Socialists by accusing them of attacking the American flag. Debs retorted: "The national flag has been polluted by the plutocracy who have used it to shield themselves in their evil doing." It had "become the flag of predatory wealth, in its exploitation of the working class." Arriving in New York City for a speech at the Hippodrome, Debs found that the ten thousand tickets for the event had been sold out ten days in advance. As he appeared on the stage, fifteen minutes of pandemonium broke loose; the audience wept, laughed, and filled the air with red flags. Even the hostile *New York Times* referred to it as the greatest political meeting in the city's history.[18]

Naturally, the nation's major newspapers—themselves wealthy

corporations—heaped scorn upon Debs and did their best to undermine Socialist electoral prospects. The Detroit *Free Press* ran the
headline:

Debs, In Luxury
Ignores Crowd
Sleeps in Magnificent Palace Car
While Followers Wait
in Vain
Flunkies Guard Leader
From the Common Herd

Of course, the reality was far different. Ernest Poole, the novelist,
recalled accompanying Debs in 1908 through the packed immigrant
ghettos of Manhattan's Lower East Side: "I stood near him for hours
one night on a truck that slowly plowed its way through a roaring
ocean of people as far as the eye could see, all up and down dark
tenement streets." There were "no loudspeakers, no brass bands. The
truck stopped and Debs leaned out with both arms raised, smiling
over the roaring crowd. Stillness came. And then only his voice was
heard—a voice that could do with a crowd what it willed, not because
of the mind behind it, but because of the great warm heart which the
crowd felt speaking there. . . . I listened to him, tingling deep."[19]

By the end of 1908, Debs and his Socialist followers had some
cause for optimism. Although the Socialist vote that year—421,000—
barely surpassed that of 1904, it was garnered despite the strong appeal
to reformers of the Democratic candidate, William Jennings Bryan.
Furthermore, Socialist Party membership had climbed to 41,000
Americans—most of them workers—organized in more than 3,000
locals. Particularly within the labor movement, Socialist influence was
growing to impressive proportions. And in cities and towns across
America, Socialists had established newspapers, built political organizations, and won public office.[20]

As they acquired a modicum of political influence in American
life, Socialists like Debs faced some difficult problems. How, for
example, were they to deal with Christianity, which often seemed to
serve as a brake on social change? Personally, Debs had little use for
organized religion, but he did find its radical elements appealing.

Thus, he sometimes drew upon Christian imagery or invoked the Christ that sought "to destroy class rule and set up the common people as the sole and rightful inheritors of the earth." Even more troublesome was the question of how to relate to organized labor. By the early twentieth century, many Socialists held important positions within the AFL. But Debs despised the increasingly conservative leadership of Samuel Gompers, who had refused the desperate ARU any assistance during the Pullman strike. Moreover, Debs saw little prospect of AFL action to create industrial unions. Therefore, in 1905, Debs helped to establish the militant Industrial Workers of the World. Here, he hoped, was a union movement that would organize the unorganized and, as its leader, Big Bill Haywood promised, "put the working class in possession of the economic power . . . without regard to capitalist masters." Despite Debs's support for the IWW, however, many Socialists continued their efforts within the AFL. A few years later, as the apolitical, anarchist aspects of the IWW came to the fore, Debs himself dropped his membership in the organization.[21]

Racism also posed a challenge to Debs and the Socialist movement. Convinced that Americans of every color would gain from a democratized economy, Debs opposed Socialist Party resolutions that focused upon the unique problems faced by blacks. "We have nothing special to offer the Negro," he insisted; "the Socialist Party is the party of the whole working class, regardless of color." In practice, however, Debs strongly opposed racial prejudice and discrimination. On his lecture tours of Southern states, he repeatedly refused to speak before segregated audiences and chided white labor leaders who excluded blacks from their unions. He publicly attacked Thomas Dixon's popular racist novel, *The Leopard's Spots*, just as he assailed D. W. Griffith's racist movie, *Birth of a Nation*. Although Debs recognized that his positions were far more advanced than those of most Americans, including some Socialists, he refused to compromise. When an anonymous letter warned him that Socialists would "lose more votes than you think" by supporting racial equality, Debs immediately printed the missive in the Socialist press, followed by his own heated reply. The Socialist Party, he wrote, "would be false to its historic mission . . . deny its philosophy, and repudiate its own teachings if, on account of race considerations, it sought to exclude any human being from political and economic freedom."[22]

Debs also staked out an advanced position on the issue of

women's rights. Although inclined toward the nineteenth-century sentimental image of women as purer and nobler than men, Debs always championed women's political and social equality. During his youth in Terre Haute, he insisted upon bringing Susan B. Anthony to that small community, where her advocacy of women's suffrage shocked local townspeople. In 1890, male readers of the *Locomotive Firemen's Magazine* repeatedly complained of stories in its Women's Department which promoted women's equality in politics and in marriage. Defending the editor of that section, Debs indicated that he not only believed she had a perfect right to such views, but that he agreed with them. In 1895, Debs announced that he welcomed equality between husband and wife, thus bringing an end to that "form of slavery." Finally, as a champion of socialism, Debs consistently supported women's suffrage and the development of a women's Socialist press. Although men outnumbered women in the leadership of the Socialist Party, many strong-minded, outspoken women did become popular party speakers and officials.[23]

If the Socialist Party underwent little internal upheaval over questions of racial and sexual equality, the issue of violence in the class struggle proved far more divisive. By 1912, Debs was sharply critical of Big Bill Haywood's emphasis upon "sabotage" and "direct action." Assailing them as "the tactics of anarchist individuals and not Socialist collectivists," Debs claimed that they played "into the hands of the enemy," for conspiracy "cannot make for solidarity." Violence would "never appeal to any considerable number" of American workers "while they have the ballot and the right of industrial and political organization." In 1912, the Socialist Party convention passed an amendment to the party's constitution making opposition to "political action" or advocacy of "sabotage of other methods of violence" grounds for expulsion. Fighting back, Haywood staunchly defended sabotage and "revolutionary action." Eventually, party members voted to expel Haywood from the Socialist Party's national executive committee, and thousands of party militants resigned in protest.[24] Debs and the Socialists, however, had clarified their position: the struggle for socialism in America would be a democratic one, waged through union solidarity in the economic realm and Socialist votes in the political.

And by 1912, all signs pointed toward further Socialist advance. Easily renominated by his party, Debs plunged into yet another campaign for president, addressing large, enthusiastic audiences. In speech after speech, his evangelical fervor set crowds ablaze. His long, angular body pulsed with energy; his blue eyes burned like flames; his arms reached out to embrace his listeners. Eighteen thousand persons crowded into Philadelphia's Convention Hall to hear him. Another 22,000 packed New York City's Madison Square Garden. Hundreds of girls—attired in white dresses with red sashes—moved through the tumultuous crowds, selling Socialist literature and red flags. As John Dos Passos noted, Debs encouraged workers to "want the world he wanted, a world . . . where everybody would split even." In the Southwest, his revivalistic zeal appealed deeply to tenant farmers and miners. In the Middle West, he captured the hearts of Polish- and German-Americans. In the East, Jewish garment workers plastered their walls with his picture. Recalling this phenomenon, the general manager of *The Forward*, New York City's Yiddish Socialist newspaper, stated: "Debs was the liberator, the first who had come from the ranks of the American workers, holding out his hand and saying, 'I am your brother.' "[25]

The election results confirmed the progress of the fledgling Socialist Party. In the 1912 Presidential campaign, Debs drew 901,000 votes—six percent of the nationwide total. Furthermore, this Socialist outpouring occurred against the backdrop of competing reform campaigns waged by Theodore Roosevelt and Woodrow Wilson. Socialist Party membership had also climbed to a new peak: 118,000 Americans. Like the Labour Party of Great Britain, the Socialist Party of America seemed on the road to power. Socialists held 1,200 offices in 340 American cities, including 79 mayors in 24 states. From Schenectady, New York, to Berkeley, California, from Reading, Pennsylvania, to Butte, Montana, Socialist administrations took office and implemented important urban reforms. Municipal ownership of utilities and transportation facilities; health and safety regulations; increased social, cultural, and recreational services; a sympathetic attitude toward unions; improved sanitation; an end to corruption—all provided for unspectacular but substantial changes in the lives of American working people. New possibilities were also emerging on the national level. In 1910, Milwaukee voters elected Victor Berger to Congress; a few years later, he was followed there by a second Socialist, Meyer London of New York.[26]

Nor was the new influence of socialism confined to government.

In 1912, the Socialist Party claimed 323 English and foreign language publications with a total circulation in excess of two million. The largest of them, the folksy and inexpensive *Appeal to Reason,* had a weekly circulation of 762,000, reaching into the poorest of tenant farmer homes. Within the unions, Socialists provided a major challenge to Gompers's staid leadership of the AFL. On the nation's campuses, an Intercollegiate Socialist Society—renamed the League for Industrial Democracy—had considerable impact upon students and faculty. Within the religious community, a Christian Socialist Fellowship, sparked by Harry F. Ward and Walter Rauschenbusch, made the case for the Kingdom of God on earth. Prominent intellectuals gravitated toward the Socialist Party, among them Sherwood Anderson, Walter Lippmann, Lincoln Steffens, John Reed, and Max Eastman. Two of their number—Upton Sinclair and Jack London— actually became best-selling novelists, providing devastating indictments of capitalism read by large numbers of Americans.[27]

Even as the Socialists extended their influence in American life, a cataclysm loomed that would dramatically alter the situation: the World War. In previous years, Debs rarely dealt with international affairs; but when he did, he invariably condemned wars, placing them within the framework of class exploitation. During the Spanish-American War of 1898, he declared that many Americans "realize that war is national murder, that the poor furnish the victims, and that . . . the effect is always the same upon the toiling class." When U.S. troops began their bloody suppression of the Filipino independence struggle, Debs told a trade union audience: "We are making a market over there in the Orient for the products of half-paid labor in this country; making a market by the force of arms and at the expense of the lives of a people whose only offense has been their love of freedom." The Wilson administration's growing military entanglement in Mexican affairs also aroused the Socialist leader's ire. "It is one thing . . . to fight for your country and another thing to fight for Rockefeller's oil derricks," he stated. To no one's surprise, then, Debs issued a stinging indictment of the World War that erupted in Europe during August 1914. The ruling class in every country, he said, had the same goal: "to extend . . . their exploitation, to increase their capacity for robbery, and to multiply their ill-gotten riches." Echoing Debs's call for U.S. neutrality, the Socialist Party issued a manifesto declaring its "opposition to this and all other wars."[28]

In the following years, as the United States drifted toward the brink of intervention, Debs and the vast bulk of his Socialist followers remained true to this position. Barnstorming across the country, the Socialist leader spoke out against the war on every possible occasion. In 1916, however, Debs had turned sixty years of age, and his health, always fragile thanks to his tireless activism, grew markedly worse. Therefore, he avoided a campaign for president that year, and happily supported the Socialist Party's nomination of Allen Benson, a journalist, for that task. Moved by appeals from his supporters, though, Debs did agree to run for Congress from his home district in Indiana. Benson waged an antipreparedness campaign, as did Debs. Indeed, the Socialist Party's 1916 platform maintained that "the competitive nature of capitalism is the cause of modern war," and that disarmament was "essential to an assured and permanent peace." The issue, Debs contended, "is socialism against capitalism, imperialism, and militarism." Actually, the election situation was far more complex—or at least confused. President Wilson also campaigned as the candidate of peace and progressivism, and many normally Socialist voters went over to the Democrats that year. Thus, the Socialist presidential vote dropped for the first time. Furthermore, in some localities, Democratic-Republican fusion tickets ousted Socialists from office. Nevertheless, Debs came in second in his race—trailing the Republican, but leading the Democrat.[29]

Although few people were aware of it, 1916 was also the year that Eugene V. Debs fell in love. The object of his affection was a Terre Haute resident with whom he had been friendly for some years: Mabel Curry. A vigorous activist for women's suffrage, Curry was a strong, intelligent, good-natured woman with a husband and three children. Debs, too, remained unhappily married, but that failed to prevent the flowering of their relationship. "You seem always to have been in my heart and my life," Debs wrote to her. I "love you with the tenderest regard, and deepest reverence, and all the passionate devotion man can have for the rarest, loveliest, and most beautiful of souls. I am reaching for you this morning, my precious love, with both arms and all my heart." Debs and Curry both considered divorce, but decided against it, apparently because of the difficulties it would cause their families. Thus, their relationship continued largely unnoticed, limited by the demands of propriety and, later, by the crisis brought about in their lives by the World War.[30]

In 1917, the storm of war broke over the nation and its hapless Socialist minority. Having won reelection as a man of peace in late 1916, Woodrow Wilson led the nation into the World War the following spring. Although much of the country was soon swept up in superpatriotic hysteria, the Socialist Party was not. In this respect, it differed from most of its Socialist and Labor Party counterparts in Europe, which—overwhelmed by nationalism—supported the war efforts of their own countries. On April 7, 1917, the day after the Congressional declaration of war, the Socialist Party of America held an emergency convention in St. Louis, Missouri, and took its stand. Reaffirming their "allegiance to the principle of internationalism and working class solidarity the world over," the delegates proclaimed their "unalterable opposition to the war," which they labeled "a crime against the people of the United States and against the nations of the world." When the convention submitted this statement to party members in a nationwide referendum, they approved it by an overwhelming vote.[31]

At first, the Socialist Party's lonely stand against the war actually seemed to augment its popularity. Although a few important writers and some prominent AFL leaders abandoned the Socialists, many new recruits—particularly from immigrant communities—flocked to the party, increasing its membership. And in the fall elections of 1917, the Socialists garnered unprecedented support in crucial urban centers. The Socialist Party's vote in Chicago rose to 34 percent, in Toledo to 35 percent, in Buffalo to 25 percent, in Cleveland to 20 percent. In fifteen cities of the Northeast, the Socialists averaged nearly 22 percent of the vote! In the nation's largest city, New York, Socialists elected ten state assemblymen, seven aldermen, and a municipal judge. Debs wrote proudly in an editorial: "The Socialist Party is rising to power."[32]

But such signs of party strength were short lived. Within a relatively brief time, fierce government repression and vigilante action smashed the laboriously built Socialist organization. Drawing upon the Espionage Act—a loosely written law prohibiting any obstruction of the war effort—the federal government began the prosecution of numerous Socialist leaders. Many were convicted, usually for speeches or writings critical of the war, and sentenced to lengthy prison terms. Meanwhile, the postmaster general banned virtually every Socialist newspaper, magazine, or other publication from the mails, wrecking the party press. Congressman Victor Berger, convicted under the Espionage Act, was expelled from the House of Representatives, reelected by the voters, and then expelled again. The New York State legislature ejected five elected Socialist members. Socialist Party headquarters in Indiana and Ohio were raided, a party convention in Mitchell, South Dakota, was broken up by force, and the Socialist Party's national office was seized and occupied for three days by government agents. Indeed, federal agents made raids upon Socialist and IWW offices around the country, carting off their records and sending thousands of Socialists and other radicals to prison. In communities throughout the nation, vigilante mobs terrorized Socialists and other suspected critics of the war—wrecking their meeting places and homes, burning their books, and occasionally lynching them.[33]

Outraged by the nationwide assault upon civil liberties, Debs was determined to act. Although sick and ailing during early 1918, he could no longer postpone a personal foray against militarism and repression. The government would either have to arrest him or open the prison gates. With the Socialist press practically extinguished by government action, Debs took to the lecture platform that June, barnstorming across the Middle West. For a time, federal authorities hesitated to arrest the famed Socialist leader. But this drove Debs all the harder. On June 16, he appeared at an outdoor rally of about a thousand people in Canton, Ohio, not far from the jail where two Socialist Party leaders had recently been hung by their wrists from a prison rafter. "It is extremely dangerous to exercise the constitutional right of free speech," Debs told his listeners, as federal agents circulated conspicuously through the crowd. For two hours, he delivered a blistering indictment of government policy. Only once, and then rather vaguely, did Debs turn to the World War, but his meaning was unmistakable: "The master class has always declared the wars; the subject class has always fought the battles. The master class has had all to gain and nothing to lose, while the subject class has had nothing to gain and all to lose."[34]

That was enough for federal authorities. A government agent had written down Debs's words in Canton, and thirteen days later a federal grand jury indicted the Socialist leader for violating the Espionage Act. At his trial, Debs freely conceded his guilt. "I have been accused of having obstructed the war," he stated. "I admit it. Gentlemen, I abhor war." He was doing "what little" he could to eliminate it by working to "establish in this country an industrial and social democracy." Facing a possible sixty-year prison sentence, the aging Socialist leader refused to flinch. "Your Honor," he said, "years ago I recognized my kinship with all living things, and I made up my mind that I was not one bit better than the meanest of the earth. . . . While there is a lower class, I am in it; while there is a criminal element, I am of it; while there is a soul in prison, I am not free."

Speaking without notes in the hushed courtroom, the Socialist leader grew ever more eloquent as he neared the conclusion of his statement. "I am thinking this morning of the men in the mills and factories," he said. "I am thinking of the women who, for a paltry wage, are compelled to work out their lives; of the little children who . . . are robbed of their childhood, and in the early, tender years, are seized in the remorseless grasp of Mammon, and forced into the industrial dungeons." They lived with "their hopes blasted, because in this high noon of our twentieth century civilization, money is still so much more important than human life." In the silent courtroom, it was a luminous, indelible moment. "I never more clearly comprehended than now," he said, "the great struggle between the powers of greed on the one hand and upon the other the rising hosts of freedom."35

To the shock and dismay of many Americans, Debs received a ten-year prison sentence. In April 1919, he began serving it at the Moundsville, West Virginia, federal prison. Soon thereafter, however, he was transferred—at Justice Department orders—to the maximum security penitentiary in Atlanta, Georgia. Debs worked in the prison warehouse and, for fifteen hours a day, was confined with five other men to a small, stiflingly hot Southern jail cell. The food was so unpalatable that he barely managed to eat. Reports began to filter out of prison that the sixty-three-year-old Socialist leader was near death, with a combination of heart ailments, lumbago, blinding headaches, and kidney trouble. Gradually, however, Debs's health improved somewhat, although Atlanta's maximum security restrictions weighed heavily upon him. Visiting privileges were limited, while Debs's letters—restricted to a single sheet of paper per week—could be written only to an authorized group of family members. Nor could Debs retain the flood of mail sent to him. Some months later, in a particularly vindictive act, the Wilson administration totally cut off

Debs's mail and visiting privileges, leaving him *incommunicado*. Throughout his prison term, Debs was isolated even further from the Socialist movement by being denied all access to Socialist literature.[36]

As in earlier days, Debs quickly won the affection of his associates. Ambling about the yard of the Atlanta penitentiary, the tall, lanky prisoner number 9653 would be surrounded by crowds of wretched inmates, all eager to tell him their stories and problems. Here, too, his generosity deeply impressed others. From his admirers in the outside world, Debs received copious quantities of tobacco, most of which he gave away to his fellow inmates. When even this supply proved insufficient to meet the needs of the prison population, he stopped smoking himself, thus enabling him to distribute it all. Among his Socialist comrades on the outside, Debs had frequently been called a "poet" and a "lover of mankind." To the prisoners in Atlanta, he was simply known as "Little Jesus."[37]

While Debs was in prison, the Socialist Party continued to disintegrate. Still reeling from the government crackdown, it suffered a disastrous internal schism in 1919. The left wing of the party, inspired by the Bolshevik revolution, demanded a "revolutionary" strategy. Bolstered by the Socialist Party's new foreign language federations, the left sought to seize control of the party apparatus and reshape it along "Bolshevik" lines. Meanwhile, the party's moderate forces, led by Berger and Hillquit, fought frantically to avert this. By late 1919, the moderates had won undisputed control of the Socialist Party, but only at the expense of the departure of virtually the entire left wing. The latter immediately formed two competing Communist organizations, whose leaders raced to Moscow to secure recognition from the new Communist International. Although Debs had initially welcomed the Bolshevik revolution—which seemed to herald the end of the war and the creation of a socialist society—the authoritarian practices of the Bolshevik government repelled him, as did this latest turn of events. He now argued that, while certainly sincere, the Communists were "mistaken in their tactics," and would "discover that the Socialist Party is best adapted for emancipating the American working class." In late 1920, he was even sharper in his strictures. "The Moscow program would commit us to a policy of armed insurrection," he said. "It is outrageous, autocratic, ridiculous." Meanwhile, with a fine impartiality, U.S. Attorney General A. Mitchell Palmer launched a new series of nationwide raids upon Communist, Socialist, anarchist and other radical organizations, further decimating and demoralizing their memberships.[38]

In an effort to reunite the splintered Socialist Party, its leaders convinced Debs to make another run for president in 1920. Confined to the Atlanta penitentiary and with his party in shambles, the aging Socialist leader could hardly wage as effective a campaign as in past years. Indeed, Debs—the first convict to ever seek the American presidency—was allowed no more than a weekly press release by prison authorities. Even so, the campaign of prisoner 9653 provided a powerful protest against political repression—a reminder to the nation of the disgraceful civil-liberties record of the Wilson administration and of the severe burdens under which Socialists labored. Thus, despite Debs's imprisonment, the devastating Palmer raids, the anti-radical preachments of politicians and the mass media, and the disintegration of the Socialist Party, Debs garnered 923,000 votes in 1920—a smaller percentage of the overall total (enhanced by women's suffrage) than he had drawn in 1912, but the largest vote ever polled by an American Socialist.[39]

The 1920 presidential campaign also heightened pressures for Debs's release from prison. Pointing out that the sixty-five-year-old Socialist leader was in poor health and could well embarrass the administration by dying behind bars, Attorney General Palmer had recommended to President Wilson that Debs's sentence be commuted to expire in February 1921. Wilson had denied this recommendation, commenting: "This man was a traitor to his country and will never be pardoned during my administration." During the 1920 presidential campaign, however, the Republican candidate, Warren G. Harding, had stated his belief in an amnesty for political prisoners. Therefore, with Harding's election, numerous prominent Americans, including many labor leaders, pressed him to pardon Debs. Assigned to review the Debs case, Attorney General Harry Daugherty ordered that Debs be placed on a train—alone and unguarded—for a visit to Washington. The attorney general talked with Debs for a good part of a day, later reporting to Clarence Darrow: "I never met a man I liked better." In the ensuing months, Debs's supporters picketed the White House and presented petitions calling for his freedom, signed by 300,000 Americans and endorsed by 700 organizations. Finally, on December 23, 1921, the White House announced that Debs and twenty-three other political prisoners would be freed on Christmas day.[40]

After nearly three grueling years in prison, Debs was returning home. Recognizing the esteem of the inmates for the Socialist leader, Atlanta's warden suspended all prison rules, and 2,300 convicts crowded against the front wall of the penitentiary. As Debs tearfully embraced his brother Theodore and other Socialist comrades at the gates, an emotional rumbling burst from the assembled inmates. And when Debs started down a path to their parked car, a great roar of love and pain shook the prison. With tears streaming down his face, Debs turned and stretched out his arms to the tumultuous prisoners. Twice more he sought to leave, only to evoke the same outpouring of affection and respect. At last, shaken, Debs made his departure.[41]

The rest was relatively easy. On his way to the train depot, Debs removed from his wallet the five-dollar bill prison authorities had given him and dispatched it to the defense committee for two imprisoned anarchists, Nicola Sacco and Bartolomeo Vanzetti. Then it was on to Washington, to meet with President Harding. When Debs entered the president's office, the jovial Harding bounded from his chair and gave the released convict a hearty handshake. "Well," said the president, "I have heard so damned much about you, Mr. Debs, that I am now very glad to meet you." From Washington, Debs caught the train to Terre Haute. Here he was greeted by a wild, cheering crowd of 25,000. Lifting him off his feet, they transported him, at last, to the front steps of his home.[42]

During his final years, Debs worked valiantly to rebuild the shattered American Socialist movement. For a time, he tried to steer clear of disputes with the Communists, but this proved impossible. Even during his prison term, they had denounced him for rejecting "the hand which Lenin extended." In turn, Debs differed sharply with the Communists over their belief in the likelihood of revolution, the value of affiliation with the Communist International, and the need for a workers' dictatorship. Eventually, he announced that he did not agree with the Communists on "anything except their right to free speech and other civil rights." Meanwhile, in the hope that Robert LaFollette's 1924 Progressive Party campaign would lead to the formation of a genuine labor party, Debs and the Socialists joined unions and other reform groups in endorsing his candidacy for president. Soon after the election, however, the Progressive Party dissolved. Moreover, although LaFollette drew almost 5 million votes, only 900,000 of them appeared on the Socialist line. Thus, the 1924 election confirmed the continued erosion of Socialist strength. Debs, however, remained feisty and determined. On January 2, 1926, in a new Socialist Party newspaper, he wrote a strong statement of support for striking coal miners, a plea for Sacco and Vanzetti, and an attack upon the Treaty of Versailles. "The word of the imperial masters is not good," he argued. "Their treaties are worthless. They lie to each other and they lie to the world to perpetuate their own vicious and debasing misrule. Down with capitalism, imperialism, and militarism."[43]

Ultimately, only death could silence him. On October 15, 1926, while convalescing at Chicago's Lindlahr Sanitarium, Debs suffered a massive heart attack. Four days later, flanked by his brother Theodore and his sister Emma, he died in his bed. The two siblings accompanied their brother's body to Terre Haute, where they were met by the president of the Central Labor Union that Debs had helped organize years earlier. Gently, the labor leader pressed for a final sacrifice—one they could not refuse: "You will have to give him to us for a while. . . . You know he belongs to us." For the next day, Debs's body lay in state at the Terre Haute Labor Temple. As thousands of workers filed by, their roughened hands thrust awkwardly in their pockets or pressing handkerchiefs against their reddened eyes, they provided an appropriate final tribute to this unrelenting champion of America's working people.[44]

Today, more than a half century after the death of Eugene V. Debs, it is certainly time to ask some hard questions about his life and its purpose. Most Americans would probably grant his courage, generosity, and ability. Many would admire his goals. Even so, some might be inclined to ask: Was Debs not really a failure? After all, the American Railway Union collapsed, the Socialist Party crumbled to insignificance, and his presidential campaigns went down to defeat. At least on the surface, this is not a record of success—particularly when combined with a couple of stiff prison terms.

But to dismiss Debs's life in this fashion is to miss the impressive elements of personal success. Throughout his long and active career, Debs thrived on the struggle for justice. How else can one explain his enormous energy and consistency, right up to his death? Unlike many of his contemporaries, Debs was never bored, disillusioned, or alienated from his work. To the contrary, he had that remarkable strength found in people who act in harmony with their beliefs. Furthermore, through his efforts to improve the lives of people around him, Debs inspired a popular affection that clearly nurtured him, in good times and bad. Thus, by embarking upon meaningful activity, Debs built for himself an extraordinarily rich and happy life.

Furthermore, despite appearances, Debs's efforts were remarkably successful. During his lifetime, or in the decades thereafter, American workers—inspired in part by Debs and the Socialists—did organize industrial unions; they did roll back the absolute power of the corporations; they did fight for and win a host of major economic reforms: minimum wages, maximum hours, unemployment insurance, the abolition of child labor, collective bargaining rights, health and safety regulations, worker's compensation, and publicly funded services that ranged from education, to health care, to adequate food, to job retraining, to day care. Nor should the pioneering nature of Debs's work be discounted in other areas—the crusade for racial justice, the fight for women's rights, and the battle for civil liberties. Of course, Debs proved incorrect in his assumption that the Socialist Party would serve as the primary instrument through which a better society would be fashioned. Instead, many a Socialist idea, having attained some measure of popularity, became incorporated into the program of the Democratic Party and, later, enacted into law. Not surprisingly, the Socialist constituency eventually gravitated toward that party's reform wing. But, in retrospect, it seems clear that Debs and the Socialists blazed the trail in the struggle for a just society.

Similarly, Debs helped forge the tradition of modern American war resistance. Although beginning as a domestic reformer, he eventually developed a trenchant class analysis of warfare and a model of unflinching resistance to it that contributed substantially to the growth of the twentieth-century American peace movement. Furthermore, unlike many Americans on the Right or the Bolsheviks on the Left, Debs had a staunch faith in democratic potentialities. Indeed, his appeal to American workers was based upon his assumption—now widely shared among peace activists—that the intelligence and decency of ordinary people constitute the surest foundations for world peace. Of all the legacies of Eugene V. Debs, this may be the most valuable.

NOTES

1. Ray Ginger, *Eugene V. Debs: A Biography* (New York: Collier Books, 1966), p. 258.

2. Ibid., pp. 18–20, 28; Nick Salvatore, *Eugene V. Debs: Citizen and Socialist* (Urbana: University of Illinois Press, 1982), pp. 10, 12.

3. Salvatore, *Eugene V. Debs*, pp. 17–18; H. Wayne Morgan, *Eugene V. Debs: Socialist for President* (Syracuse: Syracuse University Press, 1962), pp. 2–3.

4. Ginger, *Eugene V. Debs*, pp. 35–36, 49–50.

5. Sidney Lens, *Radicalism in America* (New York: Thomas Y. Crowell Company, 1969), p. 198; Salvatore, *Eugene V. Debs*, pp. 42–43, 53.

6. Ginger, *Eugene V. Debs*, pp. 96–97.

7. Ibid., p. 82; Salvatore, *Eugene V. Debs*, pp. 59–60, 81, 102, 106.

8. Ginger, *Eugene V. Debs*, pp. 105–107, 111–13; Morgan, *Eugene V. Debs*, pp. 5–6.

9. Salvatore, *Eugene V. Debs*, pp. 114–15, 121–25; Lens, *Radicalism in America*, p. 197.

10. Almont Lindsey, *The Pullman Strike* (Chicago: University of Chicago Press, 1964), pp. 19–105; Ginger, *Eugene V. Debs*, pp. 123–26.

11. Lindsey, *The Pullman Strike*, pp. 124–31; Ginger, *Eugene V. Debs*, pp. 126–35; Salvatore, *Eugene V. Debs*, pp. 128–29.

12. Lindsey, *The Pullman Strike*, pp. 132–44, 308–18; Ginger, *Eugene V. Debs*, pp. 136–43.

13. Salvatore, *Eugene V. Debs*, pp. 130–32, 135; Lindsey, *The Pullman Strike*, pp. 147–75, 203–70; Ginger, *Eugene V. Debs*, pp. 141, 145–67.

14. Salvatore, *Eugene V. Debs*, pp. 137–38; Ginger, *Eugene V. Debs*, pp. 171–72; Lindsey, *The Pullman Strike*, pp. 274–304.

15. Ginger, *Eugene V. Debs*, pp. 86, 189–97. Debs's address in Chicago is reprinted in Stephen M. Reynolds, ed., *Debs: His Life, Writings and Speeches* (Chicago: Charles H. Kerr and Company, 1908), pp. 327–44.

16. Lens, *Radicalism in America*, pp. 206–207; Salvatore, *Eugene V. Debs*, pp. 157–62.

17. Howard H. Quint, *The Forging of American Socialism: Origins of the Modern Movement* (Columbia: University of South Carolina Press, 1953), pp. 319–88; Lens, *Radicalism in America*, pp. 207–10; Morgan, *Eugene V. Debs*, pp. 17–57.

18. Milton Cantor, *The Divided Left: American Radicalism, 1900–1975* (New York: Hill and Wang, 1978), pp. 26–27; Ginger, *Eugene V. Debs*, pp. 248–49, 279, 285–86, 295–301; Morgan, *Eugene V. Debs*, pp. 59–113.

19. Ginger, *Eugene V. Debs*, pp. 297, 299.

20. Salvatore, *Eugene V. Debs*, pp. 220–21; David A. Shannon, *The Socialist Party of America* (New York: The Macmillan Company, 1955), pp. 4–5.

21. Salvatore, *Eugene V. Debs*, pp. 206, 311–12; Ginger, *Eugene V. Debs*, pp. 253–61, 272–73; Reynolds, ed., *Debs*, pp. 119–41.

22. Morgan, *Eugene V. Debs*, pp. 77–78; Ginger, *Eugene V. Debs*, pp. 276–77; Salvatore, *Eugene V. Debs*, pp. 226–27.

23. Ginger, *Eugene V. Debs*, p. 41; Salvatore, *Eugene V. Debs*, pp. 103, 215.

24. Cantor, *The Divided Left*, p. 41; Salvatore, *Eugene V. Debs*, 254–56; Shannon, *The Socialist Party*, pp. 70–73, 77–79.

25. Morgan, *Eugene V. Debs*, pp. 123–38; Salvatore, *Eugene V. Debs*, pp. 225, 231–33; John P. Diggins, *The American Left in the Twentieth Century* (New York: Harcourt Brace Jovanovich, 1973), p. 64.

26. James Weinstein, *The Decline of Socialism in America* (New York: Monthly Review Press, 1967), pp. 93, 103; Salvatore, *Eugene V. Debs*, p. 242.

27. Weinstein, *The Decline of Socialism,* pp. 84–85; Lens, *Radicalism in America,* pp. 210–11.

28. Ginger, *Eugene V. Debs,* pp. 219, 342–46; Shannon, *The Socialist Party,* pp. 81–82.

29. Ginger, *Eugene V. Debs,* pp. 346, 352–56; Cantor, *The Divided Left,* pp. 32–33, 52, 57.

30. Salvatore, *Eugene V. Debs,* pp. 277–80.

31. Shannon, *The Socialist Party,* pp. 93–98; Ginger, *Eugene V. Debs,* pp. 359–60; Cantor, *The Divided Left,* pp. 58–59.

32. Shannon, *The Socialist Party,* pp. 99–105; Lens, *Radicalism in America,* p. 211; Weinstein, *The Decline of Socialism,* pp. 145–59, 173–76.

33. H. C. Peterson and Gilbert C. Fite, *Opponents of War, 1917–1918* (Seattle: University of Washington Press, 1968), pp. 43–247; William Preston, Jr., *Aliens and Dissenters: Federal Suppression of Radicals, 1903–1933* (New York: Harper & Row, 1966), pp. 88–207; Shannon, *The Socialist Party,* pp. 108–14.

34. Ginger, *Eugene V. Debs,* pp. 370–77; Salvatore, *Eugene V. Debs,* pp. 291–93.

35. Ginger, *Eugene V. Debs,* pp. 377–79, 393–94; Peterson and Fite, *Opponents of War,* pp. 251–54.

36. Ginger, *Eugene V. Debs,* pp. 412–13; Salvatore, *Eugene V. Debs,* pp. 309–10, 316

37. Ginger, *Eugene V. Debs,* p. 411; Diggins, *The American Left,* p. 65.

38. Shannon, *The Socialist Party,* pp. 126–49; Weinstein, *The Decline of Socialism,* pp. 177–233; Salvatore, *Eugene V. Debs,* p. 324; Preston, *Aliens and Dissenters,* pp. 208–37.

39. Eugene V. Debs, *Walls and Bars* (Chicago: Charles H. Kerr Company, 1973), pp. 137–46; Morgan, *Eugene V. Debs,* pp. 169–90.

40. Ginger, *Eugene V. Debs,* pp. 425–28, 434; Peterson and Fite, *Opponents of War,* pp. 273–79.

41. Debs, *Walls and Bars,* pp. 159–64; Salvatore, *Eugene V. Debs,* p. 328.

42. Salvatore, *Eugene V. Debs,* pp. 328–29; Ginger, *Eugene V. Debs,* p. 436.

43. Salvatore, *Eugene V. Debs,* pp. 329–37; Ginger, *Eugene V. Debs,* pp. 458, 468–71, 476.

44. Salvatore, *Eugene V. Debs,* p. 341.

FURTHER READING

There is no thoroughly satisfactory biography of Debs, but the two best are Ray Ginger's very sympathetic *Eugene V. Debs: A Biography* (New York: Collier Books, 1966) and Nick Salvatore's quite critical *Eugene V. Debs: Citizen and Socialist* (Urbana: University of Illinois Press, 1982). H. Wayne Morgan's *Eugene V. Debs: Socialist for President* (Syracuse, N.Y.: Syracuse University Press, 1962) is also helpful, although limited by its focus upon presidential campaigns. Unfortunately, Stephen M. Reynolds (ed.), *Debs: His Life, Writings and Speeches* (Chicago: Charles H. Kerr and Company, 1908) is quite dated; it does, however, contain some interesting documents.

Almont Lindsey's *The Pullman Strike* (Chicago: University of Chicago Press, 1964) provides a solid study of that crucial labor upheaval, while three books are vital for understanding the history of the Socialist Party: Howard H. Quint, *The Forging of American Socialism: Origins of the Modern Movement* (Columbia: University of South Carolina Press, 1953); David A. Shannon, *The Socialist Party of America* (New York: Macmillan Company, 1955); and James Weinstein, *The Decline of Socialism in America, 1912–1925* (New York: Monthly Review Press, 1967). Other writings which cast light upon Debs and the Socialists include: Milton Cantor, *The Divided Left: American Radicalism, 1900–1975* (New York: Hill and Wang, 1978); John P. Diggins, *The American Left in the Twentieth Century* (New York: Harcourt Brace Jovanovich, 1973); Bernard Johnpoll, *The Impossible Dream: The Rise and Demise of the American Left* (Westport, Conn.: Greenwood Press, 1981); Christopher Lasch, *The Agony of the American Left* (New York: Random House, 1969); and Sidney Lens, *Radicalism in America* (New York: Thomas Y. Crowell Company, 1969).

The federal government's suppression of the Socialists and other wartime dissidents is treated thoroughly in: H. C. Peterson and Gilbert C. Fite, *Opponents of War, 1917–1918* (Seattle: University of Washington Press, 1968); William Preston, Jr., *Aliens and Dissenters: Federal Suppression of Radicals, 1903–1933* (New York: Harper & Row, 1966); and Eugene Debs's own *Walls and Bars* (Chicago: Charles H. Kerr Company, 1973).

CHARLES CHATFIELD

Norman Thomas

Harmony of Word and Deed

Norman Mattoon Thomas was the thirty-year-old pastor of a Presbyterian church and an immigrant parish in East Harlem, New York, when, in the summer of 1914, Europe went to war. An undertow of violence soon pulled even the United States into the maelstrom. The war swept Thomas out of the mainstream of progressive reform and into a career, unique in American annals, as "the nation's conscience."[1] In the twenties he revived the moribund Socialist party, only to preside over its demise in the following decade. Six times he ran as its presidential candidate. As the party disintegrated, it became increasingly clear that Norman Thomas had achieved a stature altogether his own.

He remained vigorously independent but never aloof from politics, a discriminating visionary widely respected even by those who disagreed with him. He granted that political leaders must respond to the shifting currents of power, but he insisted that they must fix direction by reference to some points of principle. Until his death at eighty-four, he sought to harmonize power and principle in national life. Beginning with a radically consistent peace ethic in World War I, Thomas developed a sophisticated interpretation of peace in relation to social change and justice in domestic and world affairs.

The Education of a Progressive

Not even Norman Thomas could have anticipated this career in 1914, for he seemed to have fit nicely into the pattern of reform carved out by progressives in church life and urban affairs. The concentration of industrial and political power and of urban population in the last quarter of the nineteenth century had led to social conditions alien to an earlier agrarian and commercial America. From a widespread reassessment of values and institutions had come a militant labor movement, an incipient Socialist party, the populism of the farmers, and the progressivism of the urban middle class. Reformers permeated virtually every aspect of society. Government on every level was being made more responsible for public welfare and more accountable to the people. By 1914 progressivism reached its apogee as a social movement and was becoming institutionalized. Its advocates looked forward to steady progress through determined work, without feeling in the least bit complacent.

They attached themselves to the Democratic and Republican parties where those seemed to be likely agents of change and, where they did not, to third parties, including the eclectic Socialist Party of America, led by the indefatigable Eugene V. Debs. A host of voluntary associations fueled and implemented reform, raising national leaders without office—men and women such as Jane Addams and Walter Rauschenbusch. Addams personified the settlement movement—a loose association of neighborhood centers which ministered to social needs, especially of immigrants, and also initiated cultural and political change. Rauschenbusch personified the "Social Gospel"—the notion that religion must minister to the whole lives of persons and that sin is a corporate and not merely individual affair. Norman Thomas emulated them both before he went his own way.

He had been lured to progressivism from a conservative background. Born (1884) in Marion, Ohio, he was reared in that town which twice had voted for populist William Jennings Bryan but was also typified by the Babbitry of newspaper editor Warren G. Harding. Thomas's father, Welling, was the minister of a substantial Presbyterian church. His mother, Mary Mattoon, was the daughter of missionaries to Siam. Norman was the oldest of four brothers and two sisters in a tightly knit family. It was a secure if narrow setting.

Plagued by frail health as a child, Thomas compensated by reading voraciously and by developing speaking and leadership skills. The summer after Norman graduated from high school, his father accepted a church position in Lewisburg, Pennsylvania, where the son entered Bucknell University. His first year of college was intellectually stifling, but the generosity of a rich uncle in Paris enabled him to escape to Princeton University, a school fabled in Thomas and Mattoon tradition.

Woodrow Wilson had just become president of the university and he still taught politics. Norman Thomas was a student in his classes, learning at least as much about speaking as about politics, which Wilson addressed in narrow terms. But that was characteristic of the curriculum as a whole, as Thomas recalled; it was not responsive to contemporary currents. Nevertheless, he developed a deep affection for Princeton. He valued his friendships there and the debating in which he excelled, and he graduated valedictorian, Phi Beta Kappa, and *magna cum laude*. Although, in retrospect, he felt that his studies had left him blissfully unprepared for reality, he perhaps underestimated the intellectual discipline with which the university had equipped him to deal with the world when he encountered it.

The shock of initiation came upon his graduation, when Thomas joined the staff of the Spring Street Presbyterian Church and Neighborhood Center on the lower west side of Manhattan. There his small-town, middle-class, and clerical world was turned upside down. He encountered a society whose norms were ethnic pluralism, poverty and ignorance, violence and apathy. He met men and women who were responding to social challenges in the spirit of progressivism. He was introduced, too, to contemporary social thought, including socialism. In 1907–08 his mentor, the pastor of Spring Street Church, took Thomas and three young colleagues on a world trip. They left tourist routes for local contacts made through missionaries, and Thomas gained special access to Siamese society where the memory of his grandparents was fresh. Within three years of his college isolation, Norman Thomas had been reeducated to international, urban, and industrial reality. Somehow, he had to make a place in this new world for the values he carried to it—truth, fairness, and progress through applied intelligence.

It was natural that he sought to pursue this goal through the church. Upon his return to New York from abroad, Thomas entered Union Theological Seminary and supported himself by taking on Christ Church, a settlement church near Hell's Kitchen on the west side of mid-Manhattan. This was the area in which Walter Rauschenbusch had worked out his pioneering exposition of the Social Gospel which, in turn, profoundly influenced Norman Thomas in his studies at Union.

In Manhattan Thomas met and fell in love with Violet Stewart. The gifted and diminutive Violet—Norman was six feet two inches tall—had founded a program for tuberculosis treatment at the church. She came from a family whose wealth would provide them both with the independence they cherished. They were married and Thomas accepted a supplementary position preaching at the genteel Brick Church on Fifth Avenue, the patron institution for his neighborhood church. He was working both sides of the track, educating rich and poor to their common social condition. His gift for "indignation over injustice" was leading him to question his assumptions, to reach back of the slums in a search for their root causes; but his association with both the wealthy members of Brick Church and the powerless people in the parish may have restrained him from polarizing his notion of society into a simple struggle between classes.

Now theologically liberal as well as committed to a social ministry, Thomas graduated from Union and was ordained in 1911. He and Violet moved into East Harlem Church, where he was given responsibility also for the American Parish, a federation of immigrant services under the Board of Home Missions. In this predominantly Italian and Hungarian community the Thomases built a strong congregational base for their extensive social services, and Norman trained younger men in the progressive version of religion.

World War I: Radical Consistency

In response to the European war, Thomas joined progressives in crossing the line from mainstream reform to dissent.

Peace had been an organized reform cause in the United States for a hundred years. It began as a largely religious phenomenon. In the latter part of the nineteenth century, however, it captured the imaginations of some liberals who put arbitration and international exchange, law, and organization on their agendas. Just prior to World War I, older peace organizations such as the American Peace Society (1828) and the Universal Peace Union (1866) grew in strength, and they were supplemented by newly endowed ones: Andrew Carnegie's Endowment for International Peace (1910) and Church Peace Union (1914), and the World Peace Foundation (1910). Together, these groups formed a kind of peace establishment. Like their European counterparts, though, they wavered with the outbreak of war and then gradually fell into line with national policy, supporting a War to End Wars.

By contrast, new peace associations were formed by progressives who were now alert to the problem of war and regarded it as yet another form of authoritarianism and injustice. The new groups included the Woman's Peace Party (1914), which pressed for mediation of the war; the American Union Against Militarism (1916), which opposed President Wilson's preparedness program and supported United States neutrality; and the Fellowship of Reconciliation (1914), which united absolute religious pacifists. Norman Thomas joined the American Union Against Militarism and the Fellowship of Reconciliation, becoming cochairman of the latter and head of the No Conscription

League. He spoke against war and militarism in streets, public halls, and colleges, fixing an image that would become increasingly familiar in the next half-century:

> His speaking voice was vibrant, musical, appealing, an instrument he manipulated with subtlety, yet capable of such volume that he could be heard on street corners over the thunder of the elevated railway. His height and impressive appearance, his obvious decency and kindliness, his mobile face and warmth of expression, his skillful marshaling of points, his quick smile and mastery of humor, combined to hold audiences. Listeners invariably had the impression of a learned but compassionate man uttering indisputable truth.[2]

Norman Thomas emerged as one of the best speakers in the nation's history.

The organizations for which he spoke brought to the peace movement a new, reformist constituency. They endured after the war, mobilizing public pressure on foreign policy issues through the crises of Vietnam and the nuclear arms race. In 1916–17 they brought Thomas into association with people who would become lifelong friends and colleagues, among them John Haynes Holmes, John Nevin Sayre, A. J. Muste, Emily Green Balch, and Roger Baldwin.[3] These and others created an antiwar literature and organized large rallies and lecture tours, challenging both the creation of a large military establishment and intervention in the European conflict. They argued: the essential problem is not Germany, it is war itself; American involvement is not inevitable; the people could choose to remain neutral and become a force for resolving the conflict and reordering the world; the idea that warfare would solve the problem of international violence is a delusion, war is an instrument of violence and injustice.

Events in the spring of 1917, notably the German antisubmarine campaign, intensified public debate and eventually led to a declaration of war. American leaders did not drift into the conflict; they made a conscious choice that had been forced by articulate opponents of war. In the following months, the crucial role of dissent in policy-making was abrogated.

Thomas's wartime service consisted of the defense of civil liberties and of the right to dissent. "Unless a people retains its liberty to discuss freely according to its conscience, it loses its soul," he wrote.[4]

One effect of mobilization was a burst of patriotic feeling: a generous national spirit gave the war an idealistic mantle. But there was also a sinister brand of patriotism woven of intolerance, hatred, and conformism that was purveyed officially and also manipulated privately to discredit dissent whether or not it was related to the war effort. During and immediately after the war this kind of patriotism was employed to threaten pacifists and socialists. Even consistent defense of their civil liberties became radical and suspect. Thomas was one of those marked as radicals precisely for consistently asserting their views.

His assertions offended wealthy contributors at Brick Church. He resigned. He even took the offensive against excessive churchly devotion to the wartime state, writing: ". . . most disheartening of all is the note of hate, of intolerance of discussion, and invitation to mob violence which is sounding from many of the pulpits."[5] Thomas was not exaggerating, nor was he alone in losing his church position for such views. In January 1918 he became the founding editor of *The World Tomorrow*, a magazine designed in part to challenge the sanctification of war. He still wrote from a Christian perspective, but his disillusionment with religious institutions was clear and his critique of them was pointed: they were violating the principles of their Christ.

Elements of secular society were violating principles, too. Patriotism was the excuse for trivial nonsense such as keeping German music off concert programs or changing German street and family names; and it also became the pretext for suppressing loyal dissent and even constructive policy proposals. A case in point was the People's Council of America for Peace and Democracy, with which Thomas was associated. The Council was founded by pacifists in the spring of 1917 in order to advance civil liberties, promote liberal treatment of conscientious objectors, and recommend democratic peace terms during the war. The Council held large meetings in the East and Midwest in the summer of 1917. It was meticulously loyal, but some of its programs were disrupted, others were refused public space, and a September assembly in Chicago was dispersed on orders from the governor of Illinois.

Thomas came under surveillance, his speeches and writings being monitored by government agents. In September 1918 an issue of his *World Tomorrow* was withheld from the mail under the Espionage Acts and was released only after the president was interviewed by

Fellowship of Reconciliation leader and minister John Nevin Sayre, whose brother was Wilson's son-in-law. Other journals fared worse, and individuals were harassed, jailed, and in at least one instance killed.

Repression was intensified after the Armistice and it merged into the infamous Red Scare. Under the approving eyes of Attorney General A. Mitchell Palmer, left-wing groups were indiscriminately labeled Bolshevik and treasonous. Socialists' parades and meetings were broken up, their offices raided; elected socialist representatives were ousted from the New York state legislature; 249 suspect aliens were deported in December 1918; and less than two weeks later some 2,700 persons were arrested in a series of raids across the country. The Industrial Workers of the World, more militant than the Socialist party, was decimated by the war and subsequent purge. The nightmare of 1918–20 confirmed Thomas's frequent warnings that the war might have repressive social consequences.

The war's divisiveness was brought home to Thomas. Of his three brothers, Ralph was a captain of engineers in the army who was wounded in France, Arthur was training with the army aviation corps, and Evan had become a conscientious objector while working with the YMCA program for German prisoners of war in England. Upon returning to New York in the spring of 1918, Evan was inducted into the army and was sent to Ft. Riley, Kansas, with other objectors. There he undertook a hunger strike in order to protest the conditions under which they were incarcerated. After six days of fasting he was transferred to a base hospital and force-fed. Subsequently, he was courtmartialed and sent to the Ft. Leavenworth military prison. When he learned of inhumane treatment being meeted out to some religious objectors there, he refused to work and was thrust into solitary confinement under grueling conditions, manacled to the bars of his cell in a standing position for eight hours a day. Word was sent to Norman, and another presidential interview by John Nevin Sayre resulted in orders mitigating the worst mistreatment in military prisons. Evan was released in January 1919, but other objectors languished under deteriorating conditions for two years after the Armistice.

His brother's experience and extensive correspondence helped Norman to crystalize his thought on conscientious objection. Evan had come to his position through a clear sense of Christian ethics, but without support from church tradition or leadership. He reasoned that, just as an individual Christian owes ultimate responsibility to his or her understanding of Christ, the church notwithstanding, so too a person should not acquiesce in the arbitrary authority of the state as epitomized in military power: authority rests on consent. The basis of his conscientious objection was the responsibility he felt to challenge authoritarianism.[6]

Norman understood this and agreed with it. He was not an absolute pacifist, he said; he believed in police power under law. However, war "knows no crime except disobedience" and, therefore, a democracy at war is a contradiction in terms.[7] Although principle is invariably compromised by power, it must be defended if it is to survive. Accordingly, the authoritarianism implicit in war, whatever might be its justification, must be challenged lest it supplant freedom in peacetime. The corollary to this was that conscientious objection on any grounds must be respected in law.

Out of this perception came Thomas's most distinguished wartime service. With Roger Baldwin he organized and led the National Civil Liberties Bureau, the forerunner of the American Civil Liberties Union, which Baldwin would build into the single most significant organization in the field of civil rights. The first concern of the Bureau was the conscientious objectors, whom it advised of legal rights, aided in camps, and defended. Beyond that, Thomas interpreted the objectors to the public. In pamphlets and *The World Tomorrow* he explained who they were, what they believed, and why their fair treatment was in the national interest:

> There is a region in human life where the commandment of the state does not run. . . . In the long run that state is most secure which recognizes this truth. . . . The heretic may be very irritating, he may be decidedly wrong, but the attempt to choke heresy or dissent from the dominant opinion by coercing the conscience is an incalculable danger to society. . . . the desperate urgency is that, in a war for democracy, America shall not kill at home that "privilege of men everywhere to choose their way of life and obedience" which she seeks to secure for the world.[8]

Following the war, Thomas wrote a judicious and comprehensive account of *The Conscientious Objector in America*, laying a sound basis for the further development of this area of civil liberties.[9]

The war drew Thomas to the Socialist party for two reasons.

First, he identified with socialist leaders who were consistently anti-war and became victims of repression. Second, socialism entertained a vision by which the Social Gospel could be extended to root causes of injustice.

The day after the United States declared war on Germany, the Socialist Party of the United States reaffirmed its antiwar stand at an emergency convention in St. Louis. Resignations resulted as war fever mounted. The antiwar resolution was presented by Morris Hillquit, Latvian-born leader of the New York section, and when Hillquit ran for mayor that fall he received public support from Norman Thomas. Here was a secular party more consistent in loyalty to its values than were all but a few churches, Thomas concluded. He campaigned for it, and a year later, in the midst of Evan's ordeal in Leavenworth, he applied for membership in the party, writing: ". . . these are days when radicals ought to stand up and be counted."[10] He was accepted despite his explicit qualms about doctrine, reservations which would return to haunt orthodox Socialists a decade later.

Thomas observed the war from East Harlem, and he concluded that international conflict was an extension of the class exploitation he saw there. The causes of war were rooted in the very organization of society. Peace required social reconstruction.[11] The young Socialist could have appropriated these ideas from a previous generation of writers and, in fact, he was much influenced by British philosopher Bertrand Russell. For his own generation, though, World War I became the textbook case of an economic interpretation of war. It was the lodestar of all Thomas's subsequent thinking about warfare, and it dramatized for him the necessity of reorganizing whole social systems. If that seems like a quixotic solution, it must be remembered that Thomas had defended a minority position which within a decade became widely validated, and this experience must have confirmed for him the wisdom of consistency in an apparently futile cause.

The American Socialist

In the decade following the war Norman Thomas became the preeminent American Socialist. To the party, he was useful as an articulate, native-born, middle-class intellectual who could broaden its constituency. To him, the party was a platform from which he could clarify his thought and articulate his convictions. It was an instrument with which he drove the knife-edge of principle into American society; but as he did so, ironically, the party itself was sliced into irreconcilable factions.

Illness plagued his family for several years after the war. The oldest son of six children died. The family moved to the country. Norman went through a kind of retrenchment. The same "inordinate concern for humankind" which had led to his disillusionment with the church now extended to theistic religion itself.[12] Henceforth, any hope of social salvation lay squarely with society. The Socialist party replaced the church as his constituency and sponsor.

It was but a shadow of the party of Eugene V. Debs. The war had taken a toll. Within two years the party was further weakened by factionalism and the desertion of Communists enamored with the Soviet experiment. A small sign of promise—and Thomas seized even the slightest hint—was the League for Industrial Democracy, formerly the Intercollegiate Socialist Society, which had a viable base in many colleges. Thomas resigned from the leadership of the religious Fellowship of Reconciliation and editorship of its *World Tomorrow* to become codirector of the League with Harry W. Laidler. He crisscrossed the country with engagements on college campuses.

Thomas was then on good terms with Morris Hillquit, whose mayoralty campaign had brought him into a working association with the Socialist party in the first place, and with B. Charney Vladek, editor of that pillar of the party, the *Jewish Daily Forward*. Hillquit and Vladek regarded Thomas as one who could help the New York section reach beyond its traditional home in the Jewish garment district. In 1924 he was nominated for governor.

He did not campaign seriously for himself. He ran to build the party and to offer New York voters an alternative to the Republican and Democratic leadership, which he regarded as equally defunct. That year Socialists endorsed the presidential candidacy of Robert LaFollette, former governor and senator from Wisconsin who had pioneered in reform politics and had voted against war with Germany. They hoped that he would generate enough support to justify a third party with a farm-labor constituency and Socialist leadership. The old progressive polled far more votes than had any Socialist presidential candidate, but Thomas ran well behind him and the party was drained by the campaign. The dream of a third party was stillborn.

Nonetheless, Thomas had demonstrated his ability to make his brand of socialism attractive. This was particularly important to members of the so-called old guard of the party in New York. They were sapped by Communists on their left and by big labor on their right, even though their ideology was tied to Marxism and their politics were linked to labor. They ran Thomas for mayor of New York in 1925. He gained liberal support but lost the election. The next year he ran for state senator and was overwhelmed by an Al Smith landslide. In 1927 he ran in vain for local office as alderman.

His campaigns had been futile only as measured by electoral politics. Within the party he developed a reputation for loyalty, commitment, and openness. He helped to shape its positions on divisive issues such as prohibition, the League of Nations, Soviet Russia, and relationships with labor and independent coalitions. By 1928 there was no other native-born Socialist of equal stature and, even though his reputation was largely confined to New York, he was nominated as the party's presidential candidate on the urgent initiative of Hillquit.

He lost the election decisively, but he proved to be an effective campaigner and he established a national constituency for himself among Socialists. Immediately after the campaign the party was reorganized in ways that reinforced his leadership. Clarence Senior, an effective administrator and close ally, became executive secretary of the national office in Chicago. Party membership gained for the first time since 1922. By 1933 it had more than doubled (to 18,548). Most of the newcomers were young, well-educated and middle-class people attracted to Norman Thomas.

With a more responsible party behind him, he moved to extend the Socialist base. He ran again for mayor in 1929, drawing support from good government elements, polling well in middle-class districts, and further increasing party membership. Incumbent Jimmy Walker won handily, but his Socialist opponent opened charges of corruption that eventually would stick. As economic depression deepened after the election, Thomas and the party proposed a major relief program for the city, which Walker rejected. Thomas also proposed a comprehensive national plan for the unemployed, most of which came to be implemented in the New Deal.

Meanwhile, he cast about for formal alliances outside the party, helping to organize the League for Independent Political Action with leading liberals and moderate Socialists. He tried to breathe intellectual vigor into the party, compiling with Laidler a symposium on *The*

Socialism of Our Times by outstanding Socialists from the United States and abroad.

Thomas allowed himself the last word in the symposium. He rejected dogmatic Marxism. The classic doctrinal debates were no longer relevant, he wrote. First, the doctrines had lost their power in the light of changes in social organization and issues since Marx had formulated them. Accordingly, Socialists could not proceed "as if they were gods beginning life on a new made world."[13] Second, Marxism was not a scientific explanation. Marx had identified crucial realities and values—the fact of universal class struggle, for example, and the value of labor. Moreover, the ideas of class struggle and the labor theory of value were important unifying myths. They contained revolutionary truths and could forge a common will. But they should not be confused with the necessarily more moderate political and economic solutions to contemporary problems.

Thomas was drawing a distinction for the party that he hoped would enable it to remain loyal to Marxist principles understood symbolically without trying to apply them literally. He was the theologian of socialism, as it were, introducing to Marxism the new criticism he had learned in seminary. Like the Social Gospel advocates, he sought to replace doctrinal disputation with the ethical imperative of social reconstruction.

What, then, were the vital issues for socialist thought and action? There were three: *to press for immediate reforms without losing the vision of a new and just social order; to establish a cooperative commonwealth without losing the democracy even imperfectly associated with capitalism;* and *to change the system that breeds war without unleashing international or class war in the process.*

In this pre-Depression statement, as no doubt in the symposium, Thomas combined two purposes. The first was to offer a principle of interpretation that might inspire Socialists of different convictions with a common vision. He wrote to no avail, for nothing could blunt the factionalism that soon would rip the party apart. The second function of the essay was to clarify his own thought. By 1929 Thomas had achieved leadership in the party and had identified the directions toward which he would tend. Through 1941 he would address national audiences on the specific, complex issues of the Depression decade; and all of his books, articles, and speeches would address the three conundrums he had identified at its outset.

Reform and Reconstruction

It is impossible to clear the New Deal from our historical imaginations, so deeply is it embedded in our institutions and ethos; and yet we must remember that the New Deal was not an election issue in 1932. The Socialist party platform contained more of it than did the Democratic platform which, in turn, was hardly distinguishable from the Republican one except that, as Thomas noted, it was briefer. His presidential candidacy that year was a foregone conclusion, for he was the party's chief spokesman on major issues. He ran in order to build the party, to lay the grounds for a broad leftwing coalition four years hence, and to persuade the public that it had a choice of direction offered by neither major party. They were, he said, "merely glass bottles with different labels, and both of them empty of any medicine for the sickness of our times."[14]

Thomas was a national figure now, with endorsement from liberal intellectuals and respect from national journals. *Time* magazine featured him in a complimentary cover story. His audiences were receptive. However, the divided Socialist party gave him inadequate support, and many of those who supported him in principle voted for Franklin Roosevelt. Thomas was left with only 2.5 percent of the vote. Although disappointed, he thought that the Depression would deepen with the halfway measures that he expected from Roosevelt, and he hoped that a left-wing coalition might surface in 1936.

The sudden initiatives of the First Hundred Days surprised him, therefore, and brought mixed emotions. He was genuinely pleased that the New Deal was appropriating programs long proposed by Socialists (and he conferred and corresponded with Roosevelt in attempts to refine and extend them). As the months passed, however, he saw liberal friends slip into the president's ranks while, at the same time, he came to the conclusion that the New Deal was accommodating capitalism to crisis rather than bringing about the cooperative commonwealth to which Socialist reform measures had been linked.

The Socialist leader granted the president's generous instincts, the odds accumulating against him, and his political skill. He freely acknowledged the achievements of the New Deal: stabilizing the economy, mitigating the worst ravages of depression, and introducing long-needed reforms, including conservation. Representative government had not been undercut in the process and, in fact, labor had a new charter of freedom. In sum, he said that the administration was replacing the chimera of laissez-faire capitalism with a form of state capitalism—a profit-based competitive economy secured by direct national intervention in return for modest regulation. However, the ameliorated system remained a stark contrast to the cooperative commonwealth of socialist principles in which capital interests would be subordinated to public interest through long-range planning and the socialization of basic industry.

In his speeches and writings, Thomas stressed that the administration was doing more for special interests than for the general public. Indeed, in every respect except perhaps the Tennessee Valley Authority, the thrust of the New Deal was to employ federal power as the instrument of capital recovery rather than to subordinate profit to public welfare. The result was drift, disparity, and the waste of natural and human resources.[15] A contest of interests is inevitable in a democracy where politics is the art of the possible, Thomas acknowledged; but overall the New Deal had failed to test the possible against the desirable. Principle was being subordinated to political power.

Nowhere was this more clear to Thomas than in the crop-sharing South. Socialist organizers in Arkansas urged him to see for himself the plight of tenant farmers there. He was already overcommitted, but he went anyway in February 1934. He talked at length with sharecroppers, sitting in their cold, rude hovels, seeing cheerless children clad in clothes made from feed sacks, sensing the hopelessness of people in bondage. Landless, they lived in shacks that belonged to their landlords and worked depleted soil at the owners' discretion, their seed, implements, and living supplies bonded from one harvest to the next. They received perhaps half their crops' income if the landlord was honest, less charges for interest and services. They were economically dependent and politically disfranchised by poll taxes, tradition, and threat. The Negroes among them suffered disproportionately.

In a world where people were starving, New Deal agricultural policy subsidized the withholding of land from production and the destruction of crops. Subsidies often were not distributed to sharecroppers as required by law, and there was no legal recourse for the illiterate, dependent peasants. Often farmers were simply put off the land not in use. Administration policy thus compounded the unjust treatment of a million and a half tenant farmers in the South.

Thomas was aroused. He arranged for a thorough study of the

area. He repeatedly wrote to Secretary of Agriculture Henry A. Wallace to no avail. He was blocked in his efforts to gain satisfaction from administration officials (the president later explained to him that the New Deal depended upon support from southern senators who, in turn, depended upon support from the planter class). Thomas persuaded a young Methodist minister, Howard Kester, to help organize an integrated Southern Tenant Farmers' Union in Arkansas, wrote extensively on the issue, and exposed it in radio broadcasts.

By 1935 the lines were drawn in Arkansas. Planters backed by local establishments were resorting to outright terror. Thomas went back at his own expense, an isolated Yankee in physical danger. A public meeting was broken up and he was forced out of the county. The campaign of terror increased. Thomas now had a national spotlight on it, however, and in Arkansas the union held firm. With some ten thousand members, it went on strike and by fall won a 40 percent raise in pay.

Thomas graphically portrayed the plight of tenant farmers in a 1934 book on *Human Exploitation in the United States*. He added chapters on the waste of families and urban resources, foresters and trees, miners and minerals, on the conditions of women in industry, children, blacks, and other depressed groups. He recast the image of social paradox drawn by Henry George in *Progress and Poverty* and Henry Demarest Lloyd in *Wealth Against Commonwealth*, and he gave the paradox a name—exploitation. The problem was not merely a failure in distribution, he wrote; it was "a failure to produce what we need" in an era when for the first time in history it was possible to do so:

> Socially more hurtful than the waste of luxury in the midst of want, is the general waste of human energy and human brains which with the aid of the machine, stand ready to produce all that the heart can desire. It is this contrast which makes modern poverty and insecurity so much more bitter and intolerable than it has ever been before. We are like men who die of thirst with the sound of running water in our ears.[16]

The core of the problem was a failure of principle, Thomas thought, the lack of a social principle against which to measure power. That, and not Marxist dogma, distinguished his New Socialism from the New Deal. The reform measures advocated by Socialists and appropriated by Roosevelt were incidental, Thomas concluded: "It is more important to observe that the essential thing about the Socialist platform has always been its purpose and its goal rather than its immediate demands."[17] Its goal was the reconstruction of society for collective, cooperative values.

Collectivism with Democracy

Arkansas was not the only place where the Socialist leader's own civil rights were violated. In Illinois he was forceably removed from a public meeting which then was dispersed by tear gas. In Jersey City his meetings were disrupted by force, he was hustled out of town, and Violet was hit in the face (she often accompanied him once the children were grown). Thomas concluded that the threat to civil liberties was as endemic to American society as was exploitation and waste; the principle of democracy was vulnerable to the power of the very special interests which it was designed to control.

He was especially troubled by mounting violence and totalitarianism abroad in the thirties: imperialist wars in China and Ethiopia, British resistance to Gandhian independence in India, ruthless regimes and the suppression of socialism in Germany and Italy, the debacle of republicanism in Spain, Stalin's purges in Russia, an arms race out of control—the litany of a collapsing world order was long. Thomas's contacts with socialists abroad were extended when he and Violet traveled in Europe and the Soviet Union in 1937. He returned to write that socialism everywhere was "on the defensive."

> Today in Germany, its classic home, and in Italy, socialism is outlawed and forbidden. In other countries in Europe, Asia and South America it is harried and persecuted. In the bourgeois democracies socialist emphasis in recent years has been . . . [on] the preservation of what democracy has already won.[18]

In fact, within the American movement Thomas's version of democratic socialism had been on the defensive since World War I. The tests of factional loyalty in its internecine battles included one's interpretation of the Soviet Union and one's position on the theoretical issue of violence in the class struggle. In both cases precisely the democratic character of socialism was at issue.

In the twenties American Socialists were sharply divided over the Soviet Union. Some believed that the Bolsheviks were so repressive as to be antisocialist. Others were altogether uncritical of the Soviet system and they left the Socialist party to emerge as a disciplined if factious Communist party. Thomas initially took the middle ground, preferring to give the Soviets a chance to prove themselves. Even in the thirties he distinguished between Soviet accomplishments in industrializing the economy and collectivising agriculture and the ruthlessness with which Stalin had pursued those goals. Whether or not Bolshevik practices were theoretically consistent with Marxist precepts, he insisted, they could not serve as a model for the United States.

Thomas's approach to Socialism was an extension of his progressive origins. It was eclectic and inclusive. Thus, he could not endorse the rigid lines separating Socialist factions, and he found it difficult to exclude Communists from the movement. For the most part, they excluded themselves by attacking Socialists in public, even resorting to direct violence to do so, until the mid-thirties when fascist Germany emerged as a clear threat to the Soviet Union. Then the Communist International directed American Communists to cooperate with Socialists in a united front. Thomas flirted with cooperation even though it alienated important Socialist leaders, but by 1935 he had become thoroughly disillusioned with Communists loyal to Moscow.

The Socialist leader was taken in, however, by Communists loyal to Leon Trotsky, the exiled leader of the Bolshevik Revolution who had become the mortal enemy of Stalin. Trotsky ordered his few but disciplined American followers to join the Socialist party and either capture or destroy it. They were admitted on the understanding that they would come in as individuals without exclusive loyalty to their own faction. Within months they had created such chaos that Thomas reversed himself and supported their expulsion.

He had been badly burned by this incident, but he learned from his experience with Communists that an inclusive movement could not successfully incorporate elements governed by absolute and exclusive loyalties. Within the party, as in the nation, inclusive democracy could be manipulated by special interests. The principle of democracy had to be adapted; but the ideal remained critically important—the sole justification for its modification.

Its blatant violation under Stalin led even the tolerant, inclusive Norman Thomas to conclude by 1938 that the direction of the Soviet

Union was "incompatible with true Socialist development."[19] Coached by knowledgeable friends such as Angelica Balabanoff, first secretary of the Communist International, he reasoned that repression in Russia and the manipulative tactics of Stalinists or Trotskyists revealed common errors in Leninism. Contrary to the Bolshevik theorist, he wrote, the state was not withering away, it was aggrandizing power absolutely; the monolithic apparatus of the revolutionary party was not temporary, it was the self-perpetuating instrument of new tyranny. In this respect, Thomas regarded the Soviet Union as a horrendous violation of the principles that socialism must be grounded in democracy and that revolution must eschew violence.

Those principles fixed Thomas's position in the factional battle which sundered the Socialist party at its national convention in May 1934. Delegates arriving in Detroit were divided into three major groups. On the right was the so-called old guard, primarily the New York section of the party. Correct and orthodox on theoretical lines, its members were conservative in action and jealous of their dominant influence. On the left were younger members impatient to become an active force for radical change and somewhat impressed by the Russian experiment. Many of them had been attracted by Thomas in whom they saw an agent of vitality. In turn, Thomas supported the militants, as they were called, especially in New York factional disputes, although he led a loosely defined third faction. Its members shared his pragmatic progressivism and included pacifist reformers with whom he had associated since World War I. Their pragmatic approach and the principle of democratic inclusiveness made them centrists, located between the old guard and militants, and preferring an eclectic party of the whole. A much smaller and peripheral fourth faction, the Revolutionary Policy Committee, was altogether radical. It defended the Soviet Union and differed with Communists mainly on tactical matters.

At the outset of the Detroit convention, an effort to define the party's theoretical position created an alliance between militants and progressives in opposition to the old guard. This was the Declaration of Principles which had been hastily written by Devere Allen—a centrist, pacifist, and friend of Thomas—who had been a principal editor of *The World Tomorrow* for a decade. Allen's Declaration sought party unity on centrist lines. For the most part, it employed conventional rhetoric in a traditional socialist critique of capitalism.

When it came to the question of the road to socialist power, though, the Declaration raised two critical issues: the questions of international conflict and class struggle. However theoretically they were couched, these issues seemed urgent in the light of events abroad.

Allen reaffirmed the party's antiwar position of 1917, adding the provision that socialist-labor resistance to war should take the form of a general strike and noncooperation. Ironically, this position was attacked by the old guard whose own late leader, Hillquit, had written the 1917 proclamation.

Allen addressed the question of class struggle by emphasizing that the alternative between fascism and democratic socialism was being sharpened with the collapse of capitalist regimes. Given the possibility of fascist control, he wrote, "the Socialist Party . . . will not shrink from the responsibility of organizing and maintaining a government under the worker's rule."[20] In a direct challenge to the radical Revolutionary Policy Committee, the Declaration committed the party to peaceful and orderly means which under duress might include a general strike. Nonetheless, it was assailed by the old guard as communist, anarchist, and illegal.

The convention was polarized when the old guard forced a vote on the Declaration without amendment. Thomas, who had been prepared for compromise, then supported Allen's statement, which carried the vote in convention and a subsequent referendum of the membership at large.

The party crumbled into discrete, warring factions. Militants and progressives eventually won control of the New York and national organizations by 1936. The old guard went its separate way. The fratricide depleted the party's ranks and split even those remaining: by 1938 membership was down to about three thousand, and it was reduced by a third in the following three years.

Norman Thomas had tried to build Socialism as a philosophy, an organization, and a program.[21] By the mid-thirties the Socialist program was essentially his own platform, but the organization was broken, apparently over questions of philosophy. In a real sense, the party was destroyed by a conflict for power within it, a contest which Thomas failed to reconcile or control. Why?

In political parties with access to economic and political power, group relationships are determined by the allocation of that power, and conflicts often can be reconciled by compromises on its distribution. In out-of-power groups such as the Socialist party, group relationships often are tested by allegiance to theoretical principles, and compromise is not possible. Theory becomes a tool with which authority is contested. That is what happened in and around the Detroit convention. Thomas would have preferred an inclusive, eclectic party, but the very principle of democratic inclusiveness posed him in opposition to groups such as Communists and the conservative old guard which would not surrender their exclusive interests. The contest with these groups was waged on the principle of democratic, nonviolent socialism. For the sake of the organization he could have compromised on almost anything except that philosophy.

Given repeated polarization among Socialists, defections to the New Deal, and raids from the radical left, the Socialist Party was doomed. To Thomas it must have seemed like a sinking platform in a rising flood of international chaos. If nothing else, its history illustrated the destructive potential of principles manipulated for the sake of power. In this respect, the party was a microcosm of the world in which its leader vainly sought tolerance and vision. Thus, the crisis of Socialism was a challenge to democratic principles in the party and in the world at large.

Peace as Change

The crisis of democracy was the ordeal of war. From the embers of Socialist disputation Thomas marshalled a coalition against American involvement in a second world war and, after Pearl Harbor, worked for decent peace. In the process he specified principles with which to assess the international uses of power and discovered that he had an independent forum for his views.

Warfare in Europe caused a realignment of the American peace movement in the thirties, as it had done from 1914 to 1917. Following World War I, internationalists pursued schemes for world cooperation such as the League of Nations, the outlawry of war, and a world court. These internationalists worked through organizations such as the Carnegie Endowment and the League of Nations Association. Although they differed sharply over questions of priority, their various projects generally were supported by liberal pacifists.

With the Japanese aggression in China in 1931 and mounting crises in Europe in the following years, both pacifist and nonpacifist internationalists cooperated in efforts to mobilize public awareness of threats to peace, to generate support for negotiated disarmament and reform of the international economy, and to revise American neutrality legislation. A series of laws reversed the nation's traditional practice of trading with belligerents in time of war and imposed stricter neutrality on the United States. Such was the tenor of public opinion that the administration found it prudent to accept them.

By 1938, however, the internationalist coalition was dissolving. Nonpacifists such as James Shotwell and Clark Eichelberger gravitated toward ever more explicit collective security and lobbied for revisions of the neutrality laws what would make it possible for the nation to help European allies to resist German aggression.[22] The Nazi invasion of Poland in the fall of 1939 increased their sense of crisis, and they set up an organization which became known the following May as the Committee to Defend America by Aiding the Allies.

The peace movement polarized as pacifists joined other advocates of strict neutrality in a campaign to Keep America Out of War. Norman Thomas coined that slogan and, beginning early in 1938, he orchestrated an antiwar coalition from what was left of his Socialist base. It was a non-Communist group which utilized the considerable legislative know-how and public contacts amassed by pacifists in their campaigns for neutrality laws. The outbreak of war in Europe in 1939 and the crushing blows which felled France and forced British troops off the continent only increased the urgency of neutralists. They sensed a deadly parallel to their experience in opposing American involvement in a European war only twenty-five years earlier.

However, by the summer of 1940 some Socialists, notably from the Jewish sections, had abandoned their party's historic position in order to support war against the Fascists. Further complicating the scene, the antiwar movement attracted Communists after the Russian-German nonaggression pact made Hitler an apparent ally of Stalin. Again Thomas had to stave off Communist infiltration until in June 1941 Germany's invasion of Russia led to a typically cynical reversal of the Communists, who then encouraged American support of the Soviet Union.

Relationships with the Left were less difficult than those with right-wing isolationists who, in the fall of 1940, organized the America First Committee. That group was able to attract strong financing and public attention unavailable to Thomas. Cooperation with it seemed to be necessary in order to avert intervention, but it was possible only on isolationist grounds. Charges of anti-Semitism in America First and its concept of a Fortress America alienated liberal pacifists and led to their withdrawal or merely nominal participation in Thomas's Keep America Out of War Congress. By the fall of 1941 the Congress was reduced to a left-wing shadow of the coalition he had envisioned.

The advocates of collective security were well organized by then, and they had the advantages of administration support and the drama of British resistance. They characterized all opponents as isolationists. They rode a swelling wave of public support for the series of steps discretely taken by Roosevelt in order to give the Allies all aid short of war. The sudden Japanese attack on Pearl Harbor caused a surge of national purpose and closed the divided ranks of the country; but it was anticlimactic for the Keep America Out of War Congress and Norman Thomas. Well before the war, his political objectives had been lost, his organization had been reduced to impotence, and his message had been thoroughly obscured.

Thomas's view of the second crisis of American intervention is important, however, because it reveals the evolution of his thinking on war and the grounds of his critique of postwar policy. He had espoused Christian pacifism in World War I, when he repudiated war altogether. Subsequently he recanted his absolute rejection of military force and, for this reason, he was understood to have reversed himself.[23] This was true only in a limited sense.

In common with other liberal, reform-oriented pacifists in the First World War, Thomas rejected war as a *method,* whatever its goal or ideal. Anticipating an important distinction later developed by Reinhold Niebuhr in *Moral Man and Immoral Society,* Thomas recognized that societies exempt themselves from the moral imperatives which may guide individuals, because groups subordinate means to ends. The test of social ethics is consequence. Although individual morality might be based on absolute principles of intrinsic worth, therefore, social ethics is based on instrumental values.

While he was an avowed Christian, Thomas had grounded his attitude to war on both a divine imperative and an assessment of political reality. When he abandoned the church, Thomas lost the absolute principle impelling his personal opposition to war, but he continued to assess war, as a political instrument, with remarkable consistency: organized violence was overwhelmingly antisocial, he held; it must never be idealized; it must always be resisted; and it can be supported only together with efforts to change the social order of which it is the ultimate method.

Thomas's understanding of the First World War was the lens through which he interpreted the Second. Indeed, he argued that war in the thirties was a resumption of conflicts unresolved in 1918. Specific aggressions were symptomatic of underlying causes of war, he wrote. German Nazism, Italian Fascism, and Japanese militarism had in common with one another and with Soviet Communism a highly militarized form of totalitarianism. Each of these states completely subordinated individuals to itself, yielded supreme economic power, and was coercive as a matter of principle. The more democratic nations differed from them in that they had distributed political and economic power broadly and had limited coercion by principles of law. However, the democracies also pursued exclusive national interests. Indeed, their short-sighted and exclusive sense of national interest following the First World War had contributed to the trend toward totalitarianism and further warfare.[24]

In the thirties this analysis was important in three respects: the question of alternatives to war, the temptation to idealize the anti-Axis alliance, and the issue of United States involvement. These were the components of an intense national debate in which Thomas was actively engaged and on which hinged momentous public choices.

As the decade opened, Thomas argued that current trends made peace improbable but not impossible. None of the schemes hailed in the twenties was a panacea, he observed, because none of them addressed the roots of war in a world where economic power was dominated by competitive, oppressive classes and where political power was divided among exclusive and ambitious nations. The dominant ideologies of capitalism and nationalism had been carried to extreme forms by both world war and depression, and they combined to strain all peaceful institutions. The alternative to war was social change leading to greater equity, democracy, and stability on a global scale. That required political will, not mere accommodation. Nor could war be regarded as a harbinger of such change, as some radicals hoped, for historically war had intensified injustice and revolutionary violence had only exchanged one ruling class for another.

Throughout the thirties Thomas found his early analysis confirmed and the alternatives to war narrowed. The democratic powers seemed no more inclined to jeopardize their exclusive national interests than were their adversaries. British and French commitments to imperialism and their self-serving responses to crises in Manchuria, Ethiopia, Spain, and Czechoslovakia only reinforced his opinion. They were peaceful in the sense that all Haves are peaceful, he wrote; they valued the present order of things. In contrast, the totalitarian states not only had the ambitions of Have-Nots, but also they had erected violent aggrandizement into a positive good.

By 1938 Thomas concluded that "the terrifying probabilities are that fascism will perish not by constructive revolution at home, but in the holocaust of Europe or worldwide war. And in that holocaust civilization may perish with it."[25] He interpreted the explosion of war in the following year as the result of old European rivalries intensified by economic competition and national ideology. Especially when he added Japan to the equation, the old rivalries were worldwide and imperialistic.

It is very important to understand that Thomas was unsparing in his denunciation of German, Italian, and Soviet totalitarianism, and that he made a sharp distinction between them and the democratic nations. Nonetheless, he included the democracies in assessing responsibility for the war. If their guilt was less immediate and direct, it was no less fundamental; for it lay in their trying to maintain an untenable world order. In this regard, the United States itself was culpable insofar as it had pursued its own economic nationalism, had refused to treat the Soviet Union as a major power or to take international responsibility, and had sought security in the status quo.

Thomas's efforts to keep America out of war from 1939 to 1941 followed from his analysis of international politics. Although he valued democracy, he did not romanticize the war aims of the democratic Allies, who were pursuing their own national interests. When the Soviet Union found itself allied against Germany, he did not idealize Stalin's self-serving regime. Indeed, he argued that war among the dictatorships mollified any threat to United States security and made British survival more likely. America could not be threatened directly, and as a neutral the nation would emerge as a major influence in the vacuum of power left in Eurasia.

Beyond national interest, however, neutrality was also necessary to insure future peace, in Thomas's view. As a belligerent, the United

States would again be tied to the war aims and national interests of the victors, and to the notion of peace as the restoration of the old order. The war itself testified to the collapse of that order, Thomas thought, and victory over the fascist dictatorships "of itself would not change the forces which produce war and facism."[26] More likely, he feared, it would bring authoritarianism to the United States by emulation. Remembering the First World War, cognizant of incipient fascism in American society, and conscious of the total mobilization required by modern warfare, Thomas warned that the nation could secure the future of democratic institutions only by remaining at peace.

At the very least, the nation should not enter war under the recurrent delusion that victory would end war itself (as supporters of intervention implied). At most, it should form a policy looking beyond the war to a new world order:

> The supreme reason for keeping America out of war . . . is the fact that only in an America spared from war can we develop for ourselves and for mankind the new techniques of conflict against the system which breeds poverty, tyranny, and war, without the wholesale murder, the mass insanity, and bitter frustration which are war's inescapable heritage.[27]

Whatever else might be its justification, war was no instrument of peace. Conversely, to Norman Thomas, a peace-seeking policy involved more than isolation from war; it required a program for a more democratic and cooperative world commonwealth.

After December 7, 1941, peace was not possible for the American people. Thomas had warned for at least three years that Roosevelt's foreign policy was "sidling up to war." The notion of being the arsenal of democracy without becoming involved in its defense was as much a sham in 1940 as it had been in 1916, he insisted, and he demanded that the people be given a clear, forthright choice between peace and war. The Japanese obviated that choice.

Thomas immediately recognized that the terms of war had changed to survival, and he adopted a policy of "critical support." He successfully negotiated this policy for the Socialist party, despite the fact that some of its members wanted somehow to withhold their support without actually opposing the war effort. Thomas regarded that as pointless obscurantism. The times demanded the defense of democracy in the United States and the formation of a constructive program for the world. Thomas refashioned the Keep America Out of War Congress into the Post War World Council.

He was chairman, and the executive secretary and office remained the same, but its scope and constituency changed. Such was the respect for Thomas that he easily shed the isolationist label that had been foisted upon him. With the new organization as his personal platform, he cooperated with many liberal internationalists in numerous civic associations. He wrote a nationally syndicated newspaper column and had weekly access to radio. His books continued to be accepted by major publishers. He spoke out freely. Thomas was now altogether independent of the Socialist party, except that he believed in it, probably because he associated the party with the vision of democratic socialism he had articulated for it. His sentiment for the party (and for the church) was like the feeling a former Socialist expressed for him, "the memory of a lost love. It never completely dies."[28]

The World as a Better Place

Happily, his dire predictions of massive wartime repression were not borne out, because, he reasoned, the Japanese had united the nation in defense. Nonetheless, individual cases of apparent injustice claimed his attention, as did the cause of conscientious objectors. Evan Thomas, now a distinguished physician, was chairman of the Metropolitan Board for Conscientious Objectors and active in the War Resisters League. Norman took a special interest in nonreligious objectors who were not protected under the law. He argued that the test of conscience could not be confined to religious affiliation, but this position was recognized by the courts only a quarter of a century later, in a more divisive war.

Thomas was aroused by the forced relocation of some 110,000 Japanese-American citizens and Japanese resident aliens from their homes on the West Coast. Many of these people lost possessions and positions earned over their lifetimes. They were victimized, Thomas believed, by wartime panic, greed, and racism. He reacted quickly, appealing to the American Civil Liberties Union which he had helped to found, and then condemning it for remaining aloof. He contacted government officials, including the president. He addressed the public through writings and radio. It was in vain. Although his efforts probably mitigated the injustice somewhat and certainly earned him the gratitude of many victims, the backwash of war trapped Japanese-Americans even more firmly than the backwaters of the New Deal had caught southern sharecroppers.

Meanwhile, Thomas criticized specific aspects of the war effort. The systematic obliteration bombing of German and Japanese cities especially drew his ire. It was unnecessary, and counterproductive, he insisted (a judgment later confirmed by military analysis). It was an immoral "massacre by bombing," in the phrase of his pacifist friend, John Nevin Sayre.[29] The use of atomic bombs on Hiroshima and Nagasaki angered him and provoked his protest: this was the culmination of that self-justifying principle of victory which had led to the holocaust of the Jews and the destruction alike of Warsaw, Tokyo, Hamburg, and Dresden.

The policy of unconditional surrender drew Thomas's severe criticism. Not only did it lengthen the war, he argued, but it also postponed the development of postwar diplomacy and facilitated Stalin's occupation of Eastern Europe and Manchuria. Negotiation was not a mere romantic attachment for Thomas. It was a process which he thought might realistically maximize peace and minimize the gains of Soviet totalitarianism. It was integral to the concept of postwar policy which he outlined in a 1944 book, *What is Our Destiny?* More accurately than it knew, probably, the publisher printed on the back of the book jacket, "This book . . . is a symbol of the liberty and the freedom for which we fight."[30]

"No peace treaty can end the war between cherished political myths and economic realities or enable men to satisfy at one and the same time their hates and their hunger," Thomas began.[31] Peace therefore could not be attained as a mere extension of the war, nor could it leap over the realities of power and conflict; rather, it must subordinate conflicts of interest to cooperative change.

Thomas dismissed two broad approaches to postwar policy which he thought did not meet this requirement. The first would impose order by the policing power of the wartime allies, the Atlantic nations, or the United States. There were several popular variations of the notion. Thomas argued that all of them extended the war in the interests of the victors. If these plans were realistic in anticipating conflict in the postwar world, he wrote, they were naive in assuming that political arrangements could contain the forces of revolutionary change or gloss over nearly irreconcilable conflicts between Stalinist Russia and the western Allies.

There were also several variations on a second approach: world government. All of them emphasized constitutional arrangements among nations. That was the problem. Governments themselves would be rent by revolutionary forces within and across national lines following the war. Thomas surveyed these currents in some detail and with prescience. He concluded that both world government and policing plans were static approaches unfit to adapt the international order to pent-up pressures for far-reaching change.

His own approach was rooted in his understanding of a world "still going through an economic and social revolution" in which "we cannot remove by any sudden act the habits, customs, interests and prejudices which have determined national organizations and their interrelations."[32] Accordingly, he advocated a series of programs, a political platform as it were, designed to sustain international order and to minimize conflict: imperialism and neocolonialism must be ended; international trade must not be stifled by arbitrary inter-ference, although it must be regulated through negotiation; scarce raw materials must be allocated by international agreement; a world fiscal system must establish parity between national currencies; capital must flow to underdeveloped areas without exploitation or external con-trol; people must be given more freedom to travel and immigrate; higher minimum wages must be established for workers in low-income countries; and the future of air space must be guaranteed by international agreement.

Thus, Thomas's primary agenda was the establishment of func-tional relationships between existing centers of power and the con-struction of a bridge between the present and preferred a world. It was process-oriented, aimed at long-term stability that might result from discovering and institutionalizing mutual interests. It required a prob-lem-solving, functional approach to international organization. In fact, during the Cold War this agenda would be addressed by a growing number of international and nongovernmental organizations which would create networks of relatively stable, functional rela-tionships. Thomas had envisioned this work, and not security issues, as being the highest priority and organizing principle of an interna-tional organization.

He did advocate a world police force capable of resisting aggression, but he added that if this were not attainable an international organization should renounce force altogether and concentrate on functional problem-solving and moral leadership. Collective security, as it eventually was built into the Security Council of the United Nations, seemed to him but a variation of the untenable policing power of dominant powers. It was guaranteed to divide and frustrate the United Nations as it had stymied the League of Nations.

International form followed from function. Thomas envisioned a confederation of nations grounded in strong regional cooperation in Europe and Latin America, with Asia free from imperialism, and Africa placed in international trusteeship en route toward national self-determination. Such an orientation would isolate Soviet totalitarianism and free other world regions to work out their own cooperative commonwealths, he argued; America's destiny was to exemplify and facilitate for others "the liberty and the freedom" for which it had fought.

In sum, Thomas's postwar policy rested on his distinction between the respective roles of power politics and social reconstruction: the United States should resist Soviet expansion precisely in order to free international and regional associations to address the practical issues of revolutionary change.

The Cold War divided Americans insofar as they emphasized either *realpolitik* or social reconstruction to the exclusion of the other. Since Thomas affirmed both terms and acknowledged the limitations of each, he became an enigma and frequent target in the national debate.

His position on domestic Communism illustrated this ambivalence. Thomas roundly condemned the self-serving manipulation of conspiracy theory by anti-Communists like Senator Joseph McCarthy. He also decried the unprincipled manipulation of truth and law by American Communists. Even though he defended their civil rights, he tried to keep them out of peace and reform organizations, and that itself became an issue—notable in the Committee for a Sane Nuclear Policy. Predictably, Thomas was criticized from both sides.

He had recanted his tentative approval of the Soviet experiment well before most disillusioned liberals formed a cohort of Cold Warriors. Even before the war's end he criticized Roosevelt for appeasing Stalin and permitting the postwar division of Europe. Thus had been polarized a region which in loose confederation might have formed its own version of a cooperative commonwealth, he lamented (and he added that Asia had been lost to imperialism). Given the fact of Soviet expansion, though, Thomas supported forthright engagement to contain it. He testified for the North Atlantic Treaty Organization in 1949 and endorsed the Korean War in the following year. The Communist states and the international Communist movement sought universal power, he thought, and they must be resisted "unless and until there is a profound modification" of their attitudes.[33]

As adamantly as he opposed Soviet Communism, however, Thomas insisted on the limits of containment: force must be applied judiciously and realistically; it must be governed by a clear sense of its limited purpose, which was to contain Soviet aggression and modify its intransigence; and its use must not undermine the very democratic values and social revolution which sanctioned it.

Thomas participated in a number of programs designed to link non-Communist cultural leaders and reinforce democratic social change around the world. He traveled to India, South-East Asia, Japan, and Mexico under the auspices of the Congress for Cultural Freedom; he went to the Middle East for the Free Europe Committee; and he organized the Institute for International Labor Research which trained non-Communist progressives in Latin America. He later learned that the sponsoring organizations had been in part funded by the CIA. He did not apologize for his work with them—it had been open and constructive; but he condemned the covert operations of the CIA. Like American support of repressive regimes, he said, these actions undermined credibility abroad and democratic institutions at home.

Just as containment should reflect democratic principles in its choice of means, so too it should be flexible and realistic, Thomas argued. In this spirit he opposed the political and military confrontation of Communism in China or Indochina even though he had supported engagement in Europe and Korea. The movements led by Mao Tse-tung and Ho Chi Minh represented countervailing powers in the Communist world, he thought, forces that would challenge the Soviet center and its Stalinist model. Recognition of China seemed realistic to Thomas as early as 1950. Intervention in Indochina never made sense to him. He became an outspoken critic of the war in Vietnam that crested in the year of his death.

Most clearly in Vietnam, military power had come to justify itself; the instrument had become policy. Like George Kennan, Thomas consistently viewed containment as a flexible and limited response to Soviet aggression in the interest of a more fluid world order. When Stalin died in 1953, Thomas urged a policy of disengagement wherever that might reinforce moderation of Stalinist intransigence. This brought him into sharp conflict with Secretary of State John Foster Dulles, whom Thomas accused of systematically increasing the polarity and rigidity of international relations. As the Communist movement evolved indigenous forms and the non-Communist world became more complex, he found disengagement seemed ever more sensible.

He coupled disengagement with disarmament. He saw the fatal propensity of power to become self-justifying in the arms race, especially the nuclear balance of terror. Thomas had urged President Truman to initiate a concerted drive in the United Nations for disarmament at the same time that he endorsed the Korean War. The Socialist appealed to the Democratic president to challenge the world with a comprehensive program including absolute prohibition of nuclear weapons, reduction of conventional forces to negotiated quota, demobilization of narrow waterways, abolition of peacetime conscription, and subordination of national military power to an international force. Critical of both unilateral disarmament and arms control, Thomas helped to found the Committee for a Sane Nuclear Policy in 1957 and contributed to growing public concern. He warned that disarmament alone offered security to the United States, and added that security of the Soviet Union also would have to be guaranteed if disarmament were to be feasible:

> Conflict there must be while communism maintains its aggressive philosophy and tactics and democracy has any life at all. But the time has come when to contain the conflict on the plane of war threatens the very race itself with destruction.[34]

He was again fighting the current. Arms build-up was accompanied by negotiated arms control in the sixties and seventies without losing momentum.

Disengagement and disarmament became increasingly important to Thomas as he sensed a growing disposition to employ force at all levels, open and convert, in order to secure national interests and influence anywhere in the world. Shortly before his death he expressed regret that "neither the United States, nor any other powerful nation has enough wisdom or strength to play policeman to the rest of the world."[35] Indeed, that approach totally contravened the principles under which Thomas had condoned the use of force in the first place: to facilitate people throughout the world in working out their own cooperative commonwealths and to adapt the international order to revolutionary change.

In fact, he linked national initiative for disarmament to a "coordinated program for economic construction throughout the earth, a peaceful war on poverty and hunger, preferably under the direction of the U.N."[36] He argued that such a program was an important corollary to even a legitimate arms policy. It would involve far more than the transfer of capital to the third World; it would require the transfer of opportunity to exchange stagnation for progress, repression for democratic participation. The real area wherein Communism must be challenged was the future, he believed, and the policeman mentality— the "tendency to declare any movement toward social revolution 'communist' "—threatened to close the future in the face of revolutionary social forces.[37]

In the final twenty-five years of his life, Thomas consistently held this challenge before the American people and their leaders. He was on his own. His beloved Violet died in 1947. The next year he conducted his last presidential campaign for the Socialist party, and then only to deny Socialist support to Henry Wallace, whom he regarded as dangerously naive. Thereafter, he worked out of his Post War World Council. He was assured of speaking engagements, radio time, outlets for his writing, and access to national leaders in many fields. Puritan that he was, he consented to have a *Playboy* interview; classic political loser, he corresponded frequently with presidents, especially John F. Kennedy; master of fact and language, he sparred effectively with the likes of Henry Kissinger; generous to a fault, he divided his energy and resources among innumerable causes and was an officer of many. A thousand friends honored him on his seventieth birthday, and he was still around twelve years later to bring eighteen thousand people to their feet in Madison Square Garden. His colleagues were his constituents—the named leadership in liberal and radical America and the thousands of unnamed people whom he inspired. A biographer rightly concluded that he appealed to the good in mankind. His hearers knew he appealed to the good in them. It elevated them. The world seemed better when one's intelligence and nobler impulses were importuned. It made some believe that a still better world was possible. . . . It was so rare that the magic of it spread across the country, though too thinly to measure.[38]

Norman Thomas developed a modern and American version of socialism, and he gave it wide currency for a decade. His was a social vision based on a discriminating sense of relative social ethics. He believed that socialist strategy should address both the goal of fundamental social revolution and the proximate steps toward it, that collective values must include the democratic process, and that violence reinforces unjust relationships. This version of democratic socialism was not a program that could command political power. It was a standard of social value against which to chart the mainstream, although in order to increase its political impact Thomas acted as though it might become political reality. His organizational work was nonetheless subsidiary to the central socialist mission as he conceived it: to be a party of dissent. When the party no longer sufficed, he carried the mission on his own.

His primary goal was peace, and he pursued it for a half century. Conflict was real enough, he believed, and it was rooted in injustice. Armed forces might secure order, but war was no instrument of peace. On the contrary, peace requires changes in the world order which at the same time minimize arbitrary, violent force and maximize justice. This version of peace was a standard against which to chart American foreign policy, and it often cast Thomas in the role of a dissenter.

Dissent was not a form of rejection for him. Thomas did not preach puritanical jeremiads. Rather, he extolled popular values—truth, fairness, and progress through applied intelligence. He urged people to approximate those virtues in the world of relative choices. Master of words, he called deeds to an accounting. In this respect, he embodied the social utility of dissent without which there is no social choice, only preferred interests. Beyond the federal principle of checking power by the open play of contending ambitions must lie an overarching social purpose. Early in American history James Madison had named that purpose: "Justice is the end of government. It is the end of civil society."[39] Norman Thomas added, it is the end of a peaceful world society.

NOTES

1. Alden Whiteman, "The Great Reformer, Unsatisfied to the End," *New York Times* (December 22, 1968), p. 2E, quoted in James C. Duram, *Norman Thomas* (Boston: Twayne, 1974), p. 140. Also, see Harry Fleischman, *Norman Thomas: A Biography* (New York: W.W. Norton, 1964, 1969) Murray B. Seidler, *Norman Thomas: Respectable Rebel* (Syracuse, N.Y.: Syracuse University Press, 1961) Bernard Johnpoll, *Pacifist's Progress: Norman Thomas and the Decline of American Socialism* (Chicago: Quadrangle, 1970) and W.A. Swanberg, *Norman Thomas: The Last Idealist* (New York: Charles Scribner's Sons, 1976).

2. Swanberg, *Norman Thomas,* p. 46.

3. John Haynes Holmes was the Unitarian pastor of the Church of the Messiah, New York, a leading preacher, pacifist, and reformer throughout his life; John Nevin Sayre lost his pastorate during the war and became the leading light in the Fellowship of Reconciliation (FOR); A. J. Muste also lost his pastorate, worked with the FOR, became a leading labor and radical activist, and returned to share the leadership of the FOR in the mid-thirties; Emily Green Balch was a settlement-house worker who became the leader of the Women's International League for Peace and Freedom and a winner of the Nobel Prize for Peace.

4. "Signs of the Times," *The World Tomorrow* 1, (October 1918): 237.

5. "What of the Church?" *The New World* (February 1918): 46. *The New World* was the original name of *The World Tomorrow.*

6. See Charles Chatfield, *The Radical "No": The Correspondence and Writings of Evan Thomas on War* (New York: Garland, 1974), pp. 104, 241–49.

7. Thomas, *The Christian Patriot* (The William Penn Lectures, 1917), p. 18, reprinted in *Norman Thomas on War: An Anthology,* Bernard K. Johnpoll, ed. (New York: Garland, 1972).

8. Thomas, *War's Heretics: A Plea for the Conscientious Objector* (New York: League for Industrial Democracy, 1924), pp. 10–12.

9. Thomas, *The Conscientious Objector in America* (New York: B.W. Huebach, 1923).

10. Quoted in full in Seidler, *Norman Thomas,* pp. 28–29.

11. Thomas, *The Challenge of War: An Economic Interpretation* (New York: League for Industrial Democracy, 1924), pp. 41–43.

12. Swanberg, *Norman Thomas,* p. 84.

13. Thomas and Laidler, *The Socialism of Our Times* (New York: Vanguard, 1929), p. 373.

14. Quoted in Swanberg, *Norman Thomas,* p. 136.

15. See especially Thomas, *The Choice Before Us: Mankind at the Crossroads* (New York: Macmillan, 1934), p. 89.

16. Thomas, *Human Exploitation in the United States* (New York: Frederick A. Stokes, 1934), p. 380.

17. Thomas, *The Choice Before Us,* p. 93.

18. Thomas, *Socialism on the Defensive* (New York: Harper, 1938), p. 9.

19. Ibid., p. 67.

20. "Declaration of Principles of the Socialist Party of the U.S.A." (Chicago: Socialist Party of the U.S.A., 1934). The declaration is printed in full in Devere Allen, "Why the Declaration Must Pass," *The World Tomorrow* 17 (June 28, 1934): 323–24.

21. Duram, *Norman Thomas,* p. 70.

22. James T. Shotwell was director of the Carnegie Endowment's Division of Economics and History and a major supporter of the League of Nations system; Clark Eichelberger was director of the League of Nations Association. The contest among peace groups over foreign policy in the thirties is recounted in Charles Chatfield, *For Peace and Justice* (Nashville: University of Tennessee Press, 1971), part 4.

23. Johnpoll, *Pacifist's Progress*, pp. 185, 232. Johnpoll's view that Thomas reversed his position on war is given seeming support by Thomas's own reflection in *A Socialist's Faith* (Port Washington, N.Y.: Kennikat Press, 1951, 1971), p. 308. The issue turns on the meaning and component assumptions of pacifism which, I believe, Johnpoll misrepresents (along with isolationism).

24. This line of thought is developed in Thomas, *America's Way Out: A Program for Democracy* (New York: Macmillan, 1931), *As I See It* (New York: Macmillan, 1932), *The Choice Before Us*, and *Socialism on the Defensive*.

25. Thomas, *Socialism on the Defensive*, p. 99.

26. Ibid., p. 208.

27. Ibid., p. 209.

28. Quoted in Swanberg, *Norman Thomas*, p. 266.

29. In 1944 Sayre and A. J. Muste of the FOR published a booklet by British author Vera Brittain on saturation bombing, but changed its title from *Seed of Chaos* to *Massacre by Bombing*. Accompanied by a signed appeal for compassion by twenty-eight religious leaders, the publication got widespread and often acrimonious attention.

30. Thomas, *What Is Our Destiny?* (Doubleday, Doran, 1944).

31. Ibid., p. 5.

32. Ibid., pp. 112, 111.

33. Thomas, *A Socialist's Faith*, p. 293.

34. Ibid., p. 292.

35. Thomas, *The Choices*, (New York: Ives Washburn, 1969), pp. 3–4.

36. Thomas, *A Socialist's Faith*, p. 293.

37. Thomas, *The Choices*, p. 8.

38. Swanberg, *Norman Thomas*, p. 454.

39. "The Federalist No. 51," in *The Federalist Papers*, ed. Roy P. Fairchild (Garden City, N.Y.: Doubleday Anchor, 1961), p. 162.

FURTHER READING

Norman Thomas reflected on aspects of his life and thought in *A Socialist's Faith* (Port Washington, NY: Kenniket Press, 1951, 1971) and in articles, but he did not write a full autobiography. *The Conscientious Objector in America* (New York: B. W. Huebsch, 1923) was a pioneering historical work. Thomas's subsequent books dealt with current affairs of society and state. Usually they were based on his speaking experience and articles. A series published by Macmillan documents his evolving socialist platform: *America's Way Out: A Program for Democracy* (1931), *As I See It* (1932), and *The Choice Before Us: Mankind at the Crossroads* (1934). *Socialism on the Defensive* (New York: Harper & Bros., 1938) rounded out this series, which was completed in 1953 with *Democratic Socialism: A New Appraisal* (New York: League for Industrial Democracy). In the same period, Thomas wrote a trenchant exposé of *Human Exploitation in the United States* (New York: Frederick A. Stokes, 1934). His perception of the nation on the world stage during and after World War II was expressed especially well in *What Is Our Destiny* (Boston: Doubleday, Doran, 1944) and *Prerequisites for Peace* (New York: Norton, 1959), the latter under the sobering impact of the Cold War and balance of terror. Just before his death, he put together the summa of his political understanding in *The Choices* (New York: Ives Washburn, 1969).

The most important biographies are W. A. Swanberg, *Norman Thomas: The Last Idealist* (New York: Charles Scribner's Sons, 1976), which is an engaging and comprehensive study of Thomas's personal and political development; James C. Duram, *Norman Thomas* (Boston: Twayne, 1974), a brief but insightful integration of Thomas's life and thought based especially on his writings; Bernard Johnpoll, *Pacifist's Progress: Norman Thomas and the Decline of American Socialism* (Chicago: Quadrangle, 1970), which treats Thomas in a strictly political context and is inordinately critical of his leadership; Murray B. Seidler, *Norman Thomas: Respectable Rebel* (Syracuse, NY: Syracuse University Press, 1961), which puts Thomas in the context of the Socialist party and is critically appreciative; Charles Gorham, *Leader at Large* (New York: Farrar, Straus & Giroux, 1970); and Harry Fleischman, *Norman Thomas: A Biography* (New York: Norton, 1964, 1969), written by a close associate in the party.

HAROLD JOSEPHSON

Albert Einstein

The Search for World Order

In 1933, shortly after Albert Einstein moved to Princeton, New Jersey, to work at the Institute for Advanced Studies, a caller telephoned the dean of the Princeton University Graduate School, requesting the physicist's address. Bombarded by interviewers' requests and desiring to minimize outside disturbances so that Einstein could proceed with his scientific research in peace, the university staff had strict orders not to release his address or telephone number. When the request was politely refused, the caller lowered his voice to a whisper and declared: "Please do not tell anybody, but I *am* Dr. Einstein. I am on my way home and have forgotten where my house is."[1]

This anecdote, one of many that circulated about Einstein's forgetfulness, his eccentricities, and his refusal to adjust to the common conventions of modern life, helped make this century's most well-known scientist a legend in his own time. His refusal to wear socks, his unkempt appearance, his long white hair, all fed a public that seemed never to tire of reading about the man who had unlocked the secrets of the universe. Einstein was the superstar of modern science, a veritable folk hero who was treated by both the public and press as a movie celebrity rather than a scientist.

Einstein's reputation as a theoretical physicist was well founded, and his insights into the nature and working of the physical laws of the universe marked him as one of the most creative intellects in human history. Most of his significant contributions to theoretical physics were made while he was in his twenties and thirties, but he continued his scientific work until his death. He is most remembered for his relativity theory, which revolutionized scientific thought with new conceptions of time, space, mass, motion, and gravitation. By treating matter and energy as exchangeable, he laid the basis for man's controlling the release of energy from the atom.

Although he always placed his scientific work above all things material and had little inclination for the frivolous or mundane, he was not entirely a cloistered scientist, unconcerned about politics or moral issues. Einstein firmly believed that scholars had a moral responsibility to make clear their position on issues that affected humankind. He wrote and spoke repeatedly on questions of war and peace, civil liberties, Zionism, and intellectual freedom. Scientific knowledge and truth, he maintained, had no geographic boundaries, and Einstein early came to believe that nationalism posed a major threat to human progress and peace. He envisioned a world where nationalism would be replaced by internationalism, where science would be used to enhance society rather than destroy it, and where intellectual freedom would never be held in check for the benefit of flag and country.

In his political convictions, Einstein often appeared paradoxical: a German who hated Germans; a pacifist who supported armed intervention against Hitler and who favored an international police force; an internationalist who supported Zionism with its strongly nationalistic overtones; a Zionist who favored placating the Arabs; an opponent of the nuclear arms race who helped initiate the American program that led to the development of the atomic bomb. Einstein at times offered his political ideas without fully thinking them through and sometimes he reversed himself on critical matters, but he remained consistent in his fundamental assumptions and retained the hope that mankind would rise above the ties of nationalism and establish an international community where peace and justice prevailed.

Born in Ulm, Germany, on March 14, 1879, the son of a nonpracticing Jewish chemical engineer, Einstein showed no particular intellectual promise as a youngster. He was so slow in learning to speak, in fact, that by the time he was three some family members worried that he might prove retarded. The concerns proved unfounded, although Einstein did not do particularly well in school and showed interest only in mathematics and science. When he was fifteen his father, whose Munich business had failed, moved the family to Milan, Italy, but left his son behind to finish his studies at the Luitpold Gymnasium, where the rudiments of Latin, Greek, history, geography, and mathematics were drummed into middle-class German youths. Disliking the regimented approach of the school and its harsh discipline, Einstein developed a deep suspicion of all forms of authority. Within six months of his family's departure, he left Munich without taking exams or receiving a diploma. Following his family across the Alps, he spent some time in Italy, completed his high school education in Aarau, Switzerland, and, in 1896, entered the Federal Polytechnic School in Zurich, where he graduated four years later, majoring in physics and mathematics.

Einstein's strong will and dislike for all things German led him to renounce his German citizenship shortly after leaving Munich. He remained a stateless person until 1901, when he applied for and received Swiss citizenship. The following year, having searched in vain for a teaching position, he was employed as a junior official at the patent office in Berne, Switzerland. Despite bureaucratic responsibilities, he found time to pursue his theoretical scientific studies. In 1905, he published a series of papers in the prestigious German physics monthly *Annalen der Physik* that profoundly altered man's view of the universe and, in their total influence, surpassed any scientific writings since the time of Sir Isaac Newton.

In one paper he presented ideas that ultimately revolutionized the theory of light and provided an explanation for what was later called the photoelectric effect. Although not generally accepted by most physicists at the time, later experiments proved his theory valid and led to Einstein's receiving the Nobel Prize in physics in 1921. In another paper he provided a theoretical explanation of Brownian movement, an irregular motion of microscopic particles suspended in a liquid or a gas. His analysis, and subsequent measurements by other physicists, confirmed the existence of atoms, convincing most remaining skeptics. In still another paper, which was submitted and accepted as his Ph.D. dissertation at the University of Zurich, he developed a method for determining the dimensions of molecules.

Einstein's major work of 1905, however, was his paper "On the Electrodynamics of Moving Bodies," in which he presented his special theory of relativity. The concept of the relativity of time and space, previously unimaginable ideas, significantly changed the Newtonian "common sense" view of time and motion and became a cornerstone of twentieth-century physics. Based on his special theory of relativity, Einstein also discovered an interrelationship between mass and energy, from which he developed his famous equation, $E = mc^2$ (energy equals mass times the velocity of light squared). Since the velocity of light is a huge quantity, the formula postulated that very small amounts of mass could produce huge amounts of energy. His theory became the basis for the development of atomic energy.

Einstein's work attracted the attention of many European physicists, and beginning in 1909 he accepted a series of teaching positions that led, in 1913, to the directorship of scientific research at the Kaiser Wilhelm Institute for Physics. He moved to Berlin in 1914 and remained connected with the Institute until 1933, when he left Germany forever and took a position at the Institute for Advanced Studies at Princeton.

Soon after moving to Berlin, Einstein completed work on his

general theory of relativity, probably his major contribution to theoretical physics. The theory provided a new description of gravitation, altering the Newtonian view that gravity was a force. Now Einstein postulated that gravitation was a curved field in the space-time continuum, created by the presence of mass. He further suggested that his theory could be tested by measuring the deflection of starlight as it traveled close by the sun, the starlight being visible only during a total eclipse. When, in November, 1919, the Royal Society of London announced that the scientific expedition it had sent to photograph the solar eclipse the previous May had completed calculations that verified the predictions made in the general theory, Einstein suddenly gained international fame and was hailed as one of history's greatest geniuses. Most people could not understand the theory of relativity, but they were quick to idolize the man who had revolutionized thinking about the universe and who seemed to be the scientists' scientist.

Einstein was amazed at the public interest in his life and work, and also somewhat displeased, for it led to constant interruptions and diverted him from his research. He directed the major thrust of his efforts towards the creation of a "unified field theory," which would link gravitation and electromagnetism. He hoped this would be a first step in discovering the common laws governing the behavior of everything in the universe, from the electron to the planets. He continued this search unsuccessfully for the rest of his life. He disagreed with the majority of his colleagues who predicted early that he would fail to discover a unified field theory. They based their opinion on the new science of quantum mechanics and the discovery of an uncertainty factor in all measurements of the movement of electrons. Einstein appreciated quantum mechanics, but argued that the lack of predictability was due to the failure to find the guiding principles of a unified theory. He preferred to believe in an exactly engineered universe and frequently declared that "God does not play dice with the world."[2]

Einstein was above all else a scientist. Prior to the outbreak of World War I in 1914, as he progressed from obscurity to renown as a physicist, he rarely discussed social or political topics. Although he seemed to care little about everyday life and politics, it is more likely that his preoccupation with science, together with the absence of international violence at the time, meant that his concerns with broader issues and with war itself had not yet been challenged. The outbreak of war brought home to him the full horror of modern armed conflict. It not only caused wholesale death and destruction in the belligerent countries, but it also caused profound upheaval in human, cultural, political, and scientific relationships throughout the world. Contacts between scientists, which had previously known no national restraints, now were curtailed sharply as nationalism colored the views of scientists and politicians alike.

Einstein was deeply shocked both by the pain and suffering of the war and by the chauvinism that accompanied it. The willingness of so many of his Berlin colleagues to lend their support to war work and to forego their worldwide scientific relationships crystallized his commitment to pacifism and internationalism. His opposition to war and his deeply felt humanism quickly rose to the surface, encouraging him to challenge the prevailing political ideology in his native Germany and the strong sense of nationalism felt throughout Europe.

Einstein's opposition to war was not the result of a carefully worked out political philosophy or intellectual theory. Instead his pacifism was an "instinctive" reaction; the thought of murdering human beings was "abhorrent" to him. His pacifism was tied to the concept that the killing of any human being was murder and that it was also murder "when it takes place on a large scale as an instrument of state policy."[3] Second only to his scientific work, Einstein's desire for peace and internationalism dominated his activities and he lent his enormous prestige and fame to promoting these twin goals.

His first public statement on these matters came as a response to a declaration issued in October, 1914, by ninety-three German intellectuals. Called a "Manifesto to the Civilized World," the document justified Germany's invasion of neutral Belgium, disclaimed German war guilt, and hailed German militarism as the saviour of German culture. The document, no doubt, represented the sentiments of most Germans, including the vast majority of intellectuals. Still, a reply was issued a few days later, written by Georg Friedrich Nicoli, a professor of physiology at the University of Berlin, and by Einstein. Signed by only two others, the "Manifesto to Europeans" emphasized the need for international cooperation, condemned the upsurge in chauvinism, and called upon men of goodwill to work for a peace settlement that would promote European unity over divisive nationalism. It was a brave message to utter in the chauvinistic environment of Berlin, and, not surprisingly, it attracted little support and much criticism. Einstein, however, would not back away. For the first time, he joined a political organization, the *Bund Neues Vaterland* (New Fatherland League). The *Bund* had been organized in November, 1914, in order to promote an early and just peace without the annexation of territories. It also supported the establishment of a supranational organization after the war. The *Bund* issued pamphlets, made public statements, and held meetings at which Einstein sometimes spoke. From the beginning the group was harrassed, and in 1916 its activities were banned. It operated clandestinely for a while, but after the armistice in 1918 it came out in the open again.

Einstein held a privileged position in wartime Germany, in part because he had retained his Swiss citizenship and was able to travel to the neutral nations and in part because his renown as a scientist allowed him to criticize the war even though his views were disliked. Despite his activities, he was somewhat circumspect in Germany, but in private conversations with those he could trust, he vented the depth of his opposition to the war. He attacked German leaders as greedy and arrogant, and criticized the German public as excessively submissive and prepared blindly to follow the dictates of state authorities. He went so far as to tell the pacifist Romain Rolland that only an Allied victory would destroy the power of Prussia and that such a defeat would be good for Germany's future. An Allied victory would serve as the basis for an enduring world organization and for the ultimate democratization of Germany. He was overjoyed, therefore, when Kaiser Wilhelm II abdicated in November, 1918, and Germany agreed to an armistice. Furthermore, he supported the Treaty of Versailles and welcomed the creation of the Weimar Republic, hoping that it would institutionalize both democracy and individual liberty in postwar Germany.

During the 1920s, Einstein's position in Germany remained ambiguous. Verification of his general theory of relativity in 1919 brought him international recognition, fame, and even hero-worship unknown to any other modern scientist. He traveled widely, not only throughout Europe, but to the Orient, to the Middle East, to South America, and to the United States. Everywhere the reaction was the same: Einstein was greeted with adulation and almost semireligious awe. In his own country, scientists recognized his accomplishments and some politicians hoped to present him to the world as typifying the "new" Germany. But others in the Weimar Republic, and especially more conservative forces, condemned him for what he was: a left-wing pacifist, internationalist, and Jew. His efforts to expose German atrocities during World War I, his aggressive attacks upon postwar German nationalism (which he called "a severe sickness"), his open avowal of Zionism and its call for the establishment of a Jewish homeland, his participation in pacifist activities, and his pronounced internationalism made him anathema to right-wing groups.

Einstein found it easy to dismiss the rantings of the right wing, but he was more concerned by the attacks in the German press and the denunciations of his political views by some of his scientific colleagues. In order to show support for the new Weimar government, and perhaps to deflect some of the harsh criticism he was receiving, he applied for and received German citizenship in 1920 (although he did not surrender his Swiss citizenship). He later regretted the decision, calling it one of the "follies" of his life. While he was willing to once again call himself a German, he was unwilling to mute his political opinions or to curtail his internationalist activities. During the early 1920s, he sought to promote internationalism by accepting lecture offers in France and Great Britain and by encouraging intellectual cooperation. He felt that it was important for "men, speaking different languages and having different political and cultural views, [to] communicate with each other across frontiers."[4]

His interest in promoting international cultural ties led him to join the Committee on Intellectual Cooperation. The Committee, originally established in 1922 in order to encourage international understanding and develop contacts between teachers, artists, scientists, and members of other intellectual professions, was an unofficial agency of the League of Nations, representing individuals rather than governments. Citizens from all nations, whether or not they belonged to the League, could participate in its work. Einstein's relationship with the Committee was rocky from the start. He resigned several times, once because German scientists were excluded from an international scientific congress and once in protest over the French invasion of the Ruhr in 1923, but each time he rejoined. He remained active on the Committee until 1930.

Einstein hoped that the Committee on Intellectual Cooperation might contribute to peace by advancing new educational theories containing antiwar values. He favored the establishment of an international university for the training of statesmen, diplomats, political writers, and political scientists. Even closer to his heart, however, was the idea of peace education. He believed that, historically, the militarism of the masses had been fostered by propaganda and that one road away from war was to teach people to resist such propaganda. "We must begin to inoculate our children against militarism," he declared, "by educating them in the spirit of pacifism. . . . Our schoolbooks glorify war and conceal its horrors. They indoctrinate children with hatred. I would teach peace rather than war, love rather than hate."5

Eventually Einstein lost faith in both the Committee and the League itself. The Committee engaged in only the most modest projects involving exchanges of literature, as well as faculty and student exchanges. It never developed the broad vision of international intellectual cooperation that Einstein supported. The League, too, disappointed him. A strong advocate of supranational organization, he did not believe that the League had lived up to its own basic principles. He was particularly irked by the League's silence during the French invasion of the Ruhr in 1923. Although he continued to advocate German membership in the world organization, he repeatedly spoke out in favor of a League that would fulfill its stated mission and become a truly international organization for the promotion of peace.

Einstein's internationalism was a crucial aspect of his pacifism, but even more central to his opposition to both war and nationalism was his belief in individual freedom. He favored complete freedom in the pursuit of truth and knowledge, and therefore favored no censorship or state-imposed restrictions on speech or press. He firmly held to the idea that the state was "made for man, not man for the state." He argued that the most important mission of the state was "to protect the individual and make it possible for him to develop into a creative personality."6

From this concept of individual freedom Einstein easily moved to the advocacy of pacifism. During the late 1920s and early 1930s, he adopted an uncompromising new pacifist position known as war resistance. When asked what he would do if another war broke out, Einstein declared that he "would unconditionally refuse all war service, direct or indirect, and would seek to persuade my friends to adopt the same position, regardless of how I might feel about the causes of any particular war." He urged all "thoughtful, well-meaning and conscientious" human beings to "assume, in time of peace, the solemn and unconditional obligation not to participate in any war, for any reason, or to lend support of any kind, whether direct or indirect."[7] These ideas led him to accept a position on the Board of Directors of the German League for Human Rights, one of the most important pacifist organizations in the country. In addition, he supported other peace groups, including the No More War Movement, the Women's International League for Peace and Freedom, and the War Resisters International.

Einstein's militant war resistance did not find much favor in Germany, in the rest of Europe, or in the United States. Vilified in Berlin, he was condemned as dangerous or naive in London, Paris, and Washington. Still, in the early 1930s, he chose to pronounce his beliefs with greater and greater vigor. "Nothing will end war," he declared, "unless the peoples themselves refuse to go to war." He desired, moreover, to move beyond rhetoric and promoted his "two per cent" idea. He told an American audience that pacifists had it within their power to initiate actioin. He suggested that if "only two per cent of those assigned to perform military service should announce their refusal to fight, as well as urge means other than war of settling international disputes, governments would be powerless" and wars would cease to be used as instruments of national policy.[8] The "two per cent" idea gained considerable attention in the United States, adding to the belief by some that Einstein was a dangerous subversive and by others that he was a pacifist hero.

Even within the peace movement, however, many had doubts about war resistance as an effective method for eliminating international armed conflict. Some, like Romain Rolland, one of the most prominent European peace leaders, pointed out that war was changing and that technicians rather than soldiers would be crucial in fighting future wars. Military equipment and inventions of mass destruction meant that governments could fight wars with much more than 2 percent of the population objecting. War resistance, argued Rolland, might be a viable moral response to war, but it would not abolish war. Advocates of disarmament, arbitration agreements, collective security, and other alternatives to war, moreover, found war resistance too impractical and uncompromising a policy to effectively curtail international conflict.

Einstein seemed impervious to the complexities of the debate within the peace movement and to the subtleties of the respective antiwar arguments. Despite the vigor with which he advocated absolute pacifism, he also recognized the value of other approaches to peace and sometimes subscribed to them despite their apparent contradiction of his own war resistance philosophy. Perhaps Einstein did not think through his political ideas as fully or as clearly as he did his scientific theories, or perhaps he realized that more than one approach was necessary to end the world's long reliance on armed might. In any case, he did not reject other alternatives to war as readily as did many advocates of absolute pacifism. They, in turn, found Einstein's eclectic approach discouraging and even harmful to their cause.

For those who did not want to serve in the armed forces but were not prepared to go to jail or suffer the consequences of absolute war resistance, Einstein supported the passage of legislation that would permit them to do alternative nonmilitary service. He rejected the argument, put forward by other advocates of war resistance, that because such services might indirectly help a nation's war-making capability it should be rejected as a legitimate alternative to serving in the armed forces. On the issue of disarmament, he had mixed feelings. He did not believe that arms limitation agreements would end war, but he did recognize the danger of arms races and saw in disarmament an appropriate first step in establishing workable peace machinery. After the Japanese invasion of Manchuria in 1931, moreover, Einstein went so far as to imply that he saw value in the idea of collective security. To most absolute pacifists, collective security directly contradicted their war resistance principles. The concept, inherent in the League of Nations, rested on the idea that the best way to prevent wars was to threaten any potential aggressor nation with the combined force of all other nations. Long an advocate of supranational organization, Einstein now suggested that for decisions reached by the League or the World Court to be effective, they might have to be backed by economic or military sanctions.

Many of Einstein's colleagues in the war resistance movement tried to dissuade him from publicly supporting alternative service or collective security, but either he did not understand the contradictions between these ideas and the principles of absolute pacifism or he chose to ignore them. In any case, for Einstein the crucial matter was to find means to end war and elevate the value of the individual regardless of the philosophical integrity of any given peace plan. His views were important not because he presented anything that was new or presented them with the force of profound reasoning, but because of who he was and the conviction with which he offered them. During the late 1920s and early 1930s, Einstein was one of the world's best known advocates of world order and peace.

The coming to power in Germany of Adolf Hitler in January, 1933, created a crisis in Einstein's life. As Germany's most prominent Jew and as one of its most outspoken pacifists, Zionists, and internationalists, he was hated by the Nazi leadership. Lecturing in the United States at the time, he immediately decided that he would not return to the country of his birth. Declaring that he would live "only in a country where civil liberty, tolerance and equality of all citizens before the law" existed, he first took up residence in the Belgian resort of Le Coq-sur-Mer and then agreed to a full-time position with the Institute for Advanced Studies and moved to Princeton, New Jersey, in October 1933. He resigned from the Prussian Academy of Sciences and began to speak out publicly against the Nazi regime. He told his friend Max Planck, the German physicist, that he had no choice but to challenge the new government, for it was waging a "war of annihilation against my defenseless fellow Jews," seeking their destruction by starvation and by depriving them of gainful employment. He reprimanded German intellectuals for their silence, warning that the Nazis would "soon succeed in destroying or paralyzing everything that is civilized in society."9

Although Einstein received a warm welcome at Princeton and was immediately made to feel at home, his arrival was not without some controversy. One Princeton University alumnus, expressing, no doubt, the feelings of many on the political right who found Einstein's pacifism, Zionism, and socialism offensive, charged that he was a "foreign sprouter of doctrines inimical to our Constitution, history and social life." He wanted Einstein barred from lecturing at the university. The charge that Einstein was a Communist or, at least, sympathetic to the Soviet Union, hounded him throughout his life. The FBI began to collect information on him as early as 1932 and for a time even believed that from 1929 to 1932 he had allowed his Berlin office to be used as a "drop" for telegraph messages from Soviet agents in the Far East. Later, even more serious charges of espionage and Communist activities would fill Einstein's FBI file, although none was ever substantiated.10

An advocate of socialism, Einstein was no Communist and never glorified the Soviet Union. In fact, he frequently took the Soviet Union to task for suppressing individual freedom. He refused, moreover, to participate in Soviet-led peace organizations and rejected an invitation to attend the International Congress Against Imperialist Wars held in Amsterdam in 1932, because he viewed it as having been manipulated by the Russians. Explaining his position, Einstein declared that he was "an adversary of Bolshevism just as much as of Fascism. I am against all dictatorships." He would not, however, subscribe to a thorough denunciation of the Soviet Union or of Communism, and the accusation that he was disloyal to his adopted country and its principles persisted.[11]

In the United States, Einstein concentrated on his scientific work, continuing to view himself as a physicist first and foremost. Although many friends in the scientific community gently suggested that he avoid public controversy, Einstein would not remain silent on international issues and soon became an advocate of "preparedness" in the United States and in Europe. It was a strange position for him to be in. Recognized as a champion of war resistance, he now demanded that the Atlantic democracies strengthen themselves against Nazi Germany. He remained constant in his abhorrence of war and in his belief that only the creation of a supranational organization would safeguard peace, but the rise of Nazism, with its glorification of war and its reckless abandonment of all ethical and moral values, forced him to alter his stand on absolute pacifism.

Einstein denied that he had changed so much as international circumstances had changed. But his advocacy of an international military force as an indispensable prerequisite for the abolition of war marked a clear-cut departure from his earlier support of absolute pacifism. Although he would have preferred an international police force under the authority of a supranational organization to the rearmament of individual states, he supported national preparedness in the absence of an international military alternative. He did not regret his earlier support of war resistance; he simply argued that methods for achieving peace must necessarily be adapted to altered conditions. As long as a majority of the nations of Europe were intent upon peace, the refusal of military service was a viable concept. The threat posed by Germany to the entire civilized world, however, could not be successfully combated by moral means; it could be met only by organized might. "To prevent the greater evil," he declared, "it is necessary that the lesser evil—the hated military—be accepted for the time being. Should German armed might prevail, life will not be worth living anywhere in Europe." To the French antimilitarist, Alfred Nahon, Einstein made clear how far he had traveled from his earlier belief in war resistance: "Were I a Belgian, I should not, in the present circumstances, refuse military service; rather, I should enter such service cheerfully in the belief that I would thereby be helping to save European civilization."[12]

Although supporters of collective security within the peace movement were glad to have Einstein on their side, many pacifists were quick to condemn him as a traitor to the cause and as a supporter of militarism. Throughout the 1930s, Einstein maintained that his position was the only reasonable and expedient way to counter Hitler. He did not want war, but he believed that Germany would resort to arms unless it was convinced that Europe was strong and united and that the United States was ready to assume a more activist and internationalist role in the world. Preparedness, according to Einstein, was the best deterrent to war. He became increasingly critical of his former pacifist colleagues, arguing that their emphasis on war resistance and disarmament "harmed rather than helped the cause of peace."

On September 1, 1939, Einstein's worst fears came true. Hitler's armies invaded Poland, and two days later England and France declared war on Germany. World War II had begun. When it was over six years later, over 30 million people had died, and the United States had dramatically ushered in the atomic age by obliterating the cities of Hiroshima and Nagasaki. Einstein was often mistakenly referred to as the father of the atomic bomb, but in truth his role was minor. Until the outbreak of war, he had doubted that his famous formula describing the equivalence of energy and mass would find any practical application during his lifetime. His reservations continued even after news reached the United States that, in Berlin, Otto Hahn had split the nucleus of a uranium atom in December, 1938.

Einstein was somewhat surprised, therefore, when he was visited by Leo Szilard of Columbia University and Eugene P. Wigner of Princeton in July, 1939 and told not only that they believed a fission chain reaction was possible, but that they feared that unless the United States accelerated atomic research, Nazi Germany might be the first to produce nuclear weapons. Convinced that the United States had to take steps to meet this threat, Einstein signed a letter on August 2

informing President Franklin D. Roosevelt of the potential for building "extremely powerful bombs of a new type," of the need for greater
contact between the government and atomic scientists, and of the
importance of federal funds being channeled to the new research.

Szilard came to Princeton because Einstein was the most famous
physicist in the world and had a better chance of impressing President
Roosevelt with the need for action than Szilard himself or any of the
other concerned scientists. Dr. Alexander Sachs, a well-known econo-
mist and friend of both Szilard and Roosevelt, delivered Einstein's
letter to the president in October. Roosevelt responded by establishing an "Advisory Committee on Uranium" and ordering it to report as
soon as possible. The committee met, but the effort was hardly on the
order hoped for by Szilard, Sachs, or Einstein. Only six thousand
dollars was appropriated for the first year of research. Einstein was
persuaded to write a second letter to Roosevelt in March, 1940, again
urging more government action, suggesting the need for secrecy in the
field of atomic research, and warning that the Germans were working
diligently to develop an atomic bomb.

As a response to this second plea, Roosevelt enlarged the committee, which eventually became the National Defense Research
Committee. The real incentive for the Manhattan Project, the name
given to the coordinated scientific effort that led to the production of
atomic bombs, however, came in the summer of 1941, when the
British convinced the Americans that a chain reaction bomb could
actually be made. The United States would certainly have developed
an atomic bomb without Einstein's letters, but his warnings doubtlessly prompted the White House into building the organizational
base that developed the bomb before the end of the war and before the
Soviet Union effected its own atomic breakthrough.

After sending his second letter to President Roosevelt, Einstein
had little direct connection with the effort to produce nuclear weapons. This was not entirely of his own choosing, for as long as Germany remained in the war, he communicated his desire to do more for
the war effort and even to help on the atomic bomb project. These
requests were largely ignored, however, mainly because his reputation
as an advocate of peace made him suspect in some quarters in Washington. To many in power, Einstein's prewar views made him a
security risk. Ironically, with the growing concern over national
security, Einstein was simply viewed as not loyal enough to work on

the very project that he helped to initiate. Few people knew that he had played a role in moving the government to develop the Manhattan Project with his letters or that he was fully aware of the potential for developing a fission bomb. Not even Dr. Vannevar Bush, chairman of the National Defense Research Committee, who made the decision to exclude Einstein from research on nuclear weapons, knew of his contribution. Such were the politics of peace and loyalty in the years following World War I.

Einstein did serve as a part-time consultant to the U.S. Navy's Bureau of Ordnance and probably knew much more about the progress of the Manhattan Project than he admitted in public after the war. His exclusion from the inner councils of the scientists working on atomic research, however, prevented his participation in the debate raging in the spring of 1945 over whether nuclear weapons should be used against Japan. Following the war, he frequently asserted that had he been consulted he would have sided with those scientists who opposed using the bomb and who favored the international control of atomic energy. Such a position was consistent with his initial view that the United States needed to produce nuclear weapons as a deterrent to the Nazis and his strong belief in world organization.

With the war over, Einstein joined in the great debate over the future of nuclear weapons and the future of the world. The postwar decade was the last of his life, and throughout the period he lent his name and immense prestige to the causes of supranational organization and the international control of atomic energy. He spoke out as a scientist-citizen, concerned about the uses governments would make of scientific discoveries and about public policy generally. To his delight, he no longer found himself alone among his scientific colleagues speaking out forcefully on public issues. No longer did physicists and other scientists feel aloof from public debate. They had been intimately involved in creating the weapons of mass destruction used during World War II and had unleashed the scientific and technological knowledge that would increase the destructiveness of future weapons even more. Now, many were willing to speak out, arguing that scientists, *because* of their knowledge, were in an excellent position to advise America and the world on these issues. Although unable, because of ill health, to attend many meetings or give many lectures, Einstein wrote extensively on issues of war and peace and became for many "the conscience of the world."[13]

Believing strongly that scientists should play a role in the discussion of the future of atomic energy and should help inform the public about the dangers and possibilities of this new force, Einstein agreed to serve as chairman of the Emergency Committee of Atomic Scientists. The Emergency Committee raised money for educational programs, supported the *Bulletin of Atomic Scientists,* and brought scientists together to discuss matters of public policy that related to atomic energy. At one such conference, held in November, 1946, Einstein and his colleagues issued a dire warning that atomic bombs would be made more cheaply and in larger numbers in the future, that there was no realistic military defense against them, that other nations would soon have the technology to make them, that if war came, they would be used and would destroy civilization, and, finally, that the only solution was the international control of atomic energy and the elimination of war.

On one crucial matter, Einstein went further than many of his colleagues on the Emergency Committee. He believed strongly that only the establishment of a supranational organization with real military power could maintain stability in the midst of international chaos and could ultimately prevent atomic holocaust. Einstein did not lament the discovery of atomic energy or feel guilty about his role in developing the atomic bomb. As a physicist he accepted the advance of science as inevitable and maintained forcefully that no restraints should be placed on scientific or technological inquiry. For him, the key was to control mankind's destructive tendencies and to channel scientific knowledge in socially beneficial directions. The only way to do this was through the establishment of world government.

Occasionally during the 1930s, Einstein had called for the creation of a supranational organization with military and legal powers to confront threats to world peace. Now, with the development of atomic weapons, his commitment to world government increased markedly. He doubted that proposals giving international control of atomic weapons to the newly formed United Nations would be sufficient. Instead he concluded that world government, with adequate power to enforce its will, was the only viable approach to establishing international peace. He warned that the "unleashed power of the atom has changed everything save our modes of thinking and we thus drift toward unparalleled catastrophe."[14] A new type of thinking was essential for survival, and for Einstein the only salvation for civilization lay "in the creation of a world government with security of nations founded upon law."[15]

The growing tension between the United States and the Soviet Union convinced Einstein that agreement between the superpowers was crucial. He challenged both those who favored giving the secret of the atomic bomb to the Russians as a stepping stone towards cooperation and those who called for UN control. Instead, Einstein advocated that the great powers concentrate their energies on establishing a world government. Recognizing that the Soviet Union might be reluctant to join such an effort, given their traditional national insecurity and fear of other nations, Einstein proposed that the Soviets be allowed to draw up the first draft of the constitution for a world government and be allowed to include the assurances necessary to convince them that their security would not be threatened. Once the United States, Great Britain, and the Soviet Union agreed upon a structure for world government, others would be invited to join. The new world government, according to Einstein, should have jurisdiction over all military matters and its only other power would be the right to interfere in countries "where a minority is oppressing the majority and, therefore, is creating the kind of instability that leads to war."[16]

Einstein anticipated the criticism that his proposal ignored the fact that minority domination was present in the Soviet Union. Admitting that minority rule existed, he seemed willing to dismiss it as not threatening to world peace and understandable given the lack of traditional democracy in the nation and the need to improve material conditions. No doubt aware of the inherent inconsistency in his position, Einstein probably felt that inclusion of the Soviet Union was so vital to the overall creation of a world government, which in turn was vital to world peace, that the internal Soviet situation had to be overlooked for the time being.

As he expected, Einstein was severely criticized for his call for world government. Sumner Welles, a former high-ranking State Department official, argued that the Soviet Union would never accept world government, as it would destroy their system. Moreover, the inconsistency in Einstein's position seemed to Welles a glaring weakness that suggested both Einstein's naiveté and his unwillingness to see the Soviet Union for what it was. Others criticized Einstein's central argument that world government would benefit mankind. They pointed out not only that the organization of the world along such lines would prove extremely difficult, if not impossible, but that there existed a grave danger that tyranny rather than liberty would dominate the new system.

Einstein's reply to such criticism was concise and direct. He feared the tyranny of world government, but feared even more the coming of another war. "Any government," he pointed out, "is certain to be evil to some extent. But a world government is preferable to the far greater evil of wars, particularly when viewed in the context of the intensified destructiveness of war."[17]

At first Einstein argued that no partial world government should be contemplated. It had to include the Soviet Union as well as the United States and Great Britain. By mid-1947, however, it became apparent that the Soviets were not interested in the concept of world government, believing that it would lead to a loss of identity and would give superiority to the capitalist majority. Einstein then came out in support of a partial supranational government, which would keep its door open to the Soviet Union and would take no action or position that might add to Soviet insecurity and fear. Once such a government was established and in operation, Einstein hoped that the Soviet Union would alter its position. To overcome the practical problem of establishing a new world organization in the midst of the Cold War, he called for the transformation of the United Nations by means of increasing the authority of the General Assembly and making it the supreme agency of the organization. He also favored doing away with the appointment of delegates by governments. Instead they should be elected by the people. Such a process, he argued, would allow delegates to follow their own conscience more easily and would result in "more statesmen and fewer diplomats." Neither the Soviet Union, nor the United States, showed any interest in either idea.

Einstein grew increasingly pessimistic about the possibility of establishing a world government and preventing future wars. He was particularly critical of the emerging Cold War and blamed both the United States and the Soviet Union for refusing to retreat from their traditional nationalism. He took America to task for stockpiling weapons and for pursuing an aggressive foreign policy that had "caused anxiety and distrust throughout the world." He criticized the Soviet Union for its total rejection of supranational organization and for its "utopian view of isolationism." Although critical of both, he seemed to feel that the United States, given its military and economic superiority, should take the first step by altering its foreign policy. He urged the United States to show more concern for Soviet security and to adopt a public policy of "no-first-use" of atomic bombs. "To maintain a stockpile of atomic bombs," he declared, "and not promise to never initiate its use is to exploit the possession of the bombs for political purposes." The United States would not be able to frighten the Soviet Union into accepting the supranational control of atomic energy, according to Einstein. On the contrary, it would simply play into their fears and "enhance the existing antagonisms and increase the danger of war."18

Einstein may have been naive, as many of his critics asserted, in believing that the Soviet Union would accept a change in American foreign policy as a sign of good faith rather than seeing it as a sign of weakness. Still, he was correct in recognizing that peace depended upon Soviet-American cooperation and that President Harry Truman's policies would only result in a dangerous arms race between two hostile and embittered nations.

Einstein's criticism of the Cold War and of American foreign policy further confirmed in the eyes of his detractors that his loyalty was questionable. The FBI, in fact, launched an official investigation in 1950 into his associations and activities. Although the investigation revealed that he belonged to some thirty "Communist-front" organizations, no evidence emerged proving Communist party membership or linking him to espionage.

The FBI investigation stemmed not only from long-term allegations about Einstein's Communist sympathies and his position on the Cold War, but also from his forthright criticism of the postwar security probes that brought dozens of intellectuals before House and Senate investigating committees and that ultimately resulted in McCarthyism. Always critical of efforts by governments to inhibit intellectual freedom, whether they be instituted by Nazi Germany, Soviet Russia, or anticommunist politicians in Washington, Einstein urged his colleagues not to succumb to the postwar "Red Scare." He suggested that they adopt a policy of Gandhian noncooperation, refusing to testify even if such refusal led to jail and economic ruin. It was a call for the same uncompromising policy that he had suggested as a war-resistance pacifist in the 1920s. He maintained that if enough intellectuals refused to cooperate with their inquisitors, they would be successful. If, however, they passively accepted the insidious investigations and cooperated with the process, they would deserve "nothing better than the slavery which is intended for them."[19] Such a stand was not designed to ease criticism from conservatives and those who already had come to hold Einstein suspect.

The last five years of Einstein's life were filled with illness and deep pessimism. He continued to believe in the necessity of world government, but came to recognize that nationalism had won the battle for men's hearts and that supranational organization would not come during his lifetime. Curiously, however, Einstein's hostility toward nationalism was tempered after 1948 by the success of one of his other life-consuming interests: the establishment of a Jewish homeland in Israel. Einstein's enthusiasm for Zionism and the cause of a Jewish homeland in Palestine first arose in early 1919, prompted by the anti-Semitism he observed in Berlin during World War I and the hostility toward Jews demonstrated by the new Weimar Republic. Always the academic, he was especially attracted to the idea of establishing a university in Jerusalem that would belong to Jews and where Jewish students and professors could pursue their intellectual interests free of the anti-Semitic tensions that prevailed in Europe. At the same time, Einstein was sensitive quite early to the apparent contradiction between his view of nationalism as one of modern man's great curses and his support of Zionism. He tried to explain away his competing commitments in this way: "When a man has both arms and he is always saying I have a right arm, then he is a chauvinist. However, when the right arm is missing, then he must do something to make up for the missing limb. Therefore I am, as a human being, an opponent of nationalism. But as a Jew I am from today a supporter of the Jewish Zionist efforts."[20]

More than this, Einstein never reconciled the two contradictory concepts. The officially sanctioned anti-Semitism of Nazi Germany and the systematic destruction of European Jews during World War II only intensified his support for the establishment of a Jewish state. He welcomed with genuine happiness, therefore, the UN resolution in 1948 establishing the State of Israel. When war broke out immediately between Israel and its Arab neighbors, Einstein was willing to support the Israeli cause. Still, he urged the government of Israel to accommodate the Arab states and to work out a peaceful arrangement. In 1952, after the death of Chaim Weizmann, informal overtures came his way offering him the presidency of Israel, but he turned them down. Ill health, a lack of political inclination, and, finally, his unwillingness to surrender his personal freedom and make the compromises necessary of every politician—all led him to reject the flattering offer.

Shortly before his death on April 13, 1955, and only some months after the introduction of the devastating new hydrogen bomb, Einstein led a group of international scientists in issuing a document known as the "Russell-Einstein Manifesto." Written by the British philosopher Bertrand Russell, with advice from Einstein, the document put the question of the thermonuclear age directly: "Shall we put an end to the human race; or shall mankind renounce war?" It once again pointed out the vast danger of nuclear weapons and urged the human race to recognize the potential threat posed by continued national sovereignty. The renunciation of nuclear weapons was not the ultimate solution, but it would lessen tensions and serve as the basis for further cooperation. "There lies before us, if we choose, continual progress in happiness, knowledge and wisdom," the Manifesto proclaimed. "Shall we, instead, choose death, because we cannot forget our quarrels? We appeal, as human beings, to human beings: Remember your humanity and forget the rest. If you can do so, the way lies open to a new paradise; if you cannot, there lies before you the risk of universal death."[21]

Such a plea was characteristic of Albert Einstein. For the moment he was able to put aside his pessimism and ask the universal questions. As he often pointed out, nuclear weapons had changed everything except man's way of thinking. Once again, he urged the adoption of a new way of thinking and of a new approach to resolving international conflicts. For Einstein, the heart and mind were not isolated; humanity had the potential for grasping higher reason intuitively and was capable of doing the sensible and the right thing. Both as a scientist and as a concerned citizen, he urged his fellow human beings to make the right choice.

Although he was born, raised, and spent his most productive years as a scientist in Europe, Einstein upheld, and, indeed, came to symbolize the best in the American tradition of dissent. His desire for peace, his support for world government, and his criticism of both American and Soviet Cold War policies were grounded in his deeply humane commitment to individual freedom. He bravely articulated his principles in Weimar Germany, even at the risk of alienating his right-wing critics. In the United States, he just as courageously challenged the prevailing anticommunist hysteria that dominated American political and intellectual life in the decade after World War II.

His commitment to peace and his opposition to the nuclear arms race also reflected a universalism characteristic of twentieth-century American dissenters. As he said in the 1920s, his belief in peace and world order were grounded in his ingrained humanism rather than any clearly defined political philosophy. Perhaps somewhat more cynical than most Americans about man's innate desire for peace, he shared with many of his adopted countrymen a belief that human destructive proclivities could be controlled through world order and a structured international system. His plea for a new world order, based on cooperation and justice, struck a spark in many of those who were frightened by the prospects of atomic holocaust and who saw in continued nationalism the threat of armed conflict and mass destruction.

Einstein's warnings about the dangers associated with the nuclear arms race were as relevant after his death as they were during the first decade of the atomic age. His readiness, moreover, to take a stand on political issues as a scientist-citizen and to challenge prevailing governmental attitudes, served as an important example for the Western scientific community. The willingness of atomic scientists to question the nuclear arms race and to go public with their concerns after 1945 would have occurred regardless of Einstein's example, but he offered them a model for responsible political activism that undoubtedly made their dissent easier.

In the end, Einstein's lifelong peace work had very limited effectiveness, especially when compared with the immense impact of his scholarly pursuits. Hailed as a scientific genius, his extraordinary insights into the physical universe revolutionized modern science. His radical scientific theories ultimately found an enthusiastic audience, and he was held in esteem precisely *because* he was willing to challenge common conventions about the nature of time, space, and motion. His challenges to common political conventions, however, were viewed as profoundly naive, when they were not denigrated as dangerous or held to be fundamentally disloyal. His rejection of nationalism and war, his desire for world government, and his deep fear of the nuclear arms race found little support in official circles. To his despair, the forces of nationalism held sway and overcame his warnings, predictions, and actions. In his final message, the Russell-Einstein Manifesto, he pointed the way toward international sanity, but he died not knowing if mankind would follow the path to world peace or the road to world destruction.

NOTES

1. Ronald W. Clark, *Einstein: The Life and Times* (New York and Cleveland: Avon, 1971), p. 512.

2. Ibid., p. 340.

3. Otto Nathan and Heinz Nordern, eds., *Einstein on Peace* (New York: Schocken, 1960), pp. 93, 98.

4. Ibid., p. 52.

5. Ibid., pp. 125–26.

6. Ibid., p. 150.

7. Ibid., p. 91, 95.

8. Ibid., p. 116–18, 125.

9. Ibid., pp. 217–18, 220.

10. Richard Alan Schwartz, "The F.B.I. and Dr. Einstein," *The Nation* 237 (September 3–10, 1983):168–73.

11. Joseph Rotblat, "Einstein the Pacifist Warrior," in Maurice Goldsmith, Alan MacKay, and James Woudhuysen, eds., *Einstein: The First Hundred Years* (Oxford: Pergamon, 1980), p. 101.

12. Nathan and Norden, eds., *Einstein on Peace*, pp. 229, 235.

13. Clark, *Einstein*, p. 587.

14. *New York Times*, May 25, 1946, p. 13.

15. Nathan and Norden, eds., *Einstein on Peace*, p. 336.

16. Ibid., p. 348.

17. Ibid., p. 349.

18. Ibid., pp. 431–34.

19. Ibid., p. 547.

20. Quoted in Clark, *Einstein*, p. 378.

21. Nathan and Norden, eds., *Einstein on Peace*, pp. 633–36.

BIBLIOGRAPHY

Einstein's papers are housed at the Institute for Advanced Studies at Princeton University. Among his books and collections of writings the most valuable for the general reader are *Why War?* (London, 1934); *The World As I See It* (London, 1935); *Out of My Later Years* (New York, 1950); and *Ideas and Opinions* (London, 1964). Also very helpful is Einstein's "Autobiographical Notes," in Paul

Arthur Schilpp, ed., *Albert Einstein: Philosopher-Scientist* (Evanston, Ill., 1949), pp. 3–94.

Numerous biographies and collections of essays evaluating his life and work have been written. These include: Philipp Frank, *Einstein: The Life and Times* (New York, 1963); Ronald W. Clark, *Einstein: The Life and Times* (New York and Cleveland, 1971); Banesh Hoffmann and Helen Dukas, *Albert Einstein: Creator and Rebel* (New York, 1972); Jeremy Bernstein, *Einstein* (New York, 1973); and Abraham Pais, *'Subtle is the Lord . . .': The Science and Life of Albert Einstein* (New York, 1982).

On Einstein's political and social views the most important work is Otto Nathan and Heinz Norden, eds., *Einstein on Peace* (New York, 1960) which contains excerpts from his correspondence as well as his speeches, writings, and interviews. An earlier attempt to compile his pacifist writings is Alfred Lief, ed., *The Fight Against War* (New York, 1933). Valuable assessments of his pacifism and his views on international politics are contained in Virgil Hinshaw Jr., "Einstein's Social Philosophy," in Paul Arthur Schilpp, ed., *Albert Einstein: Philosopher-Scientist* (London, 1949), pp. 647–61; Joseph Rotblat, "Einstein the Pacifist Warrior," in Maurice Goldsmith, Alan McKay, and James Woudhuysen, eds., *Einstein: The First Hundred Years* (Oxford, 1980), pp. 99–116; Paul Doty, "Einstein and International Security," and Bernard T. Feld, "Einstein and the Politics of Nuclear Weapons," both in Gerald Holton and Yehuda Elkana, eds., *Albert Einstein: Historical and Cultural Perspectives* (Princeton, N.J., 1982), pp. 347–68, 369–93.

JO ANN ROBINSON

A. J. Muste

Prophet in the Wilderness
of the Modern World

Abraham John Muste was born in 1885, two years after the death of Karl Marx. He died in 1967, two years before the first moon landing. In between, he lived through the last of the Indian wars, America's turn-of-the-century lunge toward overseas empire, the Great Depression, two world wars, Cold War contests among superpowers, a monstrous nuclear arms race, and revolutionary upheaval across the globe. In the swirl of these disasters, the great majority of Muste's contemporaries, thinking of themselves as realists, took the view that these events were the tragic but unavoidable expressions of "human nature."

A. J. Muste, however, saw things otherwise. As he once put it, "Joy and growth come from following our deepest impulses, however foolish they may seem or dangerous, and even though the apparent outcome may be defeat."[1] In fact, the deepest impulses within Muste led him to challenge the forces of disaster and to proclaim that different—just and nonviolent—outcomes were possible. His challenges and proclamations seemed foolish. His acts of resistance and his invitations to others to join in resistance seemed dangerous. He died without wealth, fame, status or power; and, since the new world in which he believed had not come to pass, the apparent outcome of his life was defeat. Yet the struggle of humankind toward a better world was undoubtedly advanced by his efforts. And his vision of the good society lives on in the dreams that he shared with and sustained in others. Muste was not a textbook protagonist who commanded armies or controlled the powers of nations. He was rather one of those unique historical figures "who offer alternatives, who seem to be on the margins of history but nevertheless have a far firmer grasp of what really matters than those who embody a flashy, meretricious and very often transient success."[2] He was, remembered a friend, "an authentic hero."[3]

Muste's grasp on what really matters was developed in his childhood and sustained throughout his life by religious principles that were central to his upbringing. He was born in the Dutch shipping port of Zierikzee in 1885. Six years later his family immigrated to the United States. Muste, with his parents, two sisters, and a brother, grew up in Grand Rapids, Michigan. He played with English-speaking children and attended public school through most of the primary grades. But at the same time he was part of a tightly-knit immigrant community with a strong Dutch Reform Church at its center. Muste was influenced ever after by the "religious and pious" home which his parents kept, where he was "soaked in the Bible and the language of the Bible," and by the teaching of his native church that "you live in the sight of God and there is no respecter of persons in Him, and pretension is a low and despicable thing."[4]

Six years of study in Holland, Michigan—three at Hope Preparatory School and three at Hope College (both Dutch Reform institutions)—reinforced Muste's religious commitments and prepared him to be trained for the ministry. He taught school in an Iowa farm town for a year after graduating from college. Then he traveled east to enter New Brunswick Theological Seminary. In 1909 the New Brunswick graduate became the Reverend Muste, married a former Hope classmate, Anna Huizenga, and was hired as pastor of Fort Washington Collegiate Church in New York City.

Thus far A. J. Muste had taken the course his family and church expected of an eldest son. He offered Anna Huizenga the security, status, and social position expected by in-laws and community from a responsible husband. Yet the young man was not quite the conformist that his orthodox credentials and professional standing suggested. He had performed well—often brilliantly—in the prescribed courses at Hope and New Brunswick. But he had not accepted all that was taught. While the church fathers denied and denounced Charles Darwin's theory of evolution, young Muste defied school rules and studied Darwin's writings in secret. While church teaching condemned public theatre as sinful, an apprehensive but willful Muste attended a performance of the great Richard Mansfield on a Grand Rapids stage. While his teachers insisted upon the sacredness of scripture and the unquestionable authority of those ordained to preach it, Muste dared to deliver a graduation speech at Hope College in praise of doubt and intellectual discontent. At New Brunswick he had protested what he considered banality in much of the Dutch Reform curriculum and sought new challenges in philosophy and religion courses at New York and Columbia Universities. At the same time he had begun to attend sermons and lectures by those who linked faith with social reform and promoted a modern, unorthodox movement known as "the Social Gospel." Consequently when the new minister took up his duties at the Fort Washington church (in the Washington Heights section of New York City) with what he described as "a very strong call to the ministry, a very strong urge to preach and a feeling that I had a lot to give," he did not believe that he had "arrived at a place where I was going to stay."[5]

Muste became progressively restless and dissatisfied in the next four years. His awareness of, and outrage over, the economic and social ills of urban, industrial America deepened as he grew to know members of his congregation who held prominent positions in law, politics, and social work. He voraciously read about ideas for change—especially the literature of the Progressive Movement, tracts by socialists and communists, and essays by the Russian pacifist and champion of the oppressed, Leo Tolstoy. He furthermore continued to explore theories and theologies that fundamentally contradicted those of his own church, while earning a masters degree at New York's Union Theological Seminary. By 1914, he could tolerate the contradictions no longer. Muste resigned his post, transferred church membership to a freer denomination and began a new ministry at Central Congregational Church in the wealthy suburb of Newtonville, Massachusetts. In this setting he was liberated from many theological constraints. But in no setting could anyone escape the horror that burst upon Europe in August 1914, five months before he had moved to Newtonville.

Immediately, Muste's growing concern over how to apply Christian precepts to political corruption and class conflict in America became compounded in the new struggle over how to come to terms with massive suffering and dying caused by the Great World War. His reading, studying, and acquaintanceships broadened to encompass the teachings of Quakerism and other traditions with strong antiwar strains. By 1917, at the very time when the United States decided to enter World War I, Muste concluded that Jesus Christ was a pacifist and that those who professed to follow him must refuse to take up arms or support military campaigns. Newtonville, however, was not a place where such views were welcome. Acquaintances began to shun Muste and his wife. The couple received threatening telephone calls. When the son of their closest neighbor died on the battlefront, his mother asked the Mustes to stay away from the funeral. It was time for them to move again.

Quakers in Providence, Rhode Island, took them in. But although the Friends understood his convictions and admired his courage, not even they were comfortable with the intensity of Abraham Muste's discontent. Within a few months of their move to Providence, the Mustes returned to Massachusetts, this time to a communal household in Boston. There Muste, who had recently assumed the role of Quaker minister, gathered with a few comrades each morning in an unheated room, "bundled in overcoats," as he later remembered, to study the Sermon on the Mount. "We analyzed the passages, meditated on each phrase, even each word, prayed and asked what obedience to these precepts meant for us then and there."[6] All members of the pacifist Fellowship of Reconciliation—an international body founded in England at the beginning of the war—they ministered to conscientious objectors, involved themselves in the defense of other opponents of war who ran afoul of sedition laws, and talked of establishing urban and rural cooperatives from which they could carry on the struggle against war and for economic justice and racial equality.

In February 1919, a more immediate course of action presented itself to the comrades when they learned that workers were on strike in nearby textile mills in Lawrence. They went to investigate. Finding the workers with a just cause and in desperate need of organizing skills and financial support, they joined the effort. The strikers welcomed them and elected Muste to head the strike committee. Translating Christian pacifist ideals into nonviolent strategies of resistance, Muste helped the workers attain a modest victory and began for himself a seventeen-year career in the labor movement.

Muste's most important work in the years 1921–33 occurred at Brookwood Labor College, where his initiatives foreshadowed the industrial union campaigns of the late 1930s. As director of Brookwood, Muste oversaw the training of many labor organizers who would go on to bring the benefits of unionization to thousands of exploited workers in the coal fields, textile mills, and steel plants of industrial America.

But not even Brookwood proved to be the place where Muste had "arrived to stay." In reaching out to unskilled workers, to blacks, women, youth, and even the unemployed, Muste threatened the labor establishment controlled by the American Federation of Labor and committed to a policy of craft unions for skilled workers only. That establishment reacted by seeking to discredit the college as a center of "subversion" and urging its financial backers to withdraw their support. Brookwood was weakened even more by internal dissension over which strategies would best promote survival in the era of the

Great Depression. Muste and his supporters entertained visions of revolution; other Brookwood faculty and students held to their accustomed ways of teaching and organizing. Differences between the two groups became exceedingly bitter. In 1933 the Muste family—now including three children—was uprooted once more. The next three years were the most uncertain and tumultous in all of Muste's controversial life.

With the country deep in the worst economic depression it had ever known, Muste flung himself into revolutionary activism and socialist organizing. He headed the Conference for Progressive Labor Action (which soon became the American Workers Party), promoted industrial unionism, established unemployed leagues and inclined toward ever more drastic and frequently violent tactics. He played a key role in victorious auto strikes in Toledo, Ohio, in 1934 and 1935; and he led his supporters in merging with the American followers of Russian exile, Leon Trotsky, to become the Workers Party of the United States. As executive secretary of the new party, Muste exchanged the religion and nonviolence from which he had been straying for several years for revolutionary Marxism. But this was no more a final destination than had been any other position in his past. Nineteen months later, a religious experience caused him to return to Christian pacifism.

In the summer of 1936 Muste and his wife traveled to Europe. After attending an international Trotskyist meeting and talking with party head Leon Trotsky, himself, the Mustes took time to vacation. "When you go sightseeing in Europe," he later wrote, "you go to see churches, even if you believe it would be better if there were no churches for anyone to visit." While visiting one particular church in Paris—St. Sulpice on the Left Bank—Muste was overcome by "a deep and singing peace," as an inner voice said to him, "This is where you belong, in the church, not outside it."7

With this revelation Muste at last arrived at the place where he would stay. Physical journeys in the future would take him through unexplored regions of modern war-resistance and civil disobedience. They would carry him as far away as the continents of Africa and Asia. But the religious faith he recovered in the Parisian church endowed him with an inner serenity that became one of the hallmarks of the remarkable activist career which he pursued for another thirty-one years.

World War II posed the most immediate test of his renewed faith. That the faith held up well is reflected in the title which the editors of *Time* magazine bestowed on him during the war—"number One U.S. Pacifist." As executive secretary of the Fellowship of Reconciliation, Muste supported opponents of conscription, both those who sought alternative service and those who went to jail. He worked to ameliorate the suffering of Japanese-Americans incarcerated in relocation camps, pled for emergency rescue measures for the targets of Nazi extermination policies, and decried the brutal excesses of such Allied policies as obliteration bombings. The atomic attacks on Hiroshima and Nagasaki which ended the war in August 1945 reinforced Muste's perception that, in making war on fascism, his countrymen and their allies had adopted some of the worst characteristics of their enemies. "It was the United States, 'Christian America' which perpetrated the [atomic] atrocities," he noted. "It was we and not the Nazi swine as they were called, the Fascist devils, the Japanese militarists or the Russian communists." This fact, he said, set the direction for his work in the years that followed.[8]

With the almost immediate onset of the Soviet-American Cold War, Muste renewed his efforts to organize movements of resistance against militarism, conscription, and warfare. Stubbornly he took a stance as prophet and protester against the U.S.-Soviet rivalry that generated cold war propaganda, brutal competition for "spheres of influence," a deadly nuclear-arms race, and outbreaks of military combat. He warned that each nation's perception of "the enemy" was critically mistaken and insisted that the threat of global annihilation—and the very habits of militarism, expansionism, nationalism, and colonialism which bolstered that threat—stood as the *real* enemy. He explained the world situation with typical simplicity: "If the human family in the little boat of civilization on a vast ocean keeps on fighting, the boat and its human freight will sink."[9]

Muste well understood that the advocacy of dissenting views in a democratic society required a constant struggle against the forces of conformity and silence and a constant defense of the fundamental right of free expression. He, therefore, devoted considerable time to civil liberties controversies and supported the rights of conscience not only for himself and fellow pacifists but for all nonconformists who voiced convictions contrary to establishment policy. He knew his struggle was consistent with the country's most basic constitutional promises. "In insisting that all views should be publicly heard," he once told FBI Director J. Edgar Hoover, "I am true to one of the most basic of American traditions."[10]

In addition to his commitment to peace and the right of dissent, Muste also labored during his last thirty years on behalf of the struggle of racial minorities for economic and social justice. A personal friend of such major black leaders as A. Philip Randolph, Martin Luther King, Jr., James Farmer, and Bayard Rustin, Muste supported and advised the nonviolent civil rights movement in America. He encouraged and helped to guide the development of the early Congress of Racial Equality (CORE) during the 1940s, when he was serving as executive secretary of the Fellowship of Reconciliation. With the support of the FOR, CORE engaged in direct action against segregation in public facilities and in interstate transportation, in a struggle that proved an early prelude to the nonviolent campaigns of Martin Luther King. When King came to leadership of those campaigns, beginning in Montgomery, Alabama, in 1955 and continuing throughout the next decade, he remained in communication with Muste, seeking, acknowledging, and valuing his support and advice. Muste reached out also to the student generation of the sixties, the shock-troops of a revived CORE and the newer Student Nonviolent Coordinating Committee (SNCC), who risked (and all too often met) injury and death trying to establish racial justice and political equality in America's Deep South and her northern ghettoes.

In his final years these commitments and connections, spun over a lifetime of working for civil rights, economic rights, justice, and peace, were woven by Muste into the strongest antiwar coalition in U.S. history—the mobilization against the war in Vietnam. He was the key figure in organizing highly disparate groups in massive coalition street protests that proved the largest and most impressive peace demonstrations ever held in a modern nation at war. Muste's position was central in the otherwise fragmented antiwar opposition because, as his friend Sidney Lens observed, "everyone trusted A.J." Fittingly, his final struggle culminated two months after his death (February 1967), when a throng estimated at one-half million people marched in April rains through New York City to UN Plaza, where Martin Luther King issued an eloquent cry for peace.

During the Vietnam war years, Muste also supported and abetted draft-resisters and draft-card burners; he understood and interpreted the suicides of protestors who burned themselves; he defended and sought public backing for rebellious soldiers grown sick of the senseless war they were ordered to fight; and he personally carried his quest for peace to the scene of war itself. In the spring of 1966 Muste was part of a pacifist team who spent a week in Saigon. The following January he and three other elderly clergymen traveled to North Vietnam, returning with a message delivered directly to them by North Vietnamese Premier Ho Chi Minh for United States President Lyndon Johnson:

> Mr. Johnson has stated that he would talk to anyone, anytime, anywhere about peace . . . Let Mr. Johnson come with his wife and daughters, his secretary, his doctor, his cook, but let him not come with a gun at his hip . . ."[11]

Soon after returning to the United States, twelve days after mailing a transcript of Ho Chi Minh's words to the White House, A. J. Muste died. An aneurism had ended his work in his eighty-second year.

Every student of biography realizes the difficulty of identifying the motives and "explaining" the life of any person. Yet if we are to place a life in its proper historical perspective some interpretation is necessary. We may ask about A. J. Muste, then: what were his reasons for taking the unbeaten paths that he followed? What exactly was the nature of the better world that he envisioned? What was the relationship between the means he employed and the ends which he sought? And what was his own final judgment about the course he had taken. By examining certain passages from Muste's own writings and looking in detail at his specific actions perhaps we can develop some tentative answers.

1. What were his reasons for taking the paths that he followed?

> The first consideration for a moral being has to be whether he is functioning morally, expressing what he is at that moment in his own life and history.[12]

Individuals troubled by questions of conscience or facing personal dilemmas who asked A. J. Muste for advice usually received this answer in one form or another. It holds several clues to his own motivation. In answering thus Muste assumed that he was addressing a "moral being"; he implied that that being would grow and change over time; and he expected the person to be capable of defining "what he is at that moment and his own life and history."

For Muste there was virtually no opportunity to conceive of himself or others as anything but moral. His strong religious upbringing precluded views of human nature other than as divinely created and morally governed. Even in the period when he was an avowed Marxist, Muste's moral leanings remained evident. His Trotskyist comrade, James Cannon, complained that Muste valued friendship over party discipline and raised questions of right and wrong when he should have been committed to expediency. From Cannon's point of view, "the terrible background of the Church" had doomed Muste's career as a revolutionary.[13]

But his roots in the church were also a major source of Muste's growth as a political activist and social prophet. In confronting each of the great crises of his age—the global wars, the nuclear peril, the recurring economic disasters—Muste turned to the history and symbols of religion. He drew parallels between his own time and such eras as those of the Hebrew prophets, of the Christians living during the disintegration of Rome, of the first Quakers struggling in the revolutionary upheavals of seventeenth- and eighteenth-century England. In every instance, he pointed out, "the world was doomed." Humans had to form new communities as the old order decayed around them. They had to seek "a transformed life . . . to serve as a nucleus for [a] new civilization . . ."[14] They had to continually grow and change.

By what means do moral persons assess the courses they are taking? How can they know if they are right? Inner spiritual promptings played an important part in the life-decisions Muste made. He had shown from a very early age a tendency to perceive and be moved by out-of-the-ordinary experiences of the kind of "sudden invading consciousness from beyond" that students of mysticism have examined. In his autobiography Muste described vivid memories of moments when, as a four- or five-year-old, he was shaken by sensations of beauty, awe, horror and "a sort of revelation" about the mysteries of human existence. He recalled a moment at the age of fourteen when "the world took on a new brightness" for him and he felt within himself an affirmation that "Christ is risen indeed."[15] With every crucial turning point in his later life, down to 1936, Muste associated some mystical experience.

At the time of his break from Dutch Reform orthodoxy he was "walking late one morning down the corridor of [a] hotel [when] suddenly came again that experience of a great light flooding in upon the world," leaving him with a "deep sense of the ultimate rightness of things." As he prepared to resign from his pulpit in Massachusetts during World War I another "mystical experience of God" occurred which made him "happy and at rest. . . . The war no longer had me by the throat."[16] And his conversion from Marxist back to pacifist began in that Catholic Church in Paris with the "deep singing peace" and the inner voice assuring him of where he belonged.

From the vantage point of the late twentieth century, in a pervasively secular America, such episodes are peculiar. But in a broader historical context, mystical experiences have an accepted and respected place. As the Quaker scholar, Rufus Jones, wrote in one of his studies of the great mystics in history: "There is no more reason for narrowing the word 'mysticism' to cover pathological cases alone, than there is for using the word 'love' for pathological love alone." Mystics were not usually "dreary and impractical people." In many cases their experiences endowed them with energies to lead "great reforms and champion movements of great moment to humanity." According to Jones's research, mystical experiences also had the common effect on those who reported them of fostering new powers and capabilities which enabled them to "stand the world better."[17] By all reports from those who knew Muste after his culminating experience in 1936, his most striking characteristics were the emotional equilibrium and personal serenity with which he negotiated every crisis and undertaking. As his son once summarized, "Whether he's at a ball game or climbing over a fence into a missile base, he's always at peace within himself. He's the *happiest* man I've ever known. I can't believe a man can *be* that happy but *he* is, he really is."[18]

Secure in his own identity and conviction, Muste exercised infinite faith and patience in his interaction with others. According to one of his comrades in the peace movement, Muste knew how to "bring his own wisdom to [an encounter] without being enslaved by it or intimidating others with it."[19] When his son joined the navy during World War II—at the peak of Muste's crusade against militarism—Muste struggled to avoid subjecting the youth to undue emotional pressure from his own disagreement and fatherly disappointment. Throughout his career of proselytizing for peace and justice, he affirmed that while he needed to persuade his opponents that his views were "more right" than theirs, he would never presume to be "more righteous." One of Muste's favorite Old Testament passages captured both the spirit and the substance of the new order he was laboring to fashion: "In returning and rest shall ye be saved; in quiet and confidence shall be your strength."

2. What exactly was the nature of the better world which Muste envisioned?

Ask first what is the image of a sane and humane future.
(Then ask) how is it to be translated into political reality?[20]

At the heart of Muste's comment on this subject was his conviction that the present political reality was decidedly insane and inhumane. After one of his reviews of world problems, which highlighted "the development of weapons of extermination" and "the extreme rigidity" of both the United States and the Soviet Union on questions of disarmament, Muste concluded, "Both aspects of the current situation make one think of mass hypnosis, mass hysteria or catalepsy."[21] The better world which he envisioned, then, would be governed by theories far different from those to which leaders of the present order subscribed. One of their chief fallacies, according to Muste, was "the mad dog theory" of national security and international action. Since 1914, he recalled, one dictator after another had appeared on the stage of western history and in each case world leaders had responded as to a mad dog. "Anybody knows what you have to do with a mad dog," Muste summarized. "You shoot him." After that theory put the Kaiser out of the way, Hitler and Tojo emerged. They "were [no sooner] licked" than Stalin became the next mad dog. "Two World Wars, war under the guise of police action in Korea, Cold War, and still we face a bigger and more powerful dictatorship than ever," Muste declared. Furthermore, the newest preparations for shooting down the Stalinist dog involved "super atom bombs . . . the risk of mass suicide and the certainty of spiritual degradation that go with atomic war." Muste concluded that "if we start out with the idea of killing a mad dog and end up with all mankind leading a mad dog's life . . . it could be that the mad dog theory was wrong all the time."

The recommendation that followed from this analysis was both radical and religious. It was clear to Muste that humankind would not be diverted from its suicidal course by a continuation of " 'I will if you will' bargaining. . . . There has to be an illumination," Muste insisted, "a vision, an act of will." Some nation must renounce the deadly game of power politics, unilaterally divest itself of its military arsenal and launch a global crusade to redistribute resources and end poverty and suffering everywhere.[22]

The most likely candidate for this initiative was, in Muste's view, the United States—the nation which bore chief responsibility for the "benumbing threat of nuclear war," the nation which controlled more of the world's wealth than any other nation on earth, the nation whose founders had professed a commitment to "liberty and justice for all." If the U.S. were to undergo a rebirth into nonviolence, the impact, he predicted, would be so dramatic that even its most dangerous enemies would be thrown off balance, toppled by, as one student of non-violence had called it, "moral ju jitsu." "It would be," in Muste's words, "a revolutionary development comparable in one sense to the Russian and Chinese revolutions themselves . . . [in short,] a 'spiritual atom bomb.' "[23]

Just as Muste's mystical experiences are not easily comprehended in a scientific and secular age, so his prophetic visions may seem hard to credit in a world of *realpolitik* and endless power struggles. He knew this and acknowledged that many would find his proposals "unrealistic, utterly fantastic, even perhaps mad." But he reminded critics that they were living in a time when revolutions were taking place commonly in the human understanding of the physical world. In view of these revolutions, Muste maintained, "it would seem absurd and extremely hazardous to bar from our minds the idea that a revolution in the behavior of people toward each other may also have to occur."[24]

Looking at Muste's life in retrospect requires a sense of historical sensitivity and perspective. As one reviewer of Muste's life has suggested, "a time adjustment" is needed to bring his goals into focus. The great qualitative changes in human experience—the birth of de-mocracy or the abolition of slavery, for example—occurred only after germinating through centuries of seemingly hopeless struggle. Muste's fellow-pacifist, Dorothy Day, understood this when she summed up the significance of Muste's life, quoting a modern church father: "We must not underestimate the creative power of the human genius. What makes the history of the human race different from that of the anthropoid ape is the rare but recurring emergence of men who can break out of the framework of their times and initiate a new departure."[25]

Muste was clear about the essential aspects of the departure that he lived for: unqualified acceptance of the ancient insight, "we are all members one of another"; sane patterns of collective action to promote reverence for life; toleration of differences; and equitable sharing of the earth's treasures. Muste did not delve into the mechanics of how these patterns would be developed and perpetuated. Preoccupation with such specifics at his point in time was premature. His task was to demonstrate that the great departure was necessary and to gather recruits to make it possible.

3. What was the relationship between the means which Muste employed and the ends which he sought?

Individual refusal to "go along" is now the beginning and the core of any realistic and practical movement against war and for a more peaceful and brotherly world. . . . The human being . . . "naked, weaponless, armourless, without shield or spear, but only with naked hands and open eyes" . . . is the one *real* thing in the face of the machines and the mechanized institutions of our age. He, by the grace of God, is the seed of all the human life there will be on earth, though he may have to die to make that harvest possible.[26]

The "mechanized institutions of our age" which Muste most abhorred were those promoting militarism and war. The places where he advocated "individual refusal to 'go along'" were places where extensions of those institutions were reaching out to swallow up the most precious and necessary of human resources: atomic testing sites where the basic elements of the creation—earth, air and water, and ultimately all living things dependent on them for survival—were poisoned by radioactive fallout; plants for the construction of nuclear weapons and cavernous silos for their storage, desecrating yet other parts of God's earth; networks of underground shelters cruelly purporting to offer security from a war which in truth would leave no place to hide; and—most hideous of all—the routine transformation of youth from creative, moral, growing and changing human beings into uniformed automatons, programmed to kill and destroy the homeland of their counterparts in other corners of the world for reasons they would never have a chance to examine.

Muste was at the forefront of nonviolent experiments in resisting these practices. One form that these experiments took was that of symbolically risking death to focus the attention of fellow citizens on the perils of nuclear weapons and war. During a national civil defense exercise in 1955, he and twenty-six others were arrested when they sat on park benches in City Hall Park in New York City with signs that said: "End War—The Only Defense Against Atomic Weapons." With members of a committee dedicated to nonviolent action against nuclear weapons, he walked in 1957 into the area near Las Vegas, Nevada, where atomic tests were about to occur and was arrested again. In 1958 he helped to organize and plan the strategy for the voyages of *The Golden Rule* and *The Phoenix*, ships whose crews purposely sailed into the Pacific waters where hydrogen bombs were being tested. He spent eight days in jail in 1959 after climbing (at age seventy-four) a four-and-one-half foot fence into a missile construction site near Omaha, Nebraska. He journeyed to Africa in 1960 to assist in the leadership of a mass protest against French atomic testing on African soil.

Aware that national governments require money to carry out their military plans, Muste also advocated and practiced tax-resistance. Taken to court by the Internal Revenue Service in 1960 for what was by then a twelve-year history of noncooperation, Muste was found guilty of nonpayment but cleared of charges of fraud. The guilty decision had no practical consequences, for Muste had no money or property for the government to collect. He was cleared of fraud because he had not hidden his action. Each year he had issued a public statement explaining his position and, on one occasion, submitted the Gospels and Henry David Thoreau's *Essay on Civil Disobedience* as "supporting material." To those who questioned such unconventional ways of dissent, Muste acknowledged that his actions might "seem unusual or extreme. Well," he added, "the times in which we live are unusual and we can hardly think that the threat of nuclear holocaust will be averted unless we find new ways of bearing a witness, summon fresh courage and are ready for sacrifice beyond what we have this far offered."[27]

Muste also pursued new ways of bearing witness against military conscription. He had tested, tempered, temporarily abandoned, and then reaffirmed his initial rejection of violence in the strife-torn era of the 1920s and 30s. When he confronted World War II his pacifism had as its central focus the lesson he had learned from these experiences: that *there is an inextricable relationship between means and ends; the way one approaches one's goals determines the final shape which those goals take.* "If I can't love Hitler, I can't love at all," Muste declared.[28] Conversely, he argued that those who would adopt Hitler's methods of hate to defeat Hitlerism would be conquered by that hate and cause it to spread. At the end of the war there were in fact signs that this had happened. The victor nations had taken on some of the worst traits of their enemy: increased militarism, gargantuan military bureaucracies, exorbitant defense budgets, permanent conscription, failure of moral scruple (as symbolized in the atomic incineration of Hiroshima and Nagasaki), and the erosion of civil liberties and free speech in the witch-hunt atmosphere of a cold war.

By the time of the military call-up for the war in Korea, humankind was ensnared in the nuclear age. At any moment conventional war could escalate toward nuclear holocaust. Muste felt more strongly than ever that refusal to adopt violent means and especially refusal to participate in organized military violence was an essential act of human survival. Although no draft-resistance movement of substantial proportions came together in the 1950s, the case against conscription, which Muste had been helping to construct since the eve of World War II, attracted a massive following in the years of the war in Vietnam. What Vietnam added to moral and religious concerns over the draft and to the threat of escalation from regular to nuclear war was the stark, visible (media-enhanced) image of the brutality of the greatest nation on earth mercilessly battering one of the tiniest nations on earth without any compelling justification for doing so. Muste spoke for millions of Americans when he declared, "I can't get it out of my head or my guts that Americans are away over there not only shooting at people but dropping bombs on them, roasting them with napalm and all the rest."[29] And his actions were more widely understood than they had ever been before as he reached out to support those of draft age who said, "We won't go."

Muste was indicted as a co-conspirator in the trials of several men who burned their draft cards. He told the judge in that case that neither he nor others on trial with him had engaged in lawless behavior. "The real lawlessness at loose in the world today is that of the President and his advisors who violate international law and outrage the moral values of all mankind by their actions in Vietnam."[30] He spoke words of encouragement from the platform of every draft-resisters' rally he could attend and marshalled legal services and support monies for nonregistrants, conscripts who refused to serve, and resisters in uniform who defied orders when they believed that war crimes were involved.

Although Muste valued resistance more than flight, he also had sympathy for draft-evaders who fled to such places as Canada. "If a lot of young Germans had refused to throw Jews in the oven and had made their way to other coutnries we would all have regarded them as heroes," he remarked, adding, "Fellows who do not want to shoot Vietnamese peasants are probably in the same category."[31]

Muste did not pretend that any decision to resist the state could be made easily or without cost. Nor did he promise that the outcome would be immediately rewarding. His own path of resistance had led him away from employment security, taken him in and out of jail, and through life-threatening dangers. His family had been stranded more than once in economic straits and limbos of anxiety, and Muste had faced bitter disappointment time and again. His last journey to Vietnam, made with full knowledge that his health was too frail to endure it, was interpreted by some as an act of final sacrifice. Not long before that trip, in the context of a discussion over the seemingly endless carnage in Vietnam, someone asked Muste if he still believed in a loving God. He replied, "You will recall the biblical saving, 'though he slay me yet will I trust him.'"[32]

While acutely conscious of the difficulties inherent in the choices he made, Muste never hesitated to commend those choices to the consideration of others. And he was never without prospects for his campaigns of persuasion. He sought to develop peace constituencies among a wide variety of groups of people—scientists, churchmen and women, social scientists and other academics, minorities, youth. The Society for Social Responsibility in the Sciences (SSRS) grew out of his overtures to nuclear physicists in the late 1940s and became a means of urging the members of that profession to seek work that held constructive consequences for humankind and to consult their consciences when faced with choices that would lead to destructive results. The Church Peace Mission (CPM) with Muste as "chief missioner," was from 1950 to 1962 at the forefront of the campaign to bring the world's religious leaders into the antiwar movement. Through the Council of Correspondence—another organization developed with the assistance of Muste—a band of worried intellectuals declared that "the concern for survival [was] an integral part of their concern as professional thinkers" and called on university communities and all workers in the world of ideas to join them in pursuing that concern.

The connection that increasing numbers of black activists made between their struggle for justice in America and opposition to the war in Asia was applauded and, to an important degree, facilitated by Muste. From the beginning of the nuclear age, he had confronted black leaders with the argument that their objectives could not be obtained in a context of war and frequently asked them, what will the struggle for civil rights avail if it ends with "equality in extinction"? By including opposition to the draft and resistance to the Vietnam war in their agenda in the mid-sixties, such groups as SNCC, CORE, and Martin Luther King's Southern Christian Leadership Conference (SCLC) indicated the Muste's message had been heard.

Most of all Muste took hope in his last days from the growing numbers of young people exhibiting concern over their government's social policies at home and military actions abroad. Unfazed by the media emphasis on their outlandish attire, unusual hairdos, psychedelic music, and delight in four-letter words, Muste saw in this generation "extremely intelligent and deeply concerned young people" whose "talents and energies" were endowing the antiwar movement with "true vitality." He shared with them his contacts and skills in fund-raising, spoke at their meetings, received their standing ovations, and counseled with them as they struggled over the same questions of conscience and strategy that had occupied him through most of his long life. "My attitude in all these things is frankly an experimental one," he conceded. Perhaps the youth would not create a "truly viable New Left or revolutionary movement," after all, but, he avowed, "I don't want to be separated from these young elements at this stage."[33]

4. What was Muste's own final judgment about the course he had taken?

Assume that [protest] is only the cry of a prophet in a political wilderness. Are prophets not needed in this age?[34]

It is the nature of a prophet that he rarely experience the fulfillment of his goals in his own time. Rather, his words of warning and insight burn deeply into the collective conscience of his society, from whence they may rise as moral guides for later, better-prepared, and more receptive generations. Knowing this, Muste did not consider his answer of last resort an admission of defeat. Furthermore, he believed that "the crucial thing about men or societies is not where they come from but where they are going. . . . [Man's] destiny and his God are not ties which bind and confine him. They are ahead of him and drawing him outward and onward."[35] Nonetheless, he did work for more immediate results, believed in the practical possibilities of every project with which he was involved, and enjoyed some victories.

Musteites pioneered the industrial unionism which triumphed under the New Deal. Muste's training and counsel guided the major leaders of the civil rights campaigns which ended segregation and strengthened the citizenship rights of black people. "Without Muste," Martin Luther King, Jr. said, "the American Negro might never have caught the meaning of nonviolence."[36] Muste's presence was a catalyst in forming the coalition which burgeoned so powerfully into the movement against the war in Vietnam. "What made such a broad-based coalition possible was the personality of A. J. Muste," reports one chronicle of the anti-Vietnam war movement. "While few of the groups had ever agreed, worked with, or much less trusted one another, they were all united in their respect for A. J."[37]

When the Vietnam War finally ended, some eight years after Muste's death, a period of political quietude settled over the United States. The intensely felt need to "resist authority" and "make love not war" which had seized his youngest comrades seemed to fade. But after another decade passed, messages like those that Muste proclaimed were echoing in the world again. In Nevada, local citizens protested the alarming numbers of deaths from cancer in their communities, tracing them to the fallout from the atomic tests which Muste had protested in 1957. In a pastoral letter issued from the highest councils of American Catholicism, bishops decried nuclear weapons as incompatible with the teachings of their church. The parallels between their statement and statements issued thirty years before by Muste and the Church Peace Mission were striking. In Amarillo, Texas, another Catholic bishop delivered sermons encouraging workers in the local atomic weapons factory to examine their consciences—the very plea that Muste had made so often to scientists, technicians, teachers and youth in his time. In major cities around the world mass demonstrations began on behalf of, this time, placing a "freeze" on the manufacture and deployment of nuclear arms. Perhaps at least a few of those carrying "freeze" banners were aware of the work that A. J. Muste had done before them. All members of the newest peace movement really ought to have known about him, for from his life there were encouragement to be taken and lessons to be learned. Above all, there was the insight, best captured in a saying Muste had borrowed from a French pacifist during World War II and had repeated so often that most of his associates thought it had originated with him: "There is no way to peace; peace is the way."[38]

NOTES

1. Muste to Cara Cook, June 21, 1936; personal files of Cara Cook.
2. Peter Stansky, "The Styles of the Seventies: History and Biography," *New York Times Book Review,* June 5, 1977, p. 10.
3. Paul Workman, *New York Review of Books,* October 1963, p. 14.
4. Muste, autobiographical lecture given at New Brunswick Theological Seminary in 1944, in Swarthmore College Peace Collection (hereafter SCPC).
5. Muste, Oral Memoir 589, Oral History Office, Columbia University, pp. 193, 199, 237.
6. Muste, "Sketches for an Autobiography," in *The Essays of A. J. Muste,* ed. Nat Hentoff (New York: Bobbs-Merrill Co., Inc., 1967), p. 57.
7. Muste, "Fragments of Autobiography," (1939?) SCPC, pp. 4–5.
8. Muste, "Sketches," pp. 11–12.
9. Muste, pamphlet, "How to Deal with a Dictator," (New York: Fellowship Publications, 1954), p. 14.
10. Muste to J. Edgar Hoover, April 2, 1957, SCPC.
11. Muste to President Lyndon Johnson, January 31, 1967, SCPC.
12. Muste to Tom Robbins, December 29, 1966, SCPC.
13. James Cannon, *History of American Trotskyism* (New York: Pioneer Publishers, 1944), pp. 198–199.
14. Muste, "Saints for This Age," in Hentoff, (ed.), p. 424.
15. Muste, "Sketches," pp. 4, 16–17; Oral Memoir, pp. 90–91; "Fragment," p. 7.
16. Muste, "Oral Memoir," p. 219; "Fragment," p. 8; Central Congregational Church Records, pp. 546–554.
17. Rufus M. Jones, *Studies in Mystical Religion* (London: Macmillan & Co., 1909), pp. xviii, xxx. *New Studies in Mystical Religion* (New York, 1928), p. 20.
18. Quoted in Nat Hentoff, *Peace Agitator* (New York: Macmillan Co., 1963), p. 148.
19. David Dellinger, *More Power Than We Know* (New York: Doubleday, 1975), p. 63.
20. Muste to David Riesman, March 11, 1963, SCPC.
21. Muste, "Getting Rid of War," in Hentoff, ed., p. 387.

22. Muste, "How to Deal with a Dictator," pp. 3–5; "Getting Rid of War," p. 390.

23. Muste, "Who Has the Spiritual Atom Bomb?", in Hentoff, (ed.), p. 501.

24. Ibid., pp. 498–499.

25. John L. Stipp, "A Buoyant Voyager for Justice," *Commonweal*, May 7, 1982.

26. Muste, "Of Holy Disobedience," in Hentoff, (ed.), p. 376.

27. Muste to Dear Friends, April 25, 1959, SCPC.

28. Milton Mayer, "The Christer," *Fellowship* (January 1952): 7.

29. Muste, "Who Has the Spiritual Atom bomb?", p. 500.

30. Muste, et al. "Statement of the Eight Persons Subpoenaed to Appear Before the Federal Grand Jury, November 6, 1965," SCPC.

31. Muste to Don McKelvey, October 5, 1966, SCPC.

32. Muste to Mildred Romer, June 11, 1965, SCPC.

33. Muste, "Memo Dealing With Lawrence Scott's 'A Desperate Appeal to American Pacifists,' " December 1962, SCPC.

34. Muste to I. F. Stone, April 20, 1965, SCPC.

35. Muste, "Sketches," p. 24.

36. Martin and Coretta King telegram to Muste, February 5, 1965, SCPC.

37. Robert Cooney and Helen Michalowski, *The Power of the People* (California: Peace Press, 1977), p. 186.

38. Muste, "Peace Is The Way," reprinted in *Fellowship* (December 1976): 3–5.

BIBLIOGRAPHY

For a complete biographical study of A. J. Muste see Jo Ann Ooiman Robinson, *Abraham Went Out, a Biography of A. J. Muste* (Philadelphia: Temple University Press, 1981). *Peace Agitator, the Story of A. J. Muste* by journalist Nat Hentoff (New York: Macmillan Co., 1963) provides a good introduction to Muste's life. Hentoff also compiled *The Essays of A. J. Muste* which include Muste's "Sketches for an Autobiography" (New York: Bobbs-Merrill Co., Inc. 1967). In addition to the material included in *The Essays* and the innumerable articles he wrote for various periodicals throughout his career, Muste was the author of two books, *Nonviolence in an Aggressive World* (New York: Harper & Brothers, 1940) and *Not By Might* (New York: Harper & Brothers, 1947; Garland Library reprint, N.Y., 1971).

MILTON S. KATZ

Norman Cousins

Peace Advocate and World Citizen

On the night after the atomic destruction of Hiroshima, Norman Cousins sat down and concluded that "Modern Man is Obsolete." In one of the most famous editorials in American history, the young editor of the weekly *Saturday Review* declared that the atomic bomb marked nothing less than "the violent death of one stage in man's history and the beginning of another." "A new age is born," Cousins wrote; and with its appearance came a "blanket of obsolescence not only over the methods and products of man but over man himself." The first responsibility of Americans was to become aware of the changes that had taken place on the day of Hiroshima's annihilation; and the first change was that "man's survival on earth is now absolutely dependent on his ability to avoid a new war."[1] With the bomb, Cousins believed, humankind reached that moment in history which required that it create instruments of world authority endowed with the necessary powers for controlling war and weaponry. In search of that authority, Cousins embarked on a struggle for world federation that would dominate the rest of his life and establish him as a central figure in the modern quest for world order under law.

Cousins was born on June 24, 1915, in Union Hill, New Jersey, just before his parents, Samuel and Sara Miller Cousins, decided to move their family to New York City. Grave and precocious, Cousins was nicknamed "The Professor" shortly after he entered the neighborhood public school. In the classroom, he excelled in English composition; and, out of the classroom, he was a standout baseball player. But not everything came easily to him. At the age of eleven, Cousins was consigned to a tuberculosis sanitarium because of a mistaken medical diagnosis. The experience gave him time for thought and, he said years later, a "respect for the precariousness of human life."[2]

The Cousins family had great difficulty in making ends meet during the Depression of the 1930s. Yet his parents managed to send young Cousins to Columbia University's Teachers College, where he continued playing baseball until serious injury forced him from the outfield and into the full-time pursuit of his other great interest— writing. He completed his degree in 1933, and, one year later, secured an editorial position as an education writer for the *New York Evening Post*. Three years later, he joined *Current History*, a journal of world affairs founded by the *New York Times*, as literary and managing editor. In 1940, Cousins joined the staff of the *Saturday Review* as executive editor and, two years later, at the age of twenty-seven, became its editor. He served in that capacity for the next thirty-five years. Under his editorship, the *Saturday Review* expanded in scope from a literary review to a review of ideas, the arts, and the human condition, and increased its circulation from 20,000 to 650,000 sub- scribers. The *Review* was revitalized with a unique sense of imme- diacy and impact that inspired its audience with a feeling of loyalty and a commitment to action.

Cousins began to develop his guiding life-philosophy in the hothouse of New York radical and cultural politics during the highly charged 1930s. Although raised in the Jewish religious tradition, Cousins had long felt more comfortable with the views of American revolutionary leaders like Thomas Jefferson and John Adams, who argued for religious tolerance and individual freedom of choice.[3] Religion, however, did not offer an adequate guidepost for Cousins' life in the thirties. He found some hope in the New Deal; but craved even more fundamental means of social transformation. Dissatisfied with the prevailing alternatives, he began to search inwardly to reex- amine his own place in society and the potentiality of the individual for effective ethical action.

Cousins's search for an ethic of right social action accelerated during America's involvement in World War II. Some weeks after Pearl Harbor, he attempted to join the armed forces; but he failed the physical examination as a result of his childhood illness. He therefore turned to the home-front war effort as a member of the editorial board for the Overseas Bureau of the Office of War Information. From 1943 to 1945, Cousins edited *U.S.A.*, a wartime government information journal intended for distribution abroad. In addition, he was cochair- man of the 1943 Victory Book Campaign.

It was also during this time that Cousins threw himself into a lifelong commitment to revitalize the main values of Western civiliza- tion through the construction of a working world federal system. Appalled by the vicious global crisis of the thirties, Cousins began in the early 1940s to argue for the enhancement of individual dignity, vindication of the law of progress, and the preservation of right moral order. For philosophical inspiration, he looked to the writings of the nineteenth-century American romantic Ralph Waldo Emerson and the twentieth-century Indian leader Mohandas Gandhi. From Emerson, Cousins reclaimed the idea of the individual's power and responsibility in a complex society. Emerson saw, according to Cousins, "a wide and fertile field for individual action in advancing the general welfare and believed that man, collectively or individually, need not be incarcerated by history." Gandhi impressed Cousins not only because of his philosophy or even the effectiveness of nonviolence, but in "the dramatic proof that the individual need not be helpless against massed power—that he need not be overwhelmed by any supposed inexorabilism or fatalism, that there was scope for free will and conviction in the shaping of society, and that history would be fluid, not fixed, if men were willing to transcend their egos in order to merge themselves with the larger body of mankind."[4]

At the same time, Cousins became absorbed in the wartime crusade to save Western values through world federation. He searched for relevant historical examples with an enthusiasm that brought him to center upon two areas: ancient Greece and late eighteenth-century America. In his first book, *The Good Inheritance* (1942), Cousins wrote a history of Greece with special reference to the experiences of the early city-states in attempting and eventually failing to federate among themselves. In the latter part of the book, he focused on the attempt of the framers of the American Constitution to learn from the Greek experience in creating the design of their own government, and how they replaced the weak and ineffective Articles of Confederation with a strong federal constitution with its system of checks and balances.[5]

The history of early Greece and the U.S. constitutional period had a profound effect on Cousins's development into a world federalist. In particular, it deepened his fast developing interest in the philosophy of universalism. The stories of both historical periods were vital, he wrote, for the way in which they joined "political form to ideological justice." They were, in his eyes, magnificent examples of the scope and power of human will and free choice in the affairs of men, and true instances that validated the very theory of human progress. Quite concretely, in Greece and America, men of principle had made victory through the deliberate creation of a structure of government possessing the form of law and the substance of justice.[6]

Cousins attempted to apply these lessons of federalism to his own time, especially in reference to the decline and fall of the League of Nations. Writing with the hindsight that he had accumulated by 1942, he concluded that the failure of the powers to invest the League with independent sovereignty and effective power had doomed it from the start. The basic historical principle, according to Cousins, was that states within a geographic unit must fight or unite. The very differences and difficulties that impeded the realization of a world federation actually defined the challenge. For these were the differences that inevitably produced war; and the challenge was to manage these differences within a larger system of order.[7]

The outbreak of World War II simultaneously gave pause and encouragement to Cousins and the advocates of a world federal order. At first, Cousins noted, the effect of the war's onset "was to give a cold chill to world government enthusiasts who now knew the absurdity and the danger of talking about a world government without also defining exactly what it was to be, and how it would operate if it was to deserve the support of the world's peoples who would have to establish it."[8] But, the war also brought unprecedented attention to the federalist cause. Initially, Cousins and other federalists were very much attracted to the ideas of Clarence K. Streit, a *New York Times* journalist who covered the League of Nations in Geneva, and whose book, *Union Now,* became extraordinarily popular after its publication in 1939. Streit's plan envisioned a federal union of some fifteen democracies, and in 1943 he established the Federal Union, Inc., to press for the full realization of his program.[9] Streit's work started an avalanche. Throughout World War II, a large number of books and articles advocating various forms of world government rolled down upon hungry American readers, eager for some means of achieving lasting peace.

In his *Saturday Review* editorials, Cousins also championed the call for world government through world citizenship. He complained as early as 1943 that "one of the greatest obstacles to world citizenship today is the lack of world consciousness, that the ideal is not only possible but mandatory if we are not to slide into a long period of retrogression."[10] During the war, he joined a group called Americans for World Order that helped shape public opinion in favor of the United Nations. After the war, the group changed its name to Americans for World Government.

While Cousins's federalist ideas developed as a result of his understanding of history and his response to the world crisis, it was the atomic bomb that gave the fullest urgency and scope to his thinking. When he heard the news about the bombing of Hiroshima, Cousins later said, he "couldn't have been hit harder than if a report had just been flashed that an interstellar collision involving the earth was possible and likely." He immediately realized that "man overnight had come face to face with the problems of human destiny, and that he had conquered nature only to discover that forces inside him were more powerful and terrifying."[11]

The shock of Hiroshima gave new impetus to the world-government movement. It also forced Cousins to reconsider the most expeditious way toward radical change. A gradualist by temperament, Cousins had been concerned before Hiroshima mostly with the requirements of a world community organized under law and justice. He assumed that it would take several generations before such a community could be brought into being. But, with Hiroshima, world government became an immediate necessity. "The need for world government was clear before August 6, 1945," Cousins declared, "but Hiroshima and Nagasaki raise that need to such dimensions that it can no longer be ignored. National sovereignty was preposterous now."[12]

Cousins tried to sort out his hopes and his fears of the nuclear age in his editorial, "Modern Man Is Obsolete." The gist of this famous piece was that modern man had become "a self-made anachronism," growing "more incongruous by the minute." Exalting change in everything but himself, modern man had leapt centuries ahead in inventing a new world; but he knew little about his own part in that world. Given time, man might be expected to bridge those gaps, Cousins believed; but, by his technological prowess, he destroyed even time itself. Communication, transportation, and war no longer waited on time. Whatever bridges had to be built and crossed to insure a peaceful world would have to be built and crossed immediately.[13]

Cousins's secular sermon created a tremendous response. Viewed as one of the most prophetic statements of its time, it became the most widely quoted editorial of the infant Atomic Age; and, when it was published as a book, it vaulted briefly to the best-seller list. Ironically, some people thought that Cousins had written a eulogy for man, condemned to a predicament from which there was neither retreat nor escape. But these critics simply misunderstood his purpose. Cousins believed there were rational grounds for hope, although he no longer believed that modern developments progressed toward the better if left to themselves. He was rather a traditional liberal and universalist who insisted on hoping, even though he had lost faith in the inevitable workings of progress. Cousins did not believe that any nation or people enjoyed a natural immunity from catastrophe or a special dispensation against disaster. "Survival depended on ideas and action," he wrote, "and before we decided what the ideas or what the action was to be, it was essential that we become supremely aware of the danger and resolved to meet it." Cousins never wavered in his confidence in the capacity of man to eliminate war and build a just peace, or to make changes in the human condition in order to triumph over dire problems and meet great opportunities. What he tried to do was to emphasize that the capacity for change rested on decision, and decision on recognition of the challenge.[14]

For Cousins, the decision to meet the challenge of atomic warfare reinforced his commitment to world federalism. Immediately after the bombings of Hiroshima and Nagasaki, he went on a barnstorming lecture tour with atomic scientists Harrison Brown, Leo Szilard, and Albert Einstein to try to educate the American people about the effects of nuclear war and the nuclear arms race. In October 1945, he joined with fifty influential persons, including the prominent New York lawyer Grenville Clark and former U.S. Supreme Court Justice Owen J. Roberts, who shared his conviction of the necessity for the extension of peace and order through a federal world structure. Meeting in Dublin, New Hampshire, the conferees acknowledged the value of the new United Nations but insisted that it did not go far enough in reordering world politics. They called instead for "a world federal government with limited but definite and adequate powers to prevent war," and prepared to galvanize a popular movement in its behalf.[15]

World federalism indeed was seen by many at this time to be a viable and workable notion. Federalists believed that world peace required a clearcut, authoritative definition both of the limits of national power and of the area of effective jurisdiction of the world body. The nations should retain the right to maintain their own cultures and political institutions, wrote Cousins; but the UN should have authority in matters related to world security and world development. This is what Cousins meant by world law. Recognizing that restructuring the UN, taking into account all the ideological, historical, political, and cultural differences within it, "may be the most difficult problem yet to be undertaken by the human mind," Cousins and other federalists explored in depth the specific problems that inhibited the UN's development into a genuine world security authority.[16]

In the immediate postwar world, Cousins was heartened by the fact that the world-government movement achieved substantial popularity. By mid-1946, seven U.S. senators openly advocated world government, while a dozen others admitted privately that they supported it. Nearly a hundred House members favored some form of world government, and sixteen state legislatures passed resolutions asking the federal government officially to endorse the achievement of world federation. In his annual message to Congress, President Truman declared:

> The United Nations Organization now being established represents a minimal essential beginning. It must be developed rapidly and steadily. . . . Our ultimate security requires that we begin now to develop the United Nations Organization as the representative of the world as one society.[17]

A Gallup poll taken in 1946 indicated that the general public in the street was not far behind its leaders. In stark contrast to the isolationist mood that followed World War I, 52 percent of the American public expressed support of U.S. participation in the liquidation of national armed forces, with an international police force to be given the responsibility of keeping the peace. Only 24 percent were opposed; and 22 percent remained undecided.[18]

Encouraged by these favorable signs, five of the groups dedicated to world government, including the Americans United for World Government, convened in February 1947, in Asheville, North Carolina, and combined to form the United World Federalists for World Government with Limited Powers Adequate to Prevent War (UWF). Identifying their common aim as the mobilization of "public opinion and action toward world government so that the local and national representatives of the people will be impelled to world federation by an irresistible political force," they announced the following credo: "We believe that peace is not merely the absence of war but the presence of justice, of law, of order—in short, of government and the institutions of government; that world peace can be created and maintained only under world law, universal and strong enough to prevent armed conflict between nations."[19] Officers in the UWF included some of the most respected and influential men in America. Cord Meyer,

Jr., a young war hero who had served as Harold Stassen's aide at the founding of the United Nations and author of the best-selling *Peace or Anarchy,* was elected president of the organization. Vice presidents included Grenville Clark; Cousins; Thomas K. Finletter, a New York attorney and future Secretary of the Air Force; W. T. Holliday, president of Standard Oil of Ohio; Robert Lee Humber, a Greenville, North Carolina, attorney; the liberal news commentator Raymond Gram Swing; and the historian Carl Van Doren.

The UWF was tremendously successful in attracting members. By the end of 1948, its membership rose to 40,000 people organized in 659 chapters; and Meyer announced the expenditure of $550,000 in an expansion program toward the goal of one chapter in every community. Jubilantly, Meyer cited a new Roper poll which showed an increase in public support to 64 percent for a UWF proposal that the United States initiate action to change the United Nations into a strong federation of nations.[20]

But the Cold War closed in rapidly upon the federalists' plans. In the years immediately following Hiroshima, federalist leaders criticized the policies of both the United States and the Soviet Union, holding these two powers the main obstacles before the coming of federal world government. Yet, in spite of the criticism that world government proponents directed at U.S. foreign policy, most accepted Washington's developing commitment to the containment of Soviet power. Thus, as the Cold War hardened into East-West polarity and Truman moved from the advocacy of a mixed economic-military response to the Soviet challenge to support of one based primarily on military power, the world-government movement began to disintegrate. In a typical statement of the federalists' dilemma, Cord Meyer, Jr., declared in December 1947 that "until world federation is established and the nations agree to disarm under its protection, we must maintain our defensive military strength."[21] By 1950, arguing simultaneously for the arms race and for world government, the world federalist position began to crack apart.

The final route of the world-government crusade began in late June 1950, when the North Korean troops crossed the 38th Parallel and set off the Korean War. Almost unanimously, federalist leaders approved American intervention in Korea on the grounds that America was participating in an "international police action," and that the nation was fighting the war under the flag of the United Nations.

Chapters of the UWF in about thirty cities and towns across the country ran an advertisement proclaiming "The UWF is wholeheartedly behind our nation in this and every fight that may darken the nation's future."22 Federalist sentiment gave way to nationalist fervor.

Unconcerned with the contradictions inherent in the notion of an anti-Communist world federalist structure, Cousins joined other federalists in supporting U.S. troops in Korea under UN sanction in order to crush Communist aggression. Enthusiastically, he avowed that America was fighting for a principle "that the peoples of the world are no longer obligated to acquiesce in anarchy but must meet the responsibilities involved in protecting the community at large." Although he criticized certain aspects of U.S. policy, he thought in the main that it was "honest and humanitarian," and called for the American people to unite in the face of national crisis. According to Cousins, only the revision of the UN into a world agency could create a workable context for getting out of the Cold War. His hope was that victory in Korea could be "a sturdy platform on which something more than a tentative peace could be built," and that the nations would finally realize the immediate relevance of world law and "create a common government with adequate and even overwhelming force, based on fixed and fair obligations, and built upon the principles of justice that would command the allegiance and hopes of the world's peoples."23

Yet, in spite of their clear nationalistic enthusiasms, world federalists failed in the early 1950s to make the American political climate more hospitable to their cause. On the contrary, a right-wing political resurgence—known generically as McCarthyism—pushed the highly respectable UWF so forcibly to the defensive that the organization nearly went out of business. In 1950, a parade of witnesses from the Women's Patriotic Council on National Defense, National Society of New England Women, National Society of Women Descendants of the Ancient and Honorable Artillery Company, Dames of the Loyal Legion of the United States of America, and the Veterans of Foreign Wars marched before the Senate Foreign Relations Committee and branded the United World Federalists as subversive. The following year the Senate Appropriations Committee, under the leadership of Pat McCarran, approved a bill banning funds for any organizations which "directly or indirectly promoted one world government or one world citizenship." In February 1953, *Newsweek* reported that "loyalty investigators are now asking would-be government employees if they were members of the United World Federalists." The question was ostensibly designed to satisfy congressional suspicions of any group involvement in international projects in which Communist nations participated.[24]

Cousins himself was branded subversive by different super-patriots. He nevertheless assumed the UWF presidency in 1952 and tried to drive world government advocates into retaking the political offensive. He refused to confront every charge that federalists were pro-Communist, and insisted instead on carrying the fight to the public and rallying sympathetic opinion. Rather than avowing our anti-Communism, Cousins wrote in 1952, "Let us say instead, that we are moving heaven and earth to create a human community on this planet, that world citizenship is the ultimate goal and no one need apologize for it."[25] Cousins denounced the extreme right as "a menace to the United States" for creating a climate of "uneasiness and insecurity," and contended that "there could be no more ghastly irony than is presented today by those who in the name of Americanism are actually helping to prepare the country for the eventual triumph of Communism," by their reckless assault on constitutional government through smears, purges, and the assigning of guilt by association. Cousins wanted to fight Communism, but by means of liberal humanitarianism. "Instead of fighting Communism by strengthening and enlarging humanitarian objectives," he complained, "we turned on humanitarianism itself."[26]

Through their counterattacks, Cousins and other world federalist leaders won some token victories in the form of public apologies or formal retraction. But the anti-Communist hysteria essentially devastated the rank-and-file of the already declining movement. In 1951, the UWF had an income of over $180,000 obtained from about 40,000 members. Within five years these figures had shrunk to about $65,000 and 17,000. Late in 1952, Cousins lamented, "Seven years ago, when world law was mentioned, people said it was too soon. Now when it is mentioned, they say it is too late."[27]

Hope within the organized peace movement nonetheless persisted through the dolorous 1950s. Although organizations like the UWF grew increasingly more conservative, different peace activists began to withdraw their support from the arms race, and asserted their emphatic opposition to any and all plans for atomic war. While concerned with the Soviet threat, these "nuclear pacifists" nurtured the post-Hiroshima spirit of species "survivalism;" but they lacked an issue that would renew liberal interest in confronting the nuclear menace.[28] Quite unexpectedly, a galvanizing issue presented itself in March 1954, when a United States H-bomb test explosion in the Pacific accidentally scattered radioactive dust on twenty-three Japanese fishermen and shocked the world into fear over the general health hazards of nuclear fallout attendant upon atmospheric testing. "If there is still a peace movement left in America," I. F. Stone pleaded a few months later, "this must be its platform. As a first step away from mutual destruction; no more tests."[29]

The conflict between the claimed U.S. security interest in atmospheric testing and the risk of attendant health dangers gripped concerned citizens and policy makers in angry quarrel for the next nine years. Cousins's concern with the issue intensified sharply in August 1956, when a small group of Washington University (St. Louis) professors, including the biologist Barry Commoner, showed him scientific studies detailing the human costs of radioactive fallout. One of the research studies, sponsored by the U.S. Atomic Energy Commission, demonstrated that radioactive fallout was causing increased contamination of milk supplies with the element strontium 90, a known carcinogen that particularly threatened children because the human body mistook radioactive strontium for calcium in the building process. Cousins emerged from this meeting determined to help bring nuclear testing under control. Testing for him was no longer an abstract issue. It powered the arms race, abetted the spread of nuclear weapons, and menaced children and the unborn.[30]

In fall 1956, Cousins was among those who succeeded in persuading Democratic candidate Adlai Stevenson to interject the test-ban issue into the national election campaign as the first step in a larger drive toward disarmament.[31] Shortly after, he visited Dr. Albert Schweitzer at his hospital in Lambaréné, French Equatorial Africa, to ask him to speak out against nuclear tests. A physician, philosopher, theologian, musician, and Nobel Peace Prize winner, Schweitzer had gone to Africa in order to tend to the health needs of the people. By the 1950s, he had earned virtually cultic status within the United States as a saintly grandfather whose very name was a synonym for humanitarianism. Cousins believed that "there was no one in the world whose voice would have greater carrying power than his own."[32]

Although Schweitzer had been concerned with the nuclear danger since Hiroshima, he hesitated at first upon hearing Cousins's request that he issue a public appeal against continued testing. But, after some reflection, he told Cousins that he would speak out in an attempt to stimulate world public opinion.

On April 24, 1957, under the auspices of the Nobel Prize Committee in Oslo, Schweitzer issued an extraordinary "Declaration of Conscience," in which he condemned the health dangers posed by nuclear fallout and contended that a test-ban "would be like the early sun rays of hope which suffering humanity is longing for." His statement produced a powerful response throughout the world. But the governments of the United States, the USSR, and the People's Republic of China refused to broadcast the full text of his message, and the American press generally ignored the appeal.[33] Indeed, as Robert Divine pointed out, Schweitzer's statement might have gone virtually unnoticed in the United States had not Atomic Energy Commissioner Willard Libby decided to give an official reply, in which he stated that the risk of radioactive fallout was slight "compared to the terrible risk of abandoning the defense effort which is so essential under present conditions to the survival of the free world."[34]

Schweitzer's statement and Libby's reaction precipitated a lively debate in the United States over the danger of fallout as measured against the claims of national security. In early June, Nobel Prize winner Linus Pauling released a petition signed by eleven thousand scientists, including three thousand Americans, which called for immediate action "to stop the testing of all nuclear weapons through an international agreement."[35] A Gallup poll in May 1957 showed 63 percent of Americans agreed that the U.S. should stop such tests. Only six months earlier, 56 percent of those Gallup asked had opposed a test ban. "Not since Hiroshima," commented *Newsweek*, "had such a bitter and fateful debate raged over the building, testing, and ultimate use of the A-bomb—and its vastly more destructive offspring, the H-bomb. Governments, scientists, military men, just plain citizens—all are caught up in the controversy."[36]

The issue, as seen by nuclear pacifists like Cousins, involved matters of morality and working democracy. Nuclear tests were by nature murderously indiscriminate. Shifting winds bore radioactive debris throughout the Northern hemisphere and across much of the world. In this way, atomic testing was not only harmful in its own terms, it also symbolized perfectly the utter vulnerability of the world's peoples to the ongoing nuclear menace and the governments' failure to bring it under control. The U.S. and the Soviet Union claimed that atomic testing was vital to their security interests, Cousins allowed. But their claims did not vitiate other people's rights to remain safe from the superpowers' poisons. Moreover, Cousins contended, continued testing eroded prospects for bringing the larger nuclear arms race under control. Indeed, testing only propelled that race forward at higher rates of speed and danger.[37]

Cousins urged the United States to undertake a unilateral suspension of tests in the belief that "world public opinion will compel all other nations to do likewise."[38] The Eisenhower administration, however, insisted that the development of bigger and better bombs contributed directly to the national security and outweighed the possible damage to human life caused by the tests. Moreover, both the administration and its supporters suggested that test-ban proponents were following the Communist party line and implied that their demands were subversive of the national security. Congressman Lawrence H. Smith identified Cousins as a Communist dupe, for example, because of Cousins's success in enlisting Schweitzer in the test-ban cause. Claiming that Communists and their apologists like Cousins were "stirring up a national hysteria," Smith appealed to the American people not to "let the superficial disputed fear of radioactivity blind us to the greatest threat of all-atheistic Communism."[39]

This time, however, not even the most vicious red-baiting could still the debate. Cousins and other nuclear pacifists understood that radiation was one topic that touched a sensitive nerve, and that the fear of fallout was capable of arousing the American people into pressing for a nuclear test-ban treaty. In a stream of editorials, Cousins poured his energy into the struggle to effect an international agreement to halt tests and contain the nuclear arms race. "It may or may not be too late," he wrote at one point, "but at least we owe it to sanity to make the effort."[40] He also helped give life to a new organization called SANE.

The National Committee for the Sane Nuclear Policy (SANE) originated in the spring of 1957 when Lawrence Scott, the American Friends Service Committee peace education director in Chicago, came east determined to put an end to nuclear testing. Scott contacted Cousins and Clarence Pickett, the secretary emeritus of the American

Friends Service Committee, and arranged with him and other Quaker activists to call leading liberals and pacifists to a meeting in New York on what citizens might do to end all tests.[41] On the first day of summer, 1957, twenty-seven national leaders, including churchmen, scientists, businessmen, labor representatives, authors, editors, and public figures met at the Overseas Press Club in New York and listened to Cousins's call for immediate and concerted action. "We cannot sit back and wait for radioactive burden to settle on us," he stated. "The cessation of tests will not in itself make peace, but it will stop something dangerous in itself and gain firmer ground to stop future problems." The famed psychoanalyst and author Erich Fromm, a refugee from Nazi Germany who had already in his lifetime watched mass madness overcome one great power, insisted that American public life first required the re-validation of simple saving sanity. According to Fromm "the normal drive for survival" had been overwhelmed by the Cold War, and the role of informed citizens was to try to bring "the voice of sanity to the people."[42]

Out of that understanding, the conferees launched the National Committee for a Sane Nuclear Policy. In support of the enterprise Cousins borrowed against the stock of the *Saturday Review* and spent more than several thousand dollars of his personal funds. Lenore Marshall, a wealthy New Yorker and peace activist, soon after became the group's sustaining patron. Trevor Thomas, who secured a three-month leave of absence from the Friends Committee on National Legislation of Northern California, was hired to be the temporary executive secretary. Cousins and Pickett were enlisted as cochairmen.

In October 1957, SANE leaders drafted a statement of its goals and purposes, which included the immediate cessation of nuclear weapons tests within terms of a United Nations monitored agreement, the international control of missiles and outerspace satellites through a UN agency, and the strengthening of all agencies connected with the UN. In addition, beyond these precise policy objectives, SANE leaders established their operation upon "a strong moral premise." In this way, SANE intended to speak intelligently about complex political and military considerations without floundering in endless technicalities. In this way, too, SANE activists planned to realize their main ambition of galvanizing "an aroused, articulate humanity that said to governments everywhere that a halt now [to nuclear testing], is not only possible, but imperative to survival."[43]

Its most successful strike toward rallying public support took place on November 15, when SANE ran a full-page advertisement in the *New York Times* beneath the banner headline "We Are Facing A Danger Unlike Any Danger That Has Ever Existed." Largely written by Cousins, the statement argued that "man has natural rights . . . to live and grow, to breathe unpoisoned air, to work on uncontaminated soil," and called on Americans to press their government for an immediate suspension of nuclear testing and proceed toward the development "of a higher loyalty—loyalty by man to the human community."[44]

The November advertisement "started a movement." Within six weeks of its appearance approximately twenty-five hundred letters, the vast majority of them enthusiastic, poured into the understaffed SANE office in New York in an altogether unexpected response. People in all parts of the country voluntarily placed reprints of the original advertisement in thirty-two different newspapers by January and donated an additional twelve thousand dollars to the new organization. There were also requests for twenty-five thousand reprints of the statement. Thousands of people wrote in to ask how they could help or join the Committee.[45] In fact, the grass roots response was so electrifying that SANE leaders, who were originally ambivalent toward the idea of a mass-membership organization, decided to redefine the SANE operation along these lines. By the summer of 1958, SANE had about 130 chapters representing approximately twenty-five thousand Americans.[46] Powerfully, SANE swept into "a vacuum in the American peace movement," energizing people to "politically relevant action on specific issues of the arms race." It "gave anxious citizens from varied backgrounds," one SANE leader recalled later, "a singly meaningful issue on which to act—the cessation of nuclear weapons testing."[47]

Before long, however, the testing issue gave way to an emphasis upon the dangers of nuclear weapons themselves. It was understandable. The weapons always represented the greatest concern of SANE disarmament advocates. In June 1958, pondering what would happen if the United States did ban nuclear weapons tests, Cousins maintained that such an action would "not represent the be-all and end-all of world peace and nuclear sanity." "A truly sane nuclear policy will not be achieved," he stated, "until nuclear weapons are brought completely under control." Two months later, Cousins's thoughts gained greater salience when the United States followed the lead of the

Soviet Union and voluntarily suspended nuclear weapons tests and agreed to meet with Soviet delegates in Geneva to begin negotiations for a test-ban treaty. With the testing issue thus in negotiations, SANE turned its attention to intercontinental ballistic missiles and to the threat of nuclear annihilation. At a fall 1958 national conference, the organization resolved to broaden its goal from a nuclear test ban to general disarmament.[48]

According to Lawrence Wittner, this growth of nuclear pacifism indicated "that while some Americans may have concerned themselves solely with the problem of avoiding a dosage of radiation, many others were re-examining the nature of war in light of the development of thermonuclear weapons."[49] Archetypical nuclear pacifists, Cousins and his allies believed that nuclear weapons and sophisticated delivery systems had made war, as an instrument of national policy, totally self-defeating, impractical, and immoral. Consequently, they argued, the best hope for a world without self-destroying war was in the achievement of universal, total disarmament with adequate inspection and control, down to levels required for maintenance of internal national order under a strengthened United Nations.

Yet these hopes were hard to maintain when even minor victories like the nuclear test-ban treaty proved so frustrating and difficult to realize. Between 1958 and 1962, as the Geneva talks dragged on, both SANE and Cousins worked to mobilize public opinion behind the need for the treaty as a first step toward defusing East-West tensions. Cousins was particularly influential in this process, even acting as unofficial liaison between President Kennedy and Soviet Premier Khrushchev in helping to break an impasse in the negotiations. In early 1963, with negotiations deadlocked over the questions of inspections and Khrushchev doubtful that the U.S. really wanted a treaty, Secretary of State Dean Rusk asked Cousins if he could advise the Soviet leader that Kennedy was acting in good faith and genuinely wanted a treaty. Cousins stood high in the Khrushchev estimation as a result of his support of joint conferences between American and Russian intellectuals and scientists. In addition, Cousins had met with the Soviet premier in Moscow in December 1962, on behalf of Pope John XXIII, and successfully negotiated the release of Cardinal Josyph Slipyi, a Roman Catholic prelate who had been interned during the Stalin regime.[50]

In late April 1963, Cousins conferred with Khrushchev at his Black Sea retreat for over seven hours. Cousins told the premier how a number of citizens' organizations had come together in the United States to develop public support for the president's position in favor of a test-ban treaty and how Kennedy encouraged this campaign from its inception. After reviewing several problems in Soviet-American relations, Khrushchev finally acknowledged his belief in Kennedy's sincere interest in a test-ban treaty, and agreed to join the United States in making a fresh start in negotiations.

After his meeting with Khrushchev, Cousins met with President Kennedy at the White House. A few days later, he drafted for Kennedy a letter that provided precious reinforcement to the president's plans to issue a breakthrough speech on the Cold War during his June commencement address at the American University in Washington. Urging a dramatic U.S. peace initiative, Cousins suggested that such a step might affect the course of Soviet policy and would certainly help the American image in the world. Responding positively to Cousins's thoughts, the president made at the American University commencement a landmark policy statement in behalf of détente. He spoke movingly of peace "as the necessary rational end of rational men," and appealed to the Soviets to join him in seeking a relaxation of tensions.[51] Kennedy's speech elicited a positive response within the Soviet Union and paved the way for the conclusion of the Partial Test-Ban Treaty (underground testing was still allowed), which was signed in Moscow on July 25. In gratitude, President Kennedy sent Cousins the UPI newswire on the treaty, along with a personal expression of appreciation. Later, the president gave him one of the original signed copies of the treaty document itself.

With the conclusion of the test-ban treaty, Kennedy and pro-treaty advocates like Cousins confronted another formidable obstacle: the constitutional requirement to secure a two-thirds vote of approval in the U.S. Senate. Fifty votes seemed certain, but another seventeen were needed. Cousins rightly worried that many senators feared that support for the test-ban treaty would appear in the public mind as a dangerous limitation on American nuclear capability and therefore injurious to the nation's military security. Private polling information indicated that the trend of public opinion was moving toward support of a test ban. But the impression garnered from congressional mailbags and visitors' tally sheets suggested that popular opposition to the test ban was running at about 10 to 1. In some weeks, it appeared as high as 20 to 1.[52]

In Washington, Cousins discussed the politics of ratification with presidential press aide Pierre Salinger. Encouraged by Salinger, Cousins organized the Ad Hoc Committee for a Nuclear Test-Ban Treaty for the purpose of rallying public opinion behind a ratification drive. With this in mind, Cousins and other leaders met with Kennedy on August 7, and advised the president of their plans for a nationwide campaign of advertising and public discussion. For nearly two months in the summer of 1963, debate over testing dominated the news. Between the administration's efforts and the work of Cousins's Ad Hoc Committee and groups like SANE, the tide of congressional mail began to turn. Public opinion polls showed a steady rise in the popular support of the treaty, and easing fear over any danger to the national security.[53]

In the course of this struggle for the public mind, Cousins had several confrontations with Dr. Edward Teller, a Hungarian physicist who had participated in the Manhattan Project and who had pressed most aggressively for development of the hydrogen bomb. An ardent opponent of the test ban, Teller made light of the health dangers of atomic fallout and warned of the threat to the nation's security that would follow from Soviet cheating on any attempted ban. Cousins, however, ignored Teller's jabs. He refused to argue whether or not nuclear testing produced dangerous radioactive fallout, or whether the Soviets might undertake atmospheric tests secretly. Rather, Cousins's abiding concern was that the life of the nation depended on the international control of nuclear weaponry, and that uncontrolled arms competition spelled inevitable disaster.[54]

The campaign over ratification of the test-ban treaty culminated in hearings before the Senate Foreign Relations Committee. The two principal witnesses against ratification were Dr. Teller and General Thomas S. Powers, Chief of the Strategic Air Command. Their opposition, however, was almost anticlimactic. Several other policy-shapers, including Cousins, testified in support of ratification, with gratifying effect.[55] As the treaty came down to a vote in the Senate, the number of votes sufficient for approval increased, while public opinion polls showed that 80 percent of the American people favored the treaty. Finally, on September 24, 1963, the Senate approved the treaty by an 80 to 19 margin, the largest vote in favor of arms control recorded in the Senate since the 1921–22 Washington Naval Treaties. Kennedy called the vote "a welcome culmination of this effort to lead the world once again to the path of peace." He said that no other single accomplishment in the White House gave him greater satisfaction.[56]

Members of SANE rejoiced at word of Senate ratification. The Partial Test-Ban Treaty capped a six-year battle against atmospheric testing; and SANE was singled out by national leaders like Kennedy's science adviser, Jerome Wiesner, as one of the key groups that had made the achievement possible. Cousins, however, was measured in his reaction. While he praised the treaty as a welcome respite from "the long stretch of unremitting failure and almost constant despair," he cautioned against the temptation for activists to withdraw from the disarmament struggle. "The treaty is not an end in itself," he contended. "It is a part of—or should be—a large delicate enterprise for making life less precarious for the humans who inhabit this planet. It is a portal to a more rational future. . . ." The treaty hardly ended the debate over nuclear war preparations. In fact, he concluded, that debate "has actually only begun."[57]

Maddeningly, however, the very success of the test-ban treaty undercut the momentum of citizen disarmament activism. Several nuclear pacifists concluded that their work was over and merged into the liberal wing of the Democratic Party.[58] Even SANE shifted its focus from demonstrations to lobbying and "responsible criticism," while some of its leaders, including Cousins, argued that the national organization should cease functioning because its original objective had been realized. Resigning from the chairmanship of SANE (although he remained on the national board), Cousins returned under the title of honorary president to the United World Federalists. The majority of the SANE directors, however, resolved to continue to work at improving the international climate and Soviet-American relations.[59]

And then came Vietnam. Cousins was an early critic of America's armed intervention in behalf of an anti-Communist regime in South Vietnam, and for many reasons. In the first place, he simply abhorred war and distrusted policies that required war for their fulfillment. In the second place, he had visited Indochina in 1961, and returned most impressed with the complexity of the region and with the misleading reports that most Americans received about developments there.

Thirdly, he had little respect for the South Vietnamese government. In 1962, Cousins and other national board members of SANE attacked the Ngo Dinh Diem regime as "unjust, undemocratic, and unpopular," and urged the United States to disengage itself from its support as soon as possible. After Diem's assassination in November 1963, however, the U.S. assumed larger responsibility for the support of a series of military governments, whose political incompetence was exceeded only by their failure to carry the war in the countryside against guerillas from the Communist-led National Liberation Front. Cousins concluded that Washington was already bogged down in a costly and futile holding operation.[60]

Unable to break the Communist resistance in the South, the United States inaugurated the sustained bombing of North Vietnam in February 1965 and effected a dramatic escalation in the struggle. Cousins blasted President Lyndon Johnson's unilateral commitment to full-scale intervention. "At some time soon," he wrote, "the United States will have to recognize that a military policy without a full ideological and social program will not only fall short of its goal but may actually boomerang." He opposed the bombing as an evasion of the main problem represented by the Communist-led insurgency within South Vietnam. He also believed that the president's bombing contradicted America's larger interest in the promotion of stability and security in Asia.[61] Bomb blasts seemed a poor way to make order.

While Johnson bombed, Cousins agonized over the prospect of finding some middle road toward peace that would preclude a movement toward either larger superpower war or total U.S. withdrawal. He believed that the war's escalation was working tragic consequences not only for the Vietnamese, but also for America's prestige and credibility. He feared that continuing escalation might bring about confrontation between the U.S. and Russia or China, and pave the way toward World War III. At the same time, Cousins opposed any unconditional U.S. withdrawal. He worried that an American defeat could set the stage for wholesale chaos and slaughter in South Vietnam, and would lead to grave consequences throughout Asia and perhaps the world. There was only one alternative, he said. The United Nations must be brought to effect a cease-fire and move the conflict from the battlefield toward a negotiated settlement.[62] He did not specify, however, what was to be negotiated.

Cousins believed that Vietnam represented much more than a

matter of mere military success or failure. The real issue involved the American character and the American capacity to help more than hurt. The humanitarian cast of Cousins's thinking showed itself most sharply in 1965, when the sight of U.S. Marines methodically burning down a South Vietnam village moved him to issue an editorial call for public contributions to rebuild the village. *Saturday Review* readers responded with $10,739 in contributions to raise the village of Cam Ne. Other antiwar critics saw slight value, however, in Cousins's campaign. "The real test of the United States in Vietnam," he wrote, "will be represented not by our ability to exterminate the Vietcong, but by our determination to save lives where we can, to make mercy just as central as military operations, and to put the individual human being first." The Congress should provide that any appropriations for war in Vietnam be made on the principle of moral balance, he contended. "Every dollar authorized for military spending should be matched by a dollar for relief, hospitals, medical care, restoration, reconstruction, and rehabilitation."[63] The liberal editor sometimes seemed altogether less interested in condemning war than in insisting it be fought in a more humanitarian manner.

By 1967, the U.S. had nearly half a million combat troops in Vietnam, had dropped more bombs than in all World War II, and was spending more than $2 billion per month in the war. Meanwhile the size of the antiwar opposition increased dramatically, and the tone of the dissent became sharper. In the middle of the year, while antiwar activists united in New York, San Francisco, and Washington in mass actions against government policy, Cousins and other liberal luminaries launched the NEGOTIATIONS NOW! campaign in an attempt to mobilize "millions of the as-yet uncommitted citizens" to pressure Lyndon Johnson into opening peace negotiations. Opposed to the idea of immediate U.S. withdrawal, NEGOTIATIONS NOW! supported UN Secretary-General U Thant's three-point peace program: a halt to U.S. bombing of North Vietnam; a request that Hanoi and the National Liberation Front respond affirmatively and join the U.S. in a standstill ceasefire; and a call for negotiations among all warring parties, including the National Liberation Front.[64] Working to advance U Thant's program, NEGOTIATIONS NOW! placed large ads in a number of daily newspapers in order to gather signatures for a massive petition in support of the proposal.

With most other liberal antiwar critics, Cousins believed that peace negotiations were possible in Vietnam if only the U.S. would initiate them through a unilateral bombing halt. Unlike most critics of the war, however, Cousins was not only openly courted by the Johnson administration, but was seen as a key link to the intellectual community and one who, according to Vice President Hubert Humphrey, "exercised a healthy, moderating influence on some of the leadership of the Vietnam protest movement." Recognizing that Cousins was the kind of man who wanted to be a friend of the administration if at all possible, national security advisor McGeorge Bundy met with him in June 1965 to discuss the situation in Vietnam. Six months later, presidential aide Jack Valenti suggested that Cousins accompany Humphrey on his trip to Southeast Asia.[65]

Accordingly, in late December 1965, Cousins traveled with Humphrey on a trip to the Far East, in the hope of adopting a negotiated settlement. According to Cousins, the trip had the potential for effecting a significant breakthrough to peace; but, whatever possibilities it possessed were aborted on January 30, 1966, when the U.S. resumed bombing of North Vietnam after a brief pause. Gradually, Cousins became convinced that U.S. military leaders were grasping for fuller control of the war, and complicating Johnson's attempts to end the war through negotiated means. He also believed that Saigon leaders were opposed to any policy other than outright military victory. In one of his many attempts to stimulate negotiations, he urged the U.S. government to condition further military and economic assistance to South Vietnam upon Saigon's demonstrated willingness to talk. According to the White House Asian affairs advisor Chester Cooper, Cousins was among the most reliable, responsible, and highly regarded citizen-diplomats who tried to help Washington's peacemaking efforts.[66]

In March 1968, a few weeks after the shocking Tet offensive, Cousins met with Johnson and tried to convince him to send Vice President Humphrey to negotiate directly with the North Vietnamese. The editor spoke of his conviction that America's position in the world was being gravely damaged by the war and by the divisive effect that the war was producing within the country. When Johnson expressed his doubt that Hanoi wanted peace, Cousins pointed out that every time exploratory talks had failed, it was not because Hanoi backed down but because the U.S. had attached impossible conditions to the Communists' participation. The real question, Cousins told the president, was not whether the North Vietnamese would accept a negotiated end to the war, but how Washington could convince them that America wished for a political settlement.[67]

Cousins failed to understand, however, that in spite of the sudden erosion in popular confidence that followed up Tet, the U.S. government had no interest in negotiating an end to the war that threatened the survival of an anti-Communist regime in Saigon. Shortly after his talk with Cousins, Johnson began to reverse the momentum of U.S. military involvement; and Richard Nixon worked for the next four years to reduce the American military presence. But the U.S. government scarcely deviated from its determination to prevent a Communist success in Saigon. Cousins continued to call for negotiations and for a UN resolution of the war. But his attempts to multilateralize the diplomacy of the war failed utterly to confront the depths of Washington's determination to win its way in Indochina. As the war spread into Laos and Cambodia in the early 1970s, Cousins's dream of transforming American foreign policy into a vehicle of humanitarianism appeared bankrupt. Painfully, his declining influence among other peaceseekers helped to reflect that reality.[68]

In January 1973, the Paris peace accords were finally signed, ending the era of large-scale U.S. military intervention in Vietnam. Cousins welcomed the accords in the understanding that the rebuilding and healing of all of Vietnam remained the most important item on the American national agenda. If Washington was able to spend over $30 billion annually for six years to destroy Vietnam, Cousins observed, the government could afford to spend a fraction of that amount in helping to build a new nation. There was one last chance to vindicate American honor in Vietnam, he contended. "We owe something to the Vietnamese people," and what "is most fortunate of all is that we also have the opportunity to remake ourselves in the process."[69]

Cousins spent considerable time and energy writing and speaking against American involvement in Vietnam. Yet he consistently maintained that the first responsibility of peacemakers was in the fight against nuclear war. He tried on several occasions to keep the nuclear issue alive in the public mind, speaking out against the attempted deployment of the anti-ballistic missile system in 1969 and in support of the 1972 SALT treaty. But the nuclear arms race nonetheless advanced at an astounding rate. During the 1970s, both the United States and the USSR more than doubled their arsenals of strategic nuclear warheads; and new weapons appeared much faster than the agreements that could control them. Yet fewer and fewer people seemed to care. In a 1976 editorial, "The Nightmare That Won't Go Away," Cousins deplored the fact that "hardly anyone talks anymore about nuclear stockpiles as the world's number one problem." "An entire generation has come of age with only a theoretical idea of the nature of atomic destructive force," he wrote. The anti-testing campaigns of the early 60s seemed "faroff and almost unreal." "Yet, he cautioned, "like it or not, the nuclear threat is still alive, ugly, more menacing than ever."[70]

In order to reignite discussion and debate on the nuclear issue, Cousins reassumed the presidency of the United World Federalists (now called the World Federalist Association, or WFA), and argued that its program posed the only convincing alternative to mutual annihilation. According to Cousins, the Federalists' commitment to the gradual development of a world authority to supervise a phased system of general disarmament "provides the only true security—a kind of security antithetical to unrestricted national sovereignty."[71] Under his leadership and that of Executive Director Bill Wickersham, there was a striking resurgence of world federalist support, with membership doubling to almost twelve thousand. Stressing education and political action, Cousins and the WFA pressed for a joint Soviet-American accord that would open the way for inspected disarmament among all nations down to nonthreatening force levels. Concurrently, the powers would conclude agreement providing methods and instrumentalities for the peaceful settlement of international disputes and the creation of a UN peace force. In the process, world politics might develop some sinews of world order and thus the beginning musculature of peace.

Cousins resigned from the editorship of the *Saturday Review* in 1978. He joined the faculty of the University of California-Los Angeles School of Medicine, and wrote two very popular books on his remarkable recoveries from serious illness: *Anatomy Of An Illness* (1979) and *The Healing Heart* (1983). Ironically, while Cousins had published more than a dozen books on the ills of nations, none provoked the popular acclaim that did these accounts of his bouts with personal illness. Both books were selected for distribution by the Book-of-the-Month Club, Inc., sold millions of copies, and established Cousins as a familiar figure on the national talk-show circuit. At the same time, neither of these books was irrelevant to Cousins's larger interest in ways of healing humankind and its world. "Humanity's greatest problem has never been the absence of solutions to complex situations," he once declared. "Its greatest problem has been the absence of belief in answers."[72] Eager to supply some faith in answers, Cousins struggled through these books and others and tried especially hard in all his writings to reinspire a general faith that progress was still possible, and that hope was not a state of mind but the very means of achieving progressive ends.

In June 1983, after three years of sharply escalating antinuclear protest, Cousins told the graduating class of Harvard Medical School that "The conquest of war and the pursuit of social justice . . . must become our grand preoccupation and magnificent obsession."[73] These certainly were the concerns that obsessed Norman Cousins throughout his life, and over the years he battled to make them matters of a more general concern. Driven by the shock and portent of Hiroshima, he worked to combat unchecked nationalism, promote federalism, and build a sense of world citizenship, in the belief that people as a whole might yet build a new world order free of war. His optimism was unquenchable. Indeed, the journalist Bill Moyers observed, Cousins was one of the few men who lived through an incredible era and was not consumed by it.[74]

Cousins himself once wrote that a man was measured in the end by the nature of his largest concerns and his definition of the ultimate question; and it seems only fair to evaluate him in the same way.[75] Cousins gave voice and hope for a generation to the human attempt to press forward in freedom and dignity toward the organization of a world of peace and justice. In this way, he can lay fair claim to success in life's measure. For, more than most, Norman Cousins fought as an individual of conscience to advance humanitarian solutions to what most agree is the ultimate question: how modern humankind might overcome its own obsolescence and realize a global order for the sake of its security and survival.

NOTES

1. Norman Cousins, *Modern Man Is Obsolete*, (New York: Viking Press, 1945), p. 10.

2. Norman Cousins, interview with the author, July 25, 1983 (cited hereon as Cousins interview).

3. Norman Cousins, letter to the author, October 27, 1983; and see Norman Cousins, *In God We Trust*, (New York: Harper and Brothers, 1958).

4. Norman Cousins, *Who Speaks For Man?*, (New York: Macmillan & Co., 1953), p. 5.

5. Norman Cousins, *The Good Inheritance*, (New York: Coward, McCann, 1942).

6. Cousins, *Who Speaks For Man?*, p. 12.

7. Ibid., p. 13.

8. Ibid., p. 13.

9. Clarence K. Streit, *Union Now: The Proposal for the Inter-Democracy Federal Union*, (New York: Harper and Brothers, 1940).

10. Norman Cousins, "A Bargain Counter for Ideals," *Saturday Review* 26 (October 16, 1943): 26.

11. Cousins, *Modern Man Is Obsolete*, p. 15.

12. Ibid., pp. 20, 23.

13. Ibid., p. 23.

14. Cousins, *Who Speaks For Man?*, pp. 15, 16.

15. Cousins interview; *New York Times*, October 11, 1945, p. 4; and Lawrence Wittner, *Rebels Against War: The American Peace Movement, 1941–1960*, (New York: Columbia University Press, 1970), p. 140.

16. Norman Cousins, "Report From Oslo," *Saturday Review* 50 (August 26, 1967): 22, 42. The standard work in this field is Grenville Clark and Louis B. Sohn, *World Peace Through World Law*, 1st ed., (Cambridge: Harvard University Press, 1958). Cousins's comments and summary of the major changes they suggest can be found in his *In Place of Folly* (New York: Washington Square Press, 1962), pp. 124–143.

17. Jon A. Yoder, "United World Federalists: Liberals For Law and Order," in Charles Chatfield, ed., *Peace Movements in America*, (New York: Schocken Books, 1973), p. 99.

18. Ibid., p. 100.

19. Ibid.

20. Ibid., p. 101.

21. Wittner, *Rebels Against War*, pp. 174, 175.

22. Ibid., pp. 201, 209.

23. Norman Cousins, "A Time of Hope," *Saturday Review* 33 (July 15, 1950): 22; and Cousins, "The Strange Banner," *Saturday Review* 33 (July 22, 1950): 22.

24. Yoder, "United World Federalists," p. 106; and Wittner, *Rebels Against War*, p. 222.

25. Norman Cousins, "The Climate of Freedom," *Saturday Review* 35 (December 13, 1952): 22.

26. Ibid.; and Norman Cousins, "No," *Saturday Review* 33 (October 7, 1950): 28, 29.

27. Norman Cousins, "Worse Than the H-Bomb," *Saturday Review* 35 (December 31, 1952): 20.

28. Charles DeBenedetti, *The Peace Reform in American History* (Bloomington: Indiana University Press, 1980), p. 151.

29. I. F. Stone, "First Call For A Test Ban," *I. F. Stone's Weekly* (November 1, 1954): 1.

30. Cousins interview; and Cousins, *Present Tense: An American Editor's Odyssey* (New York: McGraw-Hill, 1967), p. 266.

31. See Robert Divine, *Blowing On The Wind: The Nuclear Test Ban Debate, 1954–1960* (New York: Oxford University Press, 1978), chap. 4, "The 1956 Campaign," pp. 84–112; and letters from Adlai Stevenson to Norman Cousins, December 15, 1956 in Walter Johnson, ed. *The Papers of Adlai Stevenson*, vol. 6 (Boston: Little, Brown, and Co., 1976). p. 346.

32. Norman Cousins, *Dr. Schweitzer of Lambarene* (New York: Harper and Row, 1960).

33. *New York Times*, April 24, 1957, p. 1; and *Saturday Review* 40 (May 18, 1957).

34. Divine, *Blowing On the Wind*, p. 122; and *New York Times*, April 26, 1957, p. 4.

35. Linus Pauling, interview with author, February 9, 1983; and Pauling, *No More War* (New York: Dodd, Mead, and Co., 1958) pp. 160–78.

36. Eugene J. Rosi, "Mass and Attentive Opinion on Nuclear Weapons Tests and Fallout, 1954–1963," *Public Opinion Quarterly* 29 (Summer 1965): 283–90; and *Newsweek* 49 (May 6, 1957): 51–58.

37. Cousins, *Present Tense*, p. 60; and Cousins interview.

38. Norman Cousins, "The Great Debate Opens," *Saturday Review* 40 (June 5, 1957): 24.

39. Divine, *Blowing On the Wind*, p. 141.

40. Norman Cousins, "The Debate is Over," *Saturday Review* 42 (April 4, 1959): 25.

41. Lawrence Scott, "Memo One—Shared Thinking," April 30, 1957, National Committee for a Sane Nuclear Policy Manuscripts, Swarthmore College Peace Collection, Swarthmore, Pennsylvania, Document Group, 58 (Hereafter cited as SANE MSS).

42. Minutes of the Provisional Committee to Stop Nuclear Tests, June 21, 1957 and September 24, 1957, SANE MSS.

43. Minutes of the Executive Committee, October 8, 1957, SANE MSS.

44. *New York Times*, November 15, 1975, p. 54.

45. Arlo Hurth, "Response to the First Statement Issued by the National Committee for a Sane Nuclear Policy: November 15–December 31, 1957," (January 1958), SANE MSS.

46. SANE's members were generally upper class white, middle- to upper-middle-professionals, from Protestant or Jewish religious traditions. Sanford Gottlieb, interview with the author, January 19, 1972.

47. Sanford Gottlieb, "National Committee for a Sane Nuclear Policy," *New University Thought* 2 (Spring 1962): 156.

48. Minutes of the Executive Committee Meeting, June 8, 1958; Minutes of the First National Conference, September 29, 1958; and Minutes of the Second National Conference, October 25, 26, 1959, SANE MSS.

49. Wittner, *Rebels Against War*, p. 253.

50. Norman Cousins, *The Improbable Triumvirate: Pope John, John F. Kennedy, Nikita Khrushchev*, (New York: W. W. Norton, 1972), pp. 48–50, 77–110.

51. Cousins interview. Ted Sorensen in his book *Kennedy*, (New York: Bantam Books, 1966), p. 822, wrote that Kennedy particularly valued the April 30 letter from Cousins in preparing for his American University speech.

52. Cousins, *Improbable Triumvirate*, p. 127.

53. Ibid., pp. 128–35.

54. Ibid., pp. 144–46.

55. Ibid., p. 147.

56. Arthur Schlesinger, Jr., *A Thousand Days: John F. Kennedy in the White House*, (New York: Fawcett Crest, 1967), p. 834.

57. Norman Cousins, "Just the Beginning," *Saturday Review* 46 (September 21, 1963): 28, 29.

58. See Wittner, *Rebels Against War*, p. 277; and Paul Boyer, "From Activism to Apathy: "The American People and Nuclear Weapons, 1963–1980," *The Journal of American History* 70 (March 1984): 821–44.

59. Norman Cousins to Homer Jack, March 7, 1963, SANE MSS; and Homer Jack, "SANE: Tasks Ahead," *SANE World* 2 (October 15, 1963): 2.

60. Norman Cousins, "Report From Laos," *Saturday Review* 44 (February 18, 1961): 10; "Policy Paper on Southeast Asia," June 27, 1962; SANE MSS; and Norman Cousins, "Vietnam: Miscalculations and Alternations," *Saturday Review* 47 (December 12, 1964): 32.

61. Norman Cousins, "Vietnam and the American Conscience," *Saturday Review* 48 (February 27, 1965): 22.

62. Norman Cousins, "Double Jeopardy: UN and Vietnam," *Saturday Review* 48 (March 27, 1965): 20.

63. Norman Cousins, "Second Front in Vietnam," *Saturday Review* 49 (October 29, 1966): 22; and see Norman Cousins, "Morale and Morality in Vietnam," *Saturday Review* 50 (March 25, 1967): 22.

64. Fred Halstead, *Out Now* (New York: Monarch Press, 1978), p. 291; and Norman Cousins, "Toward National Unity Over Vietnam," *Saturday Review* 50 (December 2, 1967): 21.

65. Memo, McGeorge Bundy to the president, July 1, 1965, Aides File, National Security File, Lyndon Baines Johnson Library, Austin, Texas (hereafter cited as LBJL); memo, Jack Valenti to the president, December 16, 1965, Norman Cousins File, White House Central File, LBJL.

66. Norman Cousins, "Journeys with Humphrey: Memoir of a Peace Mission That Failed," *Saturday Review* 61 (March 4, 1978): 11; and Transcript, Chester Cooper, Oral History Interview, 2, p. 45, LBJL.

67. George Christian, "Notes of the President's Meeting with Norman Cousins," March 15, 1968, Meeting Notes Files, LBJL. Also see Norman Cousins to the President, March 25, 1968, Name File, White House Central File, LBJL.

68. See Norman Cousins, "A Respectful Suggestion for Ending the War," *Saturday Review* 51 (June 1, 1968): 20; Cousins, "Death and Deadlock," *Saturday Review* 52 (November 1, 1969): 26; and Cousins, "Who Dies For What?" *Saturday Review* 54 (April 3, 1971): 20.

69. Norman Cousins, "Vietnam: Let Us Begin," *World* 1 (February 27, 1973): 14.

70. Norman Cousins, "The Nightmare That Won't Go Away," *Saturday Review* 59 (April 17, 1976): 14.

71. "Norman Cousins Returning as President," *World Federalist Newsletter,* I (July 1976), pp. 1, 3; and Bill Wickersham, Interview, November 15, 1983.

72. Norman Cousins to Carll Tucker, *Saturday Review* 61 (April 15, 1978): 7.

73. Norman Cousins, Commencement Talk at Harvard Medical School, June 9, 1983.

74. Bill Moyers, "An American Editor's Odyssey: N.C.'s Twenty-Five Years at SR," *Saturday Review* 50 (November 11, 1967): 30.

75. Norman Cousins, "The Men of the Golden Rule," *Saturday Review* 41 (May 17, 1958): 24.

FURTHER READING

Among his many writings, Cousins most impressively set down his thinking on war/peace issues in the following books: *The Good Inheritance* (New York: Coward, McCann, 1942); *Modern Man Is Obsolete* (New York: Viking Press, 1945); *Dr. Schweitzer of Lambarene* (New York: Harper and Brothers, 1960); and *The Improbable Triumvirate: Pope John, John F. Kennedy, Nikita Khrushchev* (New York: W. W. Norton, 1972). Moreover, in a work called *Who Speaks for Man?* (New York: Macmillan Co., 1953), Cousins anticipated the globalization of world problems and argued for the development of world institutions that would act on behalf of the human interest. Finally, in the book *In Place of Folly* (New York: Harper and Brothers, 1961), he considered the implications of modern mass warfare and proposed that security in the Atomic Age could only be achieved through the control of—and not the pursuit of—force.

Although no biography has yet been published of Cousins and his work, he has assembled two books indicative of his evolving concerns: *Present Tense: An American Editor's Odyssey* (New York: McGraw-Hill, 1967) and *Human Options: An Autobiographical Notebook* (New York: W. W. Norton, 1981).

RALPH B. LEVERING

Martin Luther King, Jr.

The Challenge of Inclusive Peacemaking

Between 1955 and 1968, a black-led civil rights movement emerged across the United States, and especially in the American South, struggling to end racial segregation and to allow blacks fuller access to the largest promises of the national life. Joining millions of people from all races, creeds, and regions, this movement grew from several deep and tangled historical roots, including: the long black quest for freedom and equality; the egalitarian values inherent in the Declaration of Independence and other fundamental American documents; the strong emphasis on social justice of many of America's religious faiths; and, most recently, the labor and liberal reform movements of the 1930s and 1940s. This movement found in Martin Luther King, Jr., a leader capable of transforming millions of inchoate aspirations into an engine of peaceful social change.

The movement's largely peaceful methods and positive results were not preordained. Almost certainly, in view of long-building black frustrations, there would have been a major civil rights movement in the 1950s and 1960s, with or without the Reverend King. Yet, without King's leadership and moral authority, this movement might well have taken a far different course, perhaps even toward a racial bloodbath and severe political repression. Instead, King stepped into history and aggressively deployed the power of Christian nonviolence to move the country away from racial injustice and toward reconciliation. As was noted in a eulogy at his funeral in April 1968, he appeared as "a peaceful warrior who built an army and a movement that is mighty without missiles, able without an atomic arsenal, ready without rockets, real without bullets; an army tutored in living and loving and not in killing." He was that rare phenomenon—"a leader who was willing to die, but not willing to kill." In the process of fighting for civil rights, he helped to shepherd his country through a time of trial and progress in race relations.[1]

Fundamentally, King was an inclusive peacemaker. He sought not only to include as many supporters as possible within the civil rights movement, but also to bring about an eventual reconciliation with their opponents. He saw the circle of support for social justice, which he termed the "beloved community," expanding until it included virtually all Americans. Furthermore, King was an inclusive peacemaker in the sense that he strove to overcome his personal limitations for the sake of greater moral and political effectiveness. Within this framework, we will first examine elements of King's personal development that enabled him to become an effective leader. We will then consider how his Christian belief in inclusiveness in building the "beloved community" informed his highly successful work for peaceful change through the middle of 1965. Finally, we will analyze why his career after 1965 was less successful than it had been earlier. In examining King's life as a whole, it seems clear that it was his combination of inward preparation and testing, on the one hand, and his outward work for justice and peace, on the other, that made possible his achievements and defined his legacy.

The basic outline of King's life before the Montgomery bus boycott of 1955–56 can be summarized briefly. He was born in Atlanta on January 15, 1929. His parents were Alberta Williams King, the daughter of the pastor of the Ebenezer Baptist Church, and Martin Luther "Daddy" King, the assistant pastor who became pastor upon the death of his father-in-law in 1931. Ebenezer was a thriving church, and Martin grew up in a family with middle-class comforts. He attended church faithfully and sang hymns at church meetings at a young age. Growing up in Atlanta, he also experienced white racism firsthand.

A precocious youth, King skipped his senior year in high school and entered the predominantly black Morehouse College in Atlanta at age fifteen. After graduating from Morehouse with a degree in sociology in spring 1948, he entered the largely white Crozier Theological Seminary in suburban Philadelphia. Three years later, as valedictorian of his graduating class, he won a scholarship to attend the graduate school of his choice. That fall King entered Boston University's prestigious School of Theology, which awarded him the Ph.D. degree in 1955. In the meantime, he married Coretta Scott, a student at the Boston Conservatory, and accepted an appointment as minister of the Dexter Avenue Baptist Church in Montgomery, Alabama, beginning in the summer of 1954.[2]

As a youth, King's most difficult problem involved the choice of a vocation. He wanted to serve others and to make his mark in the world, but he was not sure how he should proceed. While attracted in some ways to the ministry, he did not like the pressure his father was putting on him to succeed him as pastor at Ebenezer; and he doubted the relevance of his church's fundamentalist religion in modern America. He toyed with the idea of becoming a doctor; and, after a bad personal experience with discrimination on a train trip, he considered becoming a lawyer so that he could help in breaking down the legal barriers that trapped blacks in a segregated subcaste.[3]

During his junior year at Morehouse, he decided to prepare for a career in the ministry, mostly as a result of the influence of two men. One was the head of the religion department, George D. Kelsey; and the other was the college's president, Benjamin Mays. Kelsey was King's favorite professor and the man who most helped him gain a new appreciation of the Bible and its relevance to modern life. In his course on the Bible, King learned from Kelsey "to see that behind the legends and myths of the Book were many profound truths which one could not escape." Implicitly criticizing preachers like Daddy King, Kelsey disparaged emotional religion and encouraged a more intellectual approach, teaching that modern ministers should include philosophical and social concerns in their preaching. Under Kelsey's influence, "the shackles of fundamentalism were removed from my body," King recalled, and a career in the ministry became a real possibility.[4]

Dr. Mays epitomized the kind of religious leader Kelsey was advocating. Highly educated, impressive in appearance, and inspiring as a speaker, Mays challenged the students to strive for integrity in their personal lives, excellence in their careers, and commitment to serving others. Active in the NAACP and a modernist in religion, Mays criticized black preachers who encouraged "socially irrelevant patterns of escape," and called the white church America's "most conservative and hypocritical institution." Impressed by Mays's combination of academic knowledge, social commitment, and religious faith, King sought him out to pursue points that the president had raised during the college's Tuesday morning chapel services. As Stephen B. Oates has observed, Mays struck King as "what he wanted a real minister to be—a rational man whose sermons were both spiritually and intellectually stimulating, a moral man who was socially involved." King realized through Mays's example that the ministry could be "a respectable force for ideas, even for social protest." At age seventeen, after years of wrestling with his future vocation, he announced to his parents that he intended to become a Baptist minister. "I came to see that God had placed a responsibility upon my shoulders," he recalled, "and the more I tried to escape it the more frustrated I would become."[5]

King's decision to accept a calling to the ministry did not require that he secure a Ph.D. degree. After all, he could have become a successful minister with his degree from Crozier and with his experience preaching in his father's church during summer vacations. While at Crozier, however, he decided that he wanted to study at Boston University with Dr. Edgar Sheffield Brightman, a leading exponent of the philosophy of personalism, whose books King had read avidly. Partly, King decided to continue his studies toward a Ph.D. because he wished to emulate the educational achievements of Dr. Mays and some of his teachers at Morehouse and Crozier. But the major reason for his decision almost certainly was the love of learning that King displayed throughout his three years at Crozier, and that he continued to exhibit in Boston.[6]

King's love of learning was grounded in his determination to use ideas as a means toward social change and racial justice. At Crozier, King became fascinated with the writings of the early twentieth-century Protestant theologian Walter Rauschenbush and other exponents of liberal Christianity, with attacks on religious liberalism by another American Protestant theologian, Reinhold Niebuhr, with the perspectives of great nineteenth-century thinkers like Hegel and Marx, and with the thought and example of Mohandas Gandhi. At Crozier, King recalled, he began "a serious intellectual quest for a method to eliminate social evil . . .," a quest greatly aided by his study of Gandhi's nonviolent movement in India.[7] He went on to Boston University mostly to deepen his intellectual understanding of Christianity, but also to study a theological/philosophical perspective, personalism, that, in King's words, "gave me metaphysical and philosophical grounding for the idea of a personal God, and it gave me a metaphysical basis for the dignity and worth of all human personality." Thus, in his graduate studies King delighted in serious intellectual pursuits while retaining his commitment to Christianity and the striving for social justice and reconciliation that he considered its central message for the world.[8]

Apart from Christian thinkers like Rauschenbush and Brightman, King appears to have been most heavily influenced by Gandhi and Hegel. King filtered the Indian's idea through his own Christian faith and personal experiences. He equated the Sanskrit word *Satayagraha* with *agape*, one of the three Greek words for love and one that appears frequently in the New Testament. Defining *agape* as an "understanding, redeeming good will for all men," King argued that Jesus and then Gandhi had lived the "love ethic" which, when combined with nonviolent resistance to evil, made social transformation possible. "Gandhi was probably the first person in history to lift the love ethic of Jesus above mere interaction between individuals to a powerful and effective social force on a large scale . . .," King wrote in *Stride Toward Freedom*. "It was in this Gandhian emphasis on love and nonviolence that I discovered the method for social reform that I had been seeking. . . ."9

King also was interested in Hegel's dialectical method of thinking, the view that truth is ascertained through the use of opposites (a thesis and an antithesis), with the combination of the two resulting in a synthesis. Indeed, Hegel maintained that history itself unfolded through the evolutionary interplay of theses, antitheses, and syntheses. As King became involved in civil rights, he quickly perceived the applicability of Hegelian ideas. He believed that an antithesis of black resistance and solidarity was needed to confront the thesis of the southern white power structure and racist ideas. Hegel's view of change in history helped King keep the civil rights movement—and white resistance to it—in perspective. Although he was deeply saddened by the deaths that occurred, he could accept them, not only because of his Christian belief in the ultimate triumph of God's love, but also because of the Hegelian tenet that "growth comes through struggle."10

Hegel's ideas may have influenced King partly because they applied to his personal experience. Alternately retiring and gregarious, King described himself as an "ambivert," a cross between an introvert and an extrovert. King also recognized that every human being has a "higher self" and a "lower self," and the danger was letting "the lower self take over." One of his favorite sermons, "A Tough Mind and a Tender Heart," begins with a dialectical analysis that could serve as an epitaph for King himself:

> A French philosopher said, "No man is strong unless he bears within his character antitheses strongly marked." The strong man holds in a living blend strongly marked opposites. Not ordinarily do men achieve this balance of opposites. The idealists are not usually realistic, and the realists are not usually idealistic. The militant are not generally known to be passive, nor the passive to be militant. . . . But life at its best is a creative synthesis of opposites in fruitful harmony.11

With his studies in Boston completed except for writing the doctoral dissertation, King wrestled with an offer to accept a Baptist pastorate in Montgomery. He was tempted by the thought of an academic career, and indeed received several offers to become a professor or a dean. He finally decided to begin his career in the ministry, however, on the assumption that he could shift after a time to higher education. In addition, Coretta, a native of rural Alabama whose family had experienced racism intensely, wished to continue living in the relative freedom of the North. King, too, remembered how much he resented segregation, and at least one northern church was interested in him. But he felt a duty to return to work among blacks in his native South; and he was convinced that educated blacks should not use their degrees to escape north. "His intense dedication compelled him toward the harder rather than the easier solution," Coretta King recalled.[12]

King had lived in Montgomery for less than eighteen months when, on December 1, 1955, a seamstress and NAACP member named Rosa Parks was arrested for refusing to give up her seat and move to the back of one of Montgomery's segregated buses. Parks immediately turned for support to E. D. Nixon, the leading black militant in the city and a man long active in both the local and state chapters of the NAACP. Nixon and others believed that the black community needed to take a strong stand against Mrs. Parks's arrest and the much broader pattern of legal segregation that it represented; accordingly, agreement was reached quickly among black leaders that the buses should be boycotted and that an organization, the Montgomery Improvement Association (MIA), should be established to coordinate the boycott. At the organizational meeting of the MIA, Nixon arranged to have the surprised King elected president. King was the best choice for at least two good reasons. He had few enemies within the black community, and he had not been in Montgomery long enough to have been bought off by the white power structure. "Somebody has to do it," King responded reluctantly to Nixon at the organizational meeting, "and if you think I can, I will serve."[13]

King did an excellent job as public leader. He spoke powerfully in defense of the boycott and in support of the demand for equal treatment, merging the seemingly contradictory themes of militancy and moderation. He responded crisply to white ministers who urged black clergy to concentrate on soul-saving and avoid social issues. And he worked effectively with Nixon and other black leaders to hold together a community in nonviolent resistance. Thanks to their efforts, the boycott was supported by virtually all blacks in the city, and the bus company felt real financial strain.

Privately, however, King was troubled. He was a young minister in the prime of life with a new family, and unsure about his own staying power. His father was urging him to come home to the relative safety of Atlanta. The constant hate letters and threatening phone calls ate at him deeply. Many of the letters and calls threatened to kill King and his wife and infant daughter, Yoki, if they did not abandon the boycott and immediately leave Montgomery. A friend told King that they had heard from reliable sources that plans were being made to assassinate him. Badly frightened, King talked with his friend Ralph Abernathy about the depression that was overtaking him. "Ralph tried to reassure me," King recalled, "but I was still afraid."[14]

Eventually, the unrelenting hatred moved King into a commitment to sustained leadership. On the night of January 27, 1956, King received a threatening phone call: "Nigger, if you aren't out of this town in three days we gonna blow your brains out and blow up your house." Unable to sleep, he made a pot of coffee and "tried to think of a way to move out of the picture without appearing a coward." He felt certain he had to quit. The pressure was becoming too great, and he could not bear the thought of losing his wife and daughter, or of being taken from them. He bowed over the table and prayed aloud: "I am here taking a stand for what I believe is right. But now I am afraid. The people are looking to me for leadership, and if I stand before them without strength and courage, they too will falter. I am at the end of my powers. I have nothing left. I've come to the point where I can't face it alone." At that point King said that he:

> experienced the presence of the Divine as I had never experienced Him before. It seemed as though I could hear the quiet assurance of an inner voice saying: "Stand up for righteousness, stand up for truth; and God will be at your side forever." Almost at once my fears began to go. My uncertainty disappeared. I was ready to face anything.[15]

Three days later, while King was speaking at a mass meeting, he received word that his house had been bombed. Not knowing whether Coretta and Yoki were alive or dead, he instructed the congregation to remain calm, and hurried home. After learning that his wife and daughter were unharmed, King went out on the porch to quiet a largely black crowd that seethed with anger and the desire to unloose retaliatory violence against whites. "We must love our white brothers, no matter what they do to us," King declared. "We must make them know that we love them. Jesus still cries out in words that echo across the centuries: Love your enemies; bless them that curse you; pray for them that despitefully use you. . . . Remember, if I am stopped, this Movement will not stop, because God is with this Movement." Afterward, a white policeman commented that "I owe my life to that nigger Preacher, and so do all the other white people who were there." King's leadership and courage helped to maintain the boycott until victory was achieved in November 1956.[16]

The death threats and the bombing forced King to face directly an issue that often confronts the peacemaker: whether one is prepared to accept death for a cause that seems greater than oneself. King did not seek martyrdom. On the contrary, he loved life and enjoyed his family and friends. Yet he and countless other civil rights workers repeatedly risked their lives, and several dozen were killed by white extremists during the 1960s. They lived in a climate of chronic fear. King managed to transcend his fear and to devote himself fully to the civil rights cause only after he had fully accepted the possibility of his own sudden death. As King said in Detroit on June 23, 1963: "And even if he [a white racist] tries to kill you, you develop the inner conviction that there are some things so dear, some things so precious, some things so eternally true that they are worth dying for. And I submit to you that if a man has not discovered something that he will die for, he isn't fit to live." King's associate Bernard Lafayette, one of millions of blacks and whites inspired by King's personal courage and religious faith, noted that "only those who are free of worrying about death can give freely of themselves."[17]

In sum, during his first twenty-seven years King developed numerous qualities that proved invaluable to him as a peacemaker. He felt a deep concern for the plight of the black masses, especially in his native South. He sustained a strong religious faith combined with a quest for greater spiritual depth and understanding. He maintained a continuing interest in his own intellectual growth and in learning about ways to bring about peaceful social change. He had an ability to communicate with people of diverse racial and educational backgrounds. And, perhaps most significant, he developed a commitment, strengthened in a time of crisis, to continue to work for social justice even if it meant forfeiting his own life.

The decade beginning with the Montgomery bus boycott in fall 1955 and ending with the Voting Rights Act in summer 1965 marked the glory days for King—and for the civil rights movement as a whole. It was during these years that King, the inclusive peacemaker, was most effective. The story of the civil rights movement during these years has been told many times; here the focus is on some key reasons for King's effectiveness, followed by a closer look at the two great events in civil rights in 1963: the springtime Birmingham campaign and King's "I Have a Dream" speech in Washington in August.

One reason for King's effectiveness during these years was his continuing personal and intellectual growth. He broadened himself by visiting West Africa in 1957 and India in 1959. The visit to the "land of my father's fathers" was memorable, and led to what King called a "nonviolent rebirth" and to a continuing interest in Africa's welfare. His trip to India deepened his commitment to Gandhian principles, including an effort upon his return to put less emphasis on material comforts in his own life. In the midst of a hectic schedule, King took time for writing and reflection. In addition to many articles, he published two books about the movement—*Stride Toward Freedom: The Montgomery Story* (1958) and *Why We Can't Wait* (1964)—and a deeply spiritual book of sermons, *Strength to Love* (1964). During these years King was especially interested in learning more about human behavior and the psychological underpinnings of racism and violence. The relatively brief periods of time that King set aside for travel and for personal renewal helped to keep his speeches and writings fresh and cogent, and helped him, at least until the mid-1960s, to avert a clear danger facing prominent peacemakers—exhaustion or burnout.[18]

King's continuing spiritual and intellectual growth made his speeches and writings more self-assured and forceful than they had been during his first years in Montgomery. In June 1963, for example, he gave an address in Detroit that illustrated his intellectual depth, his eloquence, and his insistence on maintaining an inclusive vision. His words also offered an excellent summary of major components of his basic argument, repeated with only minor changes to audience after audience:

> We're coming to see now, the psychiatrists are saying to us, that many of the strange things that happen in the subconscious, many of the inner

conflicts, are rooted in hate, and so they are saying, love or perish. Jesus told us this a long time ago. . . . History is replete with the bleached bones of nations, history is cluttered with the wreckage of communities that failed to follow this command. And isn't it wonderful to have a method of struggle that makes it possible to stand up against an unjust system, fight it will all of your might, never accept it, and yet not stoop to violence and hatred in the process? This is what we have. . . .

. . . I hope that you will allow me to say to you this afternoon, that God is not interested merely in the freedom of black men and brown men and yellow men; God is interested in the freedom of the whole human race. I believe that with this philosophy and with this determined struggle, we will be able to go on in the days ahead and transform the jangling discords of our nation into a beautiful symphony of brotherhood.[19]

A second, vitally important reason for King's effectiveness was his relationship with whites, especially with northern liberals. Ever since his Morehouse days, when he had served on the interracial Atlanta Intercollegiate Council, King believed in the possibility of working with whites to improve race relations and economic conditions for blacks. His postgraduate years in the North had involved positive relationships with white professors and fellow students. King felt strongly that liberal whites wished to support educated blacks who issued reasonable demands for racial justice and who appreciated white support in the struggle for an integrated America. In his speeches and actions during these years, King perfectly addressed these white wishes. Indeed, historian August Meier noted in 1965, King's "most important function" in the civil rights movement "is that of effectively communicating Negro aspirations to white people, of making nonviolent direct action respectable in the eyes of the white majority."[20]

From the standpoint of the movement, the most important northern whites were potential financial contributors and journalists. King's organization, the Southern Christian Leadership Conference (SCLC), and other civil rights organizations needed substantial contributions in order to sustain and enlarge their work in the South. And King proved to be an excellent fund-raiser. Urbane and convivial, he showed himself to be comfortable with whites whether in frequent speeches to potential contributors or in small-group meetings with wealthy Jews and other northern liberals. It was an essential task. Without the substantial support that poured into its Atlanta headquarters, SCLC almost certainly could not have mounted the large-scale civil rights campaigns of the early and middle 1960s.[21]

Favorable media coverage was essential to winning solid support from northern liberals, federal officials, and even southern moderates. Fortunately for the movement, the leading national media were solidly on King's side; and he returned their favor by making himself and his family available for photographs and interviews by both print and broadcast journalists. King showed the movement at its best. His deep baritone voice, good looks, and obvious sincerity and educational achievements contributed to a highly positive image in prestige newspapers like the *New York Times* and the *Washington Post*, in magazines like *Time* and *Newsweek*, and on television-radio news and special broadcasts. King appeared on the cover of *Time* on February 18, 1957; seven years later, on January 3, 1964, he became the first black to be named *Time's* "Man of the Year." King's relationship with the major media was reciprocal: he needed them to get his story across and to emphasize, through the size of headlines and the length of film clips, the importance and urgency of the movement. The media needed him because journalists tend to personify social movements in order to make them come alive for their audiences, and King ideally personified the moderate, intelligent, determined black demanding equal citizenship.[22]

One of King's bitter disappointments was the movement's failure to receive widespread and open support from southern white moderates, especially the white clergy. King made repeated appeals to fellow ministers—most memorably in his 1963 "Letter from Birmingham Jail"—but with meager results. Many southern whites were not overtly hostile toward the movement. But there were extreme segregationists, including those who violently attacked black and white civil rights workers, whose influence was not offset by moderates. King thought that the South could do better. As a southerner who loved his region and took pride in his ability to work with whites, it was especially difficult for him to accept the silence and apparent indifference of most self-styled moderates.[23]

A third and perhaps most important reason for King's effectiveness from 1955 to 1965 was his positive relationship with blacks, notably in the South but also in the North as well. Meier noted that King "functions within the movement by occupying a vital center position between its 'conservative' and 'radical' wings. . . ." This was a position that King was able to maintain during the early 1960s, but not after the rise of the black power movement from 1965 onward.[24]

Although King received warm receptions in northern black communities, especially at the crest of his influence in the early 1960s, he always felt more at home among southern blacks. They were closer to the practices and values of the black church; they were more likely to respond instinctively to his biblical language and appeal; and they were more respectful of the traditional role of the black minister as leader of the community. When one watches the footage of his speeches and sermons in the South, one is struck by the remarkable bond between King and his audience. It is impossible to recapture this mutual affection and dependence on the printed page, for the sound-tracks contain too many simultaneous chants, shouts, and responses to hear fully, much less reproduce. But one can begin to appreciate the power of King's Christian language, as in this section from a speech in Montgomery in March 1965:

> I know you are asking today, "How long will it take?" I come to say to you this afternoon, however difficult the moment, however frustrating the hour, it will not be long, because truth pressed to earth will rise again. How long? Not long, because no lie can live forever. How long? Not long, because you will reap what you sow. How long? Not long, because the arc of the moral universe is long but it bends toward justice. How long? Not long, 'cause mine eyes have seen the glory of the coming of the Lord. . . . Our God is marching on.
>
> Glory, glory hallelujah!
> Glory, glory hallelujah!
> Glory, glory hallelujah![25]

From the perspective of King as peacemaker, what was more crucial than King's oratorical bond with southern blacks was the liberating vision he helped them to achieve. King came into a world in which hate was a more powerful emotion than love in combatting oppression, and a person with a gun was more potent than a person without one. Likewise, imprisonment seemed in the eyes of southern blacks to be socially unacceptable if it resulted from one's own short-comings, and humiliating if it stemmed from white racism. But King turned these perspectives inside out. He taught that "love is something strong that organizes itself into powerful direct action," and that the method of nonviolent resistance "has a way of disarming the opponent: it exposes his moral defenses, it weakens his morale and at the same time it works on his conscience, and he just doesn't know what to do." If the white man "puts you in jail, you transform it from a dungeon of shame to a haven of freedom and human dignity." To southern blacks who had never found violence to be an effective method for lessening white oppression, King's was a message of hope and a plan of action that, by the early 1960s, was developing a track-record of success. Under King's tutelage, Christianity applied not only to personal salvation and interactions with other individuals; it also offered a formula for peaceful social change.[26]

Finally, King and his SCLC associates were effective between 1955 and 1965 because of the care that they took in planning their campaigns (except in Albany, Georgia, during 1961–62), and because King had an excellent sense of timing and knew how hard to push in particular situations, and when to back off. King could be cautious as well as militant, a "responsible and moderate" black leader to northern whites at the same time that he was pushing hard for change in particular southern cities. He was skillful in pressuring the Kennedy administration for stronger support of civil rights, while not alienating the president and his brother, Attorney General Robert Kennedy. Those who view King as primarily a prophet and activist outside the power structure tend to overlook his ability to work simultaneously within the system and outside it.[27]

The Birmingham campaign was vital to King's success. The earlier desegregation campaign in Albany had ended in failure, throwing King's leadership ability into question. He could not afford a similar failure in Birmingham, which he correctly described as "the most thoroughly segregated city in the country." Moreover, some of the younger black activists in the Student Nonviolent Coordinating Committee (SNCC) and the Congress on Racial Equality (CORE) were becoming more critical of King for several reasons. They questioned the practicality of his belief in nonviolence as a way of life. They resented the large financial contributions and the heavy media coverage he received. They believed that he was too hesitant and too willing to compromise with whites. And they noted that he had not gotten the Kennedy administration to act forcefully in support of civil rights. Birmingham thus was not only an important episode in the civil rights struggle as a whole, it was also a personal test for King, a challenge to reaffirm his leadership and moral authority within the movement.[28]

King's goals in Birmingham were much broader than they had been in Montgomery, and the difficulties he faced were greater. Instead of having a single target like public transportation, the Birmingham campaign had a wide range of objectives, including the thorough desegregation of downtown stores and other public facilities and greater economic opportunities for blacks in local businesses. More broadly, King saw the effort as a means of pressuring Kennedy and Congress to move forward on a comprehensive civil rights bill to bring about desegregation throughout the South. Among the difficulties King faced were a determined and sometimes vicious white opposition, led by Police Commissioner Eugene "Bull" Connor; a divided and violence-prone black community; and suggestions from the Kennedy administration and some northern newspapers that the campaign was ill-timed.[29]

But King went ahead. Believing that "creative tension" was needed to make progress in civil rights, King and his associates masterfully organized and carried out their campaign during the spring of 1963. They first worked to unite the local black community behind the movement and then to train blacks from diverse socioeconomic backgrounds in nonviolent techniques. At evening mass meetings, King had a particular gift for convincing young black men to turn in their weapons. Before going downtown for demonstrations, each demonstrator signed a "commitment card" in which he or she pledged "myself—my person and body—to the nonviolent movement." The pledge consisted of "ten commandments," the first four of which reflected the centrality of Christianity in the movement:

    1. MEDITATE daily on the teachings and life of Jesus.
    2. REMEMBER always that the nonviolent movement in Birmingham seeks justice and reconciliation, not victory.
    3. WALK AND TALK in the manner of love, for God is love.
    4. PRAY daily to be used by God in order that all men might be free.[30]

Three decisions—two by King, one by Connor—contributed heavily to the campaign's success. On April 11, King decided, for the first time in his career, to ignore a court injunction and continue to demonstrate, an action that resulted in his arrest two days later. Placed in solitary confinement without access to family or friends, King wrote "Letter from Birmingham Jail," an eloquent defense of the moral necessity of disobeying unjust laws. Widely reprinted and admired by both blacks and white liberals, the letter quickly became the movement's informal manifesto. In addition to focusing media attention on Birmingham and increasing northern sympathy for King's cause, his arrest got Kennedy more directly involved in the situation.[31]

Late in April, at the urging of SCLC staffers, King made the momentous decision to permit black school children to be trained in nonviolence and join the demonstrations. Mass arrests had depleted the number of adults available; and, because they did not hold jobs, young people could not be threatened with economic retaliation. The enthusiasm and courage of the high school and grade school children, some as young as six, revitalized the campaign. "What do you want?" a gruff policeman asked an eight-year-old girl walking in a demonstration with her mother. "Fee-dom," she responded forcefully. With large numbers of young people, King could now fill the jails, as Gandhi had done in India, and bring a whole new range of pressures to bear upon unyielding defenders of the status quo.[32]

The third key decision was made by Connor, whose behavior became increasingly impetuous as the campaign proceeded. On May 3, the second day in which young people were involved, Connor ordered the city's firefighters to turn their high-pressure hoses on the demonstrators; and he ordered police with German police dogs to sic them onto the children while other police clubbed unarmed demonstrators. The heavy media coverage of this naked official violence produced spasms of outrage across the country and, at long last, action in Washington. The next day, Kennedy sent the Assistant Attorney General for Civil Rights to Birmingham to seek a settlement. King, however, did not quit. He kept up the pressure until, on May 10, the city's white merchants worked out an agreement with black leaders that met the movement's demands. Economic pressure— a sharp decline in business in downtown stores for more than a month—contributed significantly to the agreement.[33]

Shortly before the settlement, there occurred a poignant moment of the kind that sustains nonviolent activists in their faith in the eventual historical triumph of their approach. Some three thousand demonstrators who were making a prayer pilgrimage to the city jail approached a police barricade. At the barricade, Chief Connor repeatedly ordered them to turn back. The marchers stopped to pray. After several seconds of growing tension, the march's leader, Reverend Charles Billups, stood up and told the police that they were not going to retreat because "We haven't done anything wrong. All we want is our freedom. . . ." Billups and the other ministers at the head of the line started forward. Connor yelled to the firefighters to "turn on the hoses." But no hoses were turned on. Instead, the police and firefighters fell back "as though hypnotized," and stepped back so that the marchers could pass through. This was "one of the most fantastic events" he had ever witnessed, King recalled. The blacks had "stared, unafraid and unmoving, at Connor's men with the hoze nozzles in their hands . . . ," and their adversaries had declined to act. "I saw there, I felt there," King said, "for the first time, the pride and the *power* of nonviolence."[34]

The events of summer 1963, beginning on June 11 with Kennedy's televised appeal for support of equality for blacks and ending with the March on Washington on August 28, constitute in retrospect the warm afterglow of Birmingham. A true hero in the black community and among white liberals, King spoke before huge audiences in Detroit and Los Angeles, led a Freedom Walk of 125,000 in Chicago, and was greeted enthusiastically in Harlem by all but a few followers of King's black nationalist rival, Malcolm X. But the highlight of the summer came at the Lincoln Memorial in Washington, where King gave one of the most powerful speeches in American history before a crowd of some 250,000 people. Fittingly, the audience was thoroughly integrated and included impressive numbers of blacks and whites; northerners and southerners; Protestants, Catholics, and Jews; professionals, industrial workers, and farm laborers. It was a truly ecumenical gathering.[35]

King's "I Have A Dream" speech was an amalgam of two central American traditions: the Declaration of Independence and political oratory on one side, and the Bible and inspired preaching on the other. At times his oratory reflected mainly the political tradition, as when he called upon America to "live out the true meaning of its creed . . . 'that all men are created equal.' " At other times the religious was paramount: "I have a dream that one day every valley shall be exalted, every hill and mountain shall be made low, and rough places will be made plains, and the crooked places will be made straight, and the glory of the Lord shall be revealed, and all flesh shall see it together." He concluded by focusing on the implications of the song "America," which perfectly combined the secular and religious themes he was emphasizing. The final paragraph summed up King's grand vision of the future:

> When we let freedom ring, when we let it ring from every village and every hamlet, from every state and every city, we will be able to speed up that day when all of God's children, black men and white men, Jews and Gentiles, Protestants and Catholics, will be able at last to join hands and sing in the words of the old Negro spiritual, "Free at last! Free at last! Thank God almighty, we are free at last!"

In applauding and shouting approval at the end of King's speech, the multitudes at the Tidal Basin were affirming their own and America's highest ideals. They also were honoring King's most eloquent expression of his inclusive vision of peace.[36]

Thanks to leadership from President Lyndon Johnson, who succeeded Kennedy in November 1963, much of the legal basis for carrying out King's dream of equality was established in the landmark Civil Rights Act of 1964. Under pressure from the successful campaign that King led in Selma, Alabama, in early 1965, Congress then passed the Voting Rights Act, which effectively gave blacks the vote in large sections of the Deep South. Combined with other Great Society programs like Head Start and Model Cities, these laws fulfilled many of the early objectives of the civil rights movement. King had helped to make possible the passage of these milestone legal advances in civil rights, principally through his struggle to persuade whites of the elementary moral rightness of such measures and blacks of their need to insist upon full citizenship.

Certainly people abroad appreciated his efforts. In fall 1964, Swedish leaders designated King the recipient of the 1964 Nobel Peace Prize for his work in peaceably combatting injustice. Gunnar Jahn, chair of the Nobel Prize Committee, called King an "undaunted champion of peace," and asked: "Is it possible that the road he and his people have charted will bring a ray of hope to other parts of the world, and hope that conflicts between races, nations, and political systems can be solved, not by fire and the sword, but in a spirit of true brotherly love?"[37]

Whereas King's career from 1955 to 1965 was marked by personal achievement and forward momentum toward equal rights for blacks, the final two-and-a-half years of his life were difficult and frustrating. Aside from his disappointment with southern whites, he had largely succeeded as an inclusive peacemaker by encouraging blacks, northern white liberals, and finally the president and Congress to work constructively for civil rights and racial equality. During his last years, however, King's liberal coalition disintegrated in the face of urban ghetto rioting and the war in Vietnam. He ended up sounding more like a prophet in the wilderness than a skillful leader of a strong movement for social change.

The events of August 1965 stand out as a watershed. On August 6, King and other civil rights leaders came to the White House for the signing of the Voting Rights Act. "Today is a triumph for freedom as huge as any victory that's ever been won on any battlefield," President Johnson announced proudly. The boast contained much truth; but those in attendance could not have known that this would be the last civil rights act until the equal-housing law passed after King's death in 1968. On August 11, only five days after the signing ceremony, a six-day-long riot broke out in the Watts section of Los Angeles. Before order was restored, thirty-four people had been killed and hundreds more had been injured, approximately four thousand had been arrested, and property damage had been put at $30 million. The Watts riot and those that followed in numerous other cities during subsequent summers weakened King's influence in both the black and white communities. So did Vietnam. On August 12 and 13, during the SCLC annual convention, King publicly and strongly opposed U.S. escalation of the war. The war was still quite popular at the time, and King took his stand against the advice of several close advisers. His statements angered Johnson and other prowar liberals, who believed that King should not criticize an administration that was doing so much for civil rights. It also angered several black civil rights leaders, who either supported the war or believed that it would be foolish politically for prominent blacks to criticize it. King's "coalition of conscience" was beginning to come apart.[38]

After visiting Watts in mid-August, King pushed forward with plans for a campaign in Chicago's ghetto in 1966 in order to call the nation's attention to poverty and other root causes of the rioting. Several SCLC staffers urged King not to proceed with the Chicago campaign, with its slim chances for success, but rather to continue to work in the South, where SCLC generally had been effective. Citing "divine guidance," King ignored his advisers and went ahead with his plans. To symbolize his commitment to improving conditions in the ghetto, in January 1966 he moved into a run-down apartment in Chicago's black ghetto; and, with the help of SCLC staffers and local black leaders, he proceeded with his campaign during most of the following eight months.[39]

The results of the Chicago campaign were mixed at best. The campaign was poorly planned, King's specific goals seemed unclear, and there proved to be less support in Chicago's black community than had been anticipated. Mayor Richard Daley and his political machine resented King's presence in the city, and many local whites were hostile. Indeed, after one demonstration King remarked that he had "never seen—even in Mississippi and Alabama—mobs as hostile and as hate-filled as I've seen in Chicago." By early August, the campaign appeared to be on the verge of total failure. But King, showing gritty determination, continued to lead demonstrations in hostile white neighborhoods. Mayor Daley, however, was more wily than Birmingham's Bull Connor. On August 26 the mayor and white civic leaders negotiated with King and other black leaders a "Summit Agreement" that promised to lessen discrimination against blacks in housing. In return, King agreed to call off a demonstration planned for suburban Cicero, thus effectively ending his campaign. King and some local black leaders believed that the somewhat vague agreement was as much as they could get the white community to concede. Other local black leaders viewed it as a sellout. From either perspective, King's only northern campaign achieved far less than he had hoped.[40]

During 1966, King largely refrained from criticizing the Vietnam War. He was preoccupied with the Chicago campaign, and distracted by growing demands of young black militants for black power. He made some guardedly critical statements regarding U.S. war policy. But it was not until early 1967, after doing careful study of the history of the conflict, that he made the war the theme of several major addresses. In February, he told an audience in Los Angeles that "the bombs in Vietnam explode at home: they destroy the hopes and possibilities for a decent America." In a sermon at his church in Atlanta, he said that he could "study war no more," and urged blacks opposed to the war to "challenge our young men with the alternative of conscientious objection." "The world now demands a maturity of

America that we may not be able to achieve," King continued. "The New Testament says, 'Repent.' It is time for America to repent now. . . ." Before a crowd of three thousand in New York's Riverside Church on April 4, he portrayed the war as a moral tragedy perpetrated by "the greatest purveyor of violence in the world today—my own government." Americans had failed to recognize the Vietnamese people as "brothers" who had suffered first under French colonialism and now under American bombs. He summarized his feelings this way:

> Somehow this madness must cease. We must stop now. I speak as a child of God and brother to the suffering poor of Vietnam. I speak for those whose land is being laid waste, whose homes are being destroyed, whose culture is being subverted. I speak for the poor of America who are paying the double price of smashed hopes at home and death and corruption in Vietnam. I speak as a citizen of the world, for the world as it stands aghast at the path we have taken. I speak as an American to the leaders of my own nation. The great initiative in this war is ours. The initiative to stop it must be ours.[41]

King's outspoken opposition to the Vietnam War grew out of longstanding concerns about U.S. foreign policy. Influenced at Crozier by Niebuhr's writings, he had rejected absolute pacifism in the international arena. Yet he felt increasingly certain during the 1950s that war was obsolete in the nuclear age, and he became less and less willing to accept America's Cold War interventionism. Concerned about the effects of Western colonialism upon Africans and other non-white peoples, King sharply criticized the Bay of Pigs invasion of Cuba in 1961 and called for greater U.S. support for revolutionary movements among impoverished peoples. "There is a revolt all over the world against colonialism, reactionary dictatorship, and systems of exploitation," King wrote at the time. "Unless we as a nation join the revolution and go back to the revolutionary spirit that characterized the birth of our nation, I am afraid that we will be relegated to a second-class power in the world with no real moral voice to speak to the conscience of humanity." King also opposed America's reliance on nuclear deterrence and brinkmanship, criticizing those who "passionately call for bigger bombs, larger nuclear stockpiles, and faster ballistic missiles."[42]

It should be kept in mind that, in 1967 as in 1965, King's strong opposition to the Vietnam War was still a minority view even among his liberal civil rights allies and supporters. Black leaders, including Roy Wilkins of the NAACP and Whitney Young of the National Urban League, attacked King's position, while normally sympathetic newspapers like the *New York Times* and the *Washington Post* blasted the SCLC leader for commenting on matters they considered irrelevant to social justice issues. King, however, believed that his opposition to the war was consistent with his concern about the oppressed and his commitment to nonviolence. He thus decided to stand on principle against a war that was draining so much of the power and potential of black America.

Like Vietnam, the rise of black nationalism presented difficult dilemmas for King. He supported many of the ideals of Stokely Carmichael and other black nationalists: pride in black history, emphasis on unity and improvement of living conditions within the black community, and constructive use of black economic and political power. But he did not like the slogan "Black Power" that had captured the imagination of many young blacks after Carmichael first used it at a Mississippi rally in 1966. King believed that the slogan had too many negative connotations, and that it would feed the growing white backlash against civil rights. He also believed that it would be impossible for blacks to continue to improve their status in American society without white support. And, even if they could make it on their own, Black Power's emphasis on separatism and its implicit endorsement of violence went against King's commitment to an inclusive Christian community.[43]

King responded in detail to Black Power ideas during winter 1967 in his last full-length book, *Where Do We Go From Here: Chaos or Community?* He was careful to acknowledge the Black Power arguments that whites had systematically oppressed blacks, and that blacks had made many gains through self-help and racial pride. But he strongly rejected black nationalism's basic premises:

> In the final analysis the weakness of Black Power is its failure to see that the black man needs the white man and the white man needs the black man. However much we may try to romanticize the slogan, there is no separate black path to power and fulfillment that does not intersect white paths, and there is no separate white path to power and fulfillment, short of social disaster, that does not share that power with black aspirations for freedom and human dignity. We are bound together in a

single garment of destiny. The language, the cultural patterns, the music, the material prosperity and even the food of America are an amalgam of black and white.[44]

King's book epitomized the changes in the black movement during the time since he had completed *Why We Can't Wait* three years earlier. In that book, King had written primarily about the black struggle for equal rights. Now he was writing much more about the systemic problem of economic inequality and the need for massive federal expenditures to "fight poverty, ignorance and slums." Equally important, in *Why We Can't Wait,* King was speaking for white liberals and for the overwhelming majority of blacks, North and South, with only the relatively small Black Muslim movement in serious opposition. Now he clearly was writing to respond to the growing nationalist movement and to rally the supporters of his nonviolent, integrationist approach. King still possessed a respected voice, but increasingly it was one voice among many.[45]

King's insistence in *Where Do We Go From Here* on large-scale federal progams to end poverty in America provided the focus for the last year of his life. Clearly his vision was now more radical, for he was advocating not only equal rights but also a coalition of the poor to demand economic justice. Earlier, as he was maintaining his coalition of blacks and white liberals (including wealthy white contributors), he had not talked about restructuring the economic system. Now he did so. As he told journalist David Halberstam in spring 1967, "I labored with the idea of reforming the existing institutions of the South, a little change here, a little change there. Now I feel quite differently. I think you've got to have a reconstruction of the entire society, a revolution of values."[46]

This vision, which David Levering Lewis recently called "the promise of nonviolent populism," informed King's planning for the Poor People's Campaign in Washington in 1968. In order to force the government to face up to the continuing problem of poverty in America, King proposed to bring poor blacks, whites, Puerto Ricans, Indians, and Chicanos to the capital. Initially, plans called for people to come from various parts of the nation and demand the passage of SCLC's $12 billion "Economic Bill of Rights," which included such things as guaranteed jobs for the able-bodied, livable incomes for the legitimately unemployed, and a firm federal commitment to open housing and integrated education. If their efforts failed, thousands more would come and create "major massive dislocations" in the city.[47]

King was determined to turn Washington into another Birmingham. He resolved to remain in the capital until federal officials agreed to end poverty once and for all. America certainly was wealthy enough to do so, King contended. What was required was the determination of the poor of all races to organize and press their claims to social justice until the power structure acceded to them. The Poor People's Campaign would be "the showdown for nonviolence," King insisted, "a 'last chance' project to arouse the American conscience toward constructive democratic change."[48]

King was unable to carry out what he had called his "last, greatest dream." He was shot down by a white racist assassin on April 4, 1968, in Memphis, Tennessee, where he had gone to lend support to the city's striking garbage workers. Yet, even if he had not been killed, the odds were against the success of the Poor People's Campaign. For one thing, the attitudes of most officials and northerners were extremely hostile. For another, it would have been very difficult to unite poor people of such diverse ethnic and regional backgrounds and to raise the funds required to sustain them in Washington until victory was achieved. But King had not gone with the odds in his other campaigns. Under incessant threat of death, he did not even have good reason to believe that he would live through them. In faith, he had strived since 1955 to help to bring about the "beloved community." In faith, he would continue to do so until he was "free at last."[49]

On Sunday, February 4, 1968, exactly two months before his death, King delivered a very personal message to the congregation at the Ebenezer Baptist Church in Atlanta, where he and his father served as co-pastors. The topic was what he would want said at his own funeral, what he believed his life added up to. Because his words bear so directly on assessing King as peacemaker, they deserve quoting at some length:

> Tell them not to mention that I have a Nobel Peace Prize. That isn't important. Tell them not to mention that I have three or four hundred other awards. That's not important. Tell them not to mention where I went to school. I'd like somebody to mention that day, that Martin

Luther King, Jr., tried to give his life serving others. I'd like for somebody to mention that day that Martin Luther King, Jr., tried to love somebody. I want you to say that day that I tried to be right on the war question. I want you to be able to say that I did try to feed the hungry. I want you to be able to say that day that I did try in my life to clothe those who were naked. . . . I want you to say that I tried to love and serve humanity. Yes, if you want to say that I was a drum major, say that I was a drum major for justice. Say that I was a drum major for peace. That I was a drum major for righteousness. And all of the other shallow things will not matter. I won't have any money to leave behind. I won't have the fine and luxurious things of life to leave behind. But I just want to leave a committed life behind. And that's all I want to say. . . .[50]

The clearest, most powerful theme in this message is King's desire to be remembered as a person who sought to live his Christian faith, to obey God's word as he understood it. Although he appears to have succeeded in this quest, King was far from perfect. He knew the ordinary pressures and temptations of life. He suffered a deep sense of guilt, and periodically knew the agony of depression. He lived through jailings, failures, hatred, and abuse, most of it delivered by his fellow Christians. Yet, as he affirmed in his sermon, he tried to remain faithful to his Christianity and to the hope for fuller human community which he believed that it nurtured.

How effective was King as a peacemaker? He surely was correct in his contention that peace within societies is not merely the absence of overt violence (what he called "negative peace"); instead, peace must involve conscious efforts to build community and bring about greater social justice ("positive peace"). He also was correct to note that means and ends are interrelated, that only nonviolent methods are likely to lead to a more just and peaceful society. Like Gandhi, King's teachings and actions are likely to be studied and discussed as long as there are nonviolent movements for social change.

King's life, and the civil rights movement generally, suggest strongly the importance of an inclusive approach in bringing about social change. At the height of the movement, King and his allies stressed the need for inclusive peacemaking that joined blacks and whites, intellectuals and the uneducated, northerners and southerners, unionized workers and the unorganized, Catholics, Jews, and Protestants. Obviously, many Americans were indifferent toward the movement, and others were openly hostile to it. Yet even these could not avoid being impressed by the power of diverse groups working together to realize King's dream of equality as human beings and as Americans. The "drum major for justice" clearly succeeded in helping the band play together and in leading it forward.

The years from 1955 to 1965 yielded genuine achievements, but King's last years were marred with frustrations. The drum major was still trying to lead, but sections of the biracial band drifted off into side streets or quarreled among themselves rather than playing their instruments. In this situation, the drum major himself began to lose direction: did the parade route follow Vietnam Street, Chicago Avenue, or Poverty Boulevard? The Chicago experience suggests that a peacemaker is not likely to be as effective outside his native milieu—in King's case, the American South—as he is working within it. His criticisms of the Vietnam War never carried the weight of his comments and actions in civil rights, where his expertise and moral authority were evident and where he repeatedly had risked his life. These final years thus point toward the conclusion that inclusive peacemaking may falter as the result of changing external circumstances, success in achieving earlier goals, shifting priorities, or uncertain leadership. King was well prepared for leadership in nonviolent resistance and often masterful in exercising it. But even he could not work miracles after the goal of equality under the law had been largely achieved and after violence escalated in Vietnam and America. The relative failures of King's final years must not be allowed to overshadow his earlier achievements or the vision of inclusive peacemaking that he maintained to the end. For the movement that King led brought needed social change to America, while faithfully adhering to his call to "love or perish." By seeking to love their white oppressors and to turn enemies into friends, and by acting on the principle that all Americans "are tied together in the single garment of destiny,"[51] black leaders established a framework in which both races could emerge as winners. As activists of the post-King era confront such issues as the intensified arms race and the continuing quest for equality for minorities and women, King's example of inclusive peacemaking based on the love ethic stands as a model of successful peaceful change. His example also endures as an imperative if people and nations are to survive and flourish in the nuclear age.

NOTES

1. The quotation is included in the film "Dr. Martin Luther King, Jr.: An Amazing Grace" (New York: WABC, 1978).

2. The best overall discussion of King's life before 1956 is Stephen B. Oates, *Let the Trumpet Sound: The Life of Martin Luther King* (New York: Harper & Row, 1982), pp. 3–51.

3. Ibid., pp. 14, 17; Lerone Bennett, Jr., *What Manner of Man: A Biography of Martin Luther King, Jr.* (Chicago: Johnson Publishing, 1964), pp. 24–26; David L. Lewis, *King: A Critical Biography* (Baltimore: Penguin, 1971), pp. 3–4, 19–20.

4. Quoted in Oates, p. 19.

5. Ibid., pp. 19–20. See also Lewis, *King*, p. 23; Bennett, p. 27; and William Robert Miller, *Martin Luther King, Jr.* (New York: Avon Books, 1969), p. 25.

6. Oates, pp. 35–36.

7. Quoted in Kenneth L. Smith and Ira G. Zepp, Jr., *Search for the Beloved Community: The Thinking of Martin Luther King, Jr.* (Valley Forge, PA: Judson Press, 1974), p. 15.

8. Smith and Zepp, pp. 99–114; Martin Luther King, Jr., *Stride Toward Freedom: The Montgomery Story* (New York: Harper & Row, 1958), p. 100; Ervin Smith, *The Ethics of Martin Luther King, Jr.* (New York: Edwin Mellen Press, 1981), p. 13.

9. Oates, pp. 32–33; King, *Stride Toward Freedom*, p. 97.

10. King, "Facing the Challenge of a New Age," *Phylon* 18 (April 1957): 25; Smith and Zepp, p. 117; King, *Stride Toward Freedom*, p. 101.

11. Oates, pp. 41, 283; King, *Strength to Love* (New York: Harper & Row, 1963), p. 9.

12. Oates, p. 49. Coretta Scott King, *My Life with Martin Luther King, Jr.* (New York: Holt, Rinehart, and Winston, 1969), pp. 94–95.

13. Oates, pp. 67–68; King, *Stride Toward Freedom*, p. 56; Lewis, p. 56. Recollections of Rosa Parks and E. D. Nixon are located in Howard Raines, *My Soul Is Rested* (New York: Putnam's, 1977), pp. 37–51.

14. King, *Stride Toward Freedom*, p. 134.

15. Ibid., pp. 133–35; Oates, p. 88.

16. Ibid., pp. 135–38; Oates, p. 90.

17. The Detroit address is reproduced in "The Great March to Freedom" (cassette tape available from the Martin Luther King, Jr. Center for Nonviolent Social Change, Atlanta, Georgia); interview with Bernard Lafayette, October 28, 1984.

18. Oates, pp. 116–18, 140–44.

19. "The Great March to Freedom" (cassette tape)

20. Oates, p. 21. August Meier, "On the Role of Martin Luther King," *New Politics* 4 (Winter 1965): 59.

21. Oates, pp. 214, 249, 270, 449, 457.

22. Ibid., pp. 115, 279, passim.

23. "Letter from Birmingham Jail" is included in King, *Why We Can't Wait* (New York: Harper & Row, 1964), pp. 76–95. A lengthy 1966 statement of his disappointment with whites is contained in the film "Dr. Martin Luther King, Jr.: An Amazing Grace," cited above.

24. Meier, p. 59.

25. Quoted in Oates, p. 364. This portion of King's speech also appears in the film "Dr. Martin Luther King, Jr.: An Amazing Grace," which clearly demonstrates King's relationship with southern black audiences.

26. Lafayette interview; the King quotations are from the videotape "The Negro and the American Promise" (New York: NET, 1963) and from "The Great March to Freedom," cited above.

27. The best study of King's relationship with the Kennedy administration is Carl M. Brauer, *John F. Kennedy and the Second Reconstruction* (New York: Columbia University Press, 1977). A recent essay on King that emphasizes his prophetic qualities is Alonzo L. Hamby, *Liberalism and Its Challengers: FDR to Reagan* (New York: Oxford University Press, 1985), pp. 139–82.

28. Quoted in Oates, p. 210. On questions about King's leadership, see Meier, pp. 52–55, and Harvard Sitkoff, *The Struggle for Black Equality, 1954–1980* (New York: Hill and Wang, 1981), pp. 127–28.

29. David L. Lewis, "Martin Luther King, Jr., and the Promise of Nonviolent Populism," in *Black Leaders of the Twentieth Century*, ed. John Hope Franklin and August Meier (Urbana: University of Illinois Press, 1982), p. 285; Oates, pp. 209–38.

30. Bennett, p. 131; King, *Why We Can't Wait*, pp. 77–100.

31. Oates, pp. 219–30.

32. Ibid., pp. 232–33.

33. Ibid., pp. 234–41.

34. Ibid., pp. 236–37; King, "Interview," *Playboy* (January 1965), p. 67.

35. Oates, pp. 253, 257.

36. Ibid., pp. 259–62.

37. The quotation is on a placard at the Martin Luther King, Jr., Center for Nonviolent Peaceful Change, Atlanta, Georgia.

38. Oates, pp. 370–80; Sitkoff, pp. 200–201.

39. Hamby, pp. 175–77; Oates, pp. 376, 387–95.

40. Oates, pp. 405–16.

41. Ibid., pp. 375, 428–36. The Atlanta speech is contained in the film "Dr. Martin Luther King, Jr.: An Amazing Grace"; the New York speech is reprinted in "Beyond Vietnam: Dr. Martin Luther King's Prophesy for the '80's" (New York: Clergy and Laity Concerned, 1982), pp. 1–10.

42. Oates, pp. 40, 173. King, *Strength to Love*, p. 29.

43. Oates, pp. 400–422; Hamby, pp. 170–71.

44. King, *Where Do We Go From Here: Chaos or Community?* (New York: Bantam, 1968), pp. 60–61.

45. Ibid., p. 7; Oates, pp. 426–27.

46. Oates, pp. 437–38, 441–42; Colman McCarthy, "King and Pacifism: The Other Dimension," *Washington Post*, October 30, 1983, p. C10.

47. Lewis, "Martin Luther King, Jr., and the Promise of Nonviolent Populism," pp. 296–302; Oates, pp. 448, 451–52, 457.

48. Oates, pp. 449–62; Lewis, "Martin Luther King, Jr., and the Promise of Nonviolent Populism," pp. 298–300.

49. Oates, p. 451.

50. Ibid., p. 458, and film "Martin Luther King, Jr.: An Amazing Grace."

51. King, quoted in Smith and Zepp, p. 121.

FURTHER READING

Those interested in learning more about King's life and thought should begin with his own writings, most of which are still available in paperback. Three of these, when read together, may be viewed as the first draft of an autobiography: *Stride Toward Freedom: The Montgomery Story* (New York, 1958); *Why We Can't Wait* (New York, 1964); and *Where Do We Go From Here: Chaos or Community?* (New York, 1967). Indispensable for understanding the religious basis of his thought is *Strength to Love* (New York, 1963); for the prophetic vision of the last year of his life, see *The Trumpet of Conscience* (New York, 1968).

The best biography of King to date is Stephen B. Oates, *Let the Trumpet Sound: The Life of Martin Luther King, Jr.* (New York, 1982). This favorable study should be read together with David L. Lewis, *King: A Critical Biography* (New York, 1970), and Lewis's excellent article "Martin Luther King, Jr., and the Promise of Nonviolent Populism," in John Hope Franklin and August Meier, eds., *Black Leaders of the Twentieth Century* (Urbana, 1982), pp. 277–303. For a somewhat critical recent assessment, see the chapter on King in Alonzo Hamby, *Liberalism and Its Challengers: FDR to Reagan* (New York, 1985). Three early biographies also remain useful: L. D. Reddick, *Crusader Without Violence: A Biography of Martin Luther King, Jr.* (New York, 1959); Lerone Bennett, Jr., *What Manner of Man: A Biography of Martin Luther King, Jr.* (Chicago, 1964), and William Robert Miller, *Martin Luther King, Jr.* (New York, 1968). David Garrow, *The FBI and Martin Luther King: From 'Solo' to Memphis* (New York, 1981) is a valuable study of King's relationship with the federal government.

Useful studies of King's thought include John Ansbro, *Martin Luther King, Jr.: The Making of a Mind* (Maryknoll, N.Y., 1982); Ervin Smith, *The Ethics of Martin Luther King, Jr.* (New York, 1981); Kenneth L. Smith and Ira G. Zepp, Jr., *Search for the Beloved Community: The Thinking of Martin Luther King, Jr.* (Valley Forge, Pa., 1974); and Hanes Walton, Jr., *The Political Philosophy of Martin Luther King, Jr.* (Westport, Conn., 1971).

ANNE KLEJMENT

The Berrigans

Revolutionary Christian Nonviolence

Shortly after dawn on September 9, 1980, eight women and men arrived by car at the gates of the General Electric Company plant in a sprawling and affluent Philadelphia suburb called King-of-Prussia. Their mission was nuclear sabotage. While two of the saboteurs distracted a security guard, the others dashed into a building where they expected to find nuclear warheads under construction. Unsure of the exact location of their targets, they happened upon a top-security room that housed nosecones for the *Mark 12A* missile. Rejoined by their two accomplices, the eight saboteurs pulled out concealed hammers and containers of their own blood and applied the hammers and blood to two warheads and some secret plans. They then stepped back and, grasping each other's hands, prayed and sang in an antinuclear ritual until security guards captured them. Charged with causing an estimated forty thousand dollars in damages, the eight were brought to trial on several counts of burglary, criminal conspiracy, and simple assault. The prosecution treated them as vandals. The defendants, however, saw themselves as the Plowshares Eight to express their fealty to the Old Testament command to beat swords into plowshares. Others thought of them as holy outlaws who tried to serve God in the face of conflicting civil and moral law.[1]

Two of the leading figures in the Plowshares Eight action were the long-time war resisters Daniel and Philip Berrigan. The two men were brothers, priests—and nonviolent revolutionaries. The story of how they progressed from members of a fairly conventional ethnic Catholic family into nonviolent revolutionaries is remarkable in itself. But it also reflects the greater drama of how wider popular involvement and more imaginative and assertive tactics have enlivened the last generation of American citizen peace activism and have moved more people than ever into saying the radical "no" against genocidal government war preparations.

The most notable characteristic of the Berrigans' youth was their deeply engrained obedience to the Catholic church and its tradition of social justice. Daniel was born in the Iron Range country town of Virginia, Minnesota, on May 9, 1921, the fifth of six sons of Thomas W. and Frida Fromhart Berrigan. Two years later, his youngest brother and closest companion, Philip, was born in Two Harbors,

The author wishes to thank Ben Morreale of SUNY College at Plattsburgh, Nancy L. Roberts and Mulford Q. Sibley, both of the University of Minnesota, who kindly offered helpful advice.

Minnesota, on the shores of Lake Superior. While the boys were still young, the family left the Midwest for Syracuse, New York, where the elder Berrigan held a succession of mostly low-wage jobs. At times he tried to supplement his meager earnings by farming with the help of his sons. The family farm, however, yielded no marked improvement in the Berrigans' standard of living. When asked what he grew on his acreage, Tom Berrigan customarily snapped: "Boys!"[2]

Both parents left lasting impressions on their children. A former railroad engineer and a staunch union man, Thomas Berrigan, or "Dado," as the boys called their father, waged a lifelong battle for labor solidarity out of a belief born from experience that only strong unions could curb the excesses of corporate power. During his early years of railroading on the Iron Range, a region known for its radicalism, he expressed admiration of socialist politics and of the Socialist party leader Eugene V. Debs, a fellow railroader and labor organizer. His youngest sons, however, mainly remembered Dado's support for Alfred E. Smith, the Catholic presidential candidate in 1928, and the populistic "Radio Priest," Father Charles E. Coughlin, whose vitriolic attacks upon President Herbert Hoover's weak response to the depression earned him great popularity. Some years later, Berrigan's politics assumed a more conventional, if not conservative mold, even though he did help unionize electrical workers and establish Syracuse's first Catholic Interracial Council. Yet Thomas Berrigan's lasting legacy to his youngest sons involved his politics less than his temperament. Even after many years, his sons remembered their father for his fierce discipline. It was his iron rule and toughness, his three youngest sons recalled, that steeled them to struggle against governmental and corporate injustices and survive the rigors of life in prison.

Frida Fromhart Berrigan was a child when her family emigrated from Germany to the pioneer Midwest in the last decade of the nineteenth century. Her brother's death in a mine-shaft accident introduced Frida firsthand to the meaning of corporate irresponsibility. But it also intensified her Catholic faith. According to family legend, Frida's devout Catholicism was so intense that Thomas Berrigan, the colorful young railroader who had little use for either institutional religion or management bosses, agreed to return to the Catholic church in order to marry her. Under Frida's gentle but insistent guidance, Tom slowly realized that religion did address contemporary labor and social problems in serious ways; and, in raising their brood, the husband and wife lived out their belief that religious duty included strict attention to social justice concerns. During hard economic times, coping to manage a large household on a marginal income, Frida provided food and occasional lodging for tramps and the unemployed. Hardly a learned political critic or a vocal social activist, she lived her faith in the ordinary ways of prayer, gentleness, and simple, personal efforts to relieve human suffering. She was a woman possessed, her son Daniel reflected, of "a practical German piety, unselfconscious, a matter of yea and nay, intellectual only in the sense of being firmly held and consequential."[3]

Daniel, physically the most frail of the Berrigan brothers, was a quiet, studious boy. He had a childhood interest in sports and became a cheerleader in spite of his older brothers' taunts; but he longed from an early age to enter the priesthood. At eighteen, he left home to enter a seminary of the Society of Jesus near Poughkeepsie, New York, on the Hudson River, and began the arduous thirteen-year regimen that prepared men for life as Jesuit priests. Leaving the ways of the world behind, Daniel immersed himself in the four-hundred-year-old routine of prayer, study, and self-denial planned by the Spanish soldier-turned-saint, Ignatius Loyola, who founded the order during the Counter-Reformation. Daniel's clerical status exempted him from military service during the Second World War, but he quietly supported the war effort and followed its progress and his brothers' activities from behind seminary walls. After a brief stint working with staff members at a local mental hospital and a few hectic years teaching at a Jesuit preparatory school in Jersey City, New Jersey, he completed his studies and was ordained a priest in 1952. His ambition—still largely unfulfilled—was to work with blacks.[4]

Philip, a sturdy youth, was more athletic and outgoing than his older brother. Hard-working like his father, Philip earned college tuition early in the forties by scrubbing down trains in the New York Central Railroad yards. After one semester of study at the College of St. Michael in Toronto, he was drafted into the army and returned to the U.S. Overseas he received a commission as an infantry second lieutenant, although he saw little action in that capacity. At the war's end, Philip returned to college at Holy Cross in Worcester, Massachusetts, where he received a degree in 1950. That summer he stunned his friends when he announced that, like his brothers Jerome and Daniel, he intended to study for the priesthood. Sickened by the racial hatred that he had witnessed during his basic training in the South and uninspired by the materialistic aspirations of his classmates, Philip chose the priesthood. He followed his brother Jerome into the Society of St. Joseph, a Catholic missionary order devoted to spiritual care of black Americans.

By the early 1950s, then, Daniel and Philip (Jerome left seminary one year before ordination in 1954) plainly had decided that they had been called to work as Christ's servants among America's dispossessed. Daniel's commitment to a social-justice priesthood intensified in the year after his ordination when he studied in France and met some of the controversial worker-priests who took factory jobs (and sometimes suggested Marxist political analyses) in their attempts to draw workers back to the Catholic church.

Back in the United States, Daniel was assigned to teach at Brooklyn Preparatory School; but he cautiously expanded his call to include a ministry to workers. He prodded students and middle-class Catholics, in such groups as the Young Christian Workers and the Walter Ferrell Guild, to work for social justice for the poor, particularly blacks and Puerto Ricans. In his preaching he pointed out to working-class worshippers that Christ, too, had been a worker and that the modern church did share the concerns of the common people. Even his own radio sermons for "The Sacred Heart Hour" emphasized the relevance of Christ and the concern of the church for ordinary working people as well as the dispossessed. In 1957, in recognition of his achievements and talents, he was named to the faculty of the Jesuits' LeMoyne College in Syracuse as a theology instructor. Still his spiritual appetite was not satisfied. While teaching at LeMoyne, a solidly middle-class institution in a self-satisfied decade, he founded International House, a religious social service group that sent students to work with the poor in the American South and Latin America.

Philip was ordained a Josephite priest in 1955, spent three years at a black church in Washington, D.C., and then five years in New Orleans teaching at a black high school. When Philip first arrived in the South, his view of the race problem mirrored the Josephites' faith in an exclusively spiritual approach to the issue. In practice, this meant that Philip and the Josephites showed less interest in civil rights activities and social reform efforts than in running the churches and religious schools that would uplift blacks through Catholicism. The evangelical Protestant civil rights movement, however, challenged the Josephites' cautious approach. Inevitably, the contradictions between hateful racism and Christian spiritual equality proved highly unsettling to Philip, who stood by and observed the violent resentment of southern white Christians and the loving nonviolent responses of the supporters of Martin Luther King, Jr. By the early sixties Philip felt estranged from the Josephites' timid course of action. He decided that the order possessed no monopoly of Christian teaching. In fact, black evangelicals appeared to live the spirit of Christian love and self-sacrifice in its purest form, while white Christians paid lip-service to the very ideals that they refused to practice.[5]

After recognizing that a purely spiritual solution to the racial issue failed the Gospel command to love one's neighbor, the two brothers started to devote more attention to political and social approaches to the question. They remained insistent, however, that these approaches stand rooted in a mature spirituality. Philip joined such groups as Urban League and the Congress of Racial Equality (CORE), which promoted racial integration and full equality for blacks. In his Catholic Sodality chapter, a group devoted to pious works, Philip also espoused integration, encouraging both blacks and whites to join. Daniel spoke out in Syracuse in favor of open housing, marched in local protests, and even considered missionary service in Africa. When whites joined black Freedom Riders in the South during 1961 in nonviolent attempts to desegregate public transportation facilities, the brothers asked their respective superiors for permission to participate. Daniel's request was denied, and he obediently remained in Syracuse. The Josephites, on the other hand, initially approved of Philip's participation; but, after a southern Catholic bishop protested the decision, Philip's superiors ordered him home. Now Philip understood more clearly how severely the Josephites compromised their commitment of service to American blacks. Furthermore, the Josephite tradition of ministering exclusively to blacks hindered the full integration of the races in the South. Although Philip could not change the policies of his order single-handedly, he did try to expand his own activities, so that he could remain faithful to his conscience and perhaps raise the consciousness of his religious community.

The Berrigans began to practice a unified spiritual and political activism during the civil rights struggles of the early sixties. Their transition from an essentially spiritual approach to a more fully politically and socially active one was undertaken with initial caution and in fear of censure from their religious orders. Curiously enough, the theological bases for their interest in fusing a deep spirituality with controversial activism stemmed from the traditionalism of their seminary training and their fascination with postwar French theology.[6] Sharing his new enthusiasms with his younger brother in a lively correspondence, Daniel outlined an incarnational theology, which emphasized the divinity and humanity of Christ. Jesus's life, death, and resurrection offered his followers special power through grace. In Daniel's eyes, Christians possessed the means of dramatically changing the world with this divine assistance. As he later discovered, mature faith required Christians to live in the world in a loving, liberating manner. Moreover, he believed that traditional church emphasis on human dignity and respect for the natural order could be greatly strengthened by practice of the new theology.

The Berrigans' theology sprang from a number of sources. They absorbed a great deal from their grammar school catechism, common to the Catholic experience of their time, and from massive exposure to the teachings of St. Thomas Aquinas, the medieval theologian and philosopher whose influence dominated seminary training through the era preceding the Second Vatican Council in the 1960s. The Jesuit's experiences with the French worker-priests, as well as his reading of such avant-garde theologians as the Dominican Henri de Lubac and the Jesuit Pierre Teilhard de Chardin, opened Daniel to a progressive, optimistic theology. Philip was not a member of this vanguard. Educated apart from the European experience and less well versed in French language and culture than his older brother, he depended instead on Daniel's enthusiasm to direct his attention to this new synthesis. But he quickly applied his brother's vision of a new priesthood to the issues he faced in the South.

Also in the early 1960s, the Berrigans expanded their concerns to include the danger of nuclear war. Their views were influenced by the writings of a well-known Trappist monk, Thomas Merton, who had recently concluded that the country was slipping into moral decline as a result of its indifference toward domestic demands for justice and its preoccupation with confronting the Soviet Union abroad. Their views were also formed in response to immediate crises. Philip felt especially alarmed by President John F. Kennedy's handling of the Cuban Missile Crisis of October 1962; and he flung himself with characteristic vigor into learning about peace possibilities. He voraciously read such magazines as the *Progressive*, searching for a better understanding of foreign policy, while he continued educating himself in the Christian nonviolence of the civil rights movement by carefully studying the writings of Martin Luther King, Jr. Furthermore, he welcomed Pope John XXIII's letter to Catholics in 1963, *Pacem in terris* (Peace on Earth), for its insistence that the arms race weakens mutual understanding and wastes resources that could build a just social order.[7] Philip justified his new concerns on the grounds that the peace issue encompassed the spiritual and physical needs of all peoples. Facing a question that involved the preservation of all human life, he threw himself with his customary exuberance into the peace cause, which gradually absorbed his civil rights interests. The shaping of the black American future seemed threatened both by the expense of the arms race and by its potential for ending all life on earth.

Daniel meanwhile proceeded along a parallel path. Moving toward nuclear pacifism, Daniel soaked up new papal teachings on war and peace in Pope John XXIII's encyclical, followed the debate of the Vatican Council on related issues, delved into the writings of the Indian nonviolent leader, Mohandas Gandhi, and interviewed Archbishop T. D. Roberts, a prominent Catholic peace leader, during a European trip in 1963–64.[8]

Late in 1962, Philip first publicly connected domestic racial strife with the nuclear arms race, when he complained that America's cold war obsessions were aggravating racial hatreds and compromising chances of living Christianity. By 1965 he condemned the arms race as "an indictment of our pious, half-believed contention that moral strength is the strongest force in the world—a contention," he added, "restricted to pharasaic preachments."[9] He questioned the value of nuclear weapons as a deterrent to another world war; and he openly condemned their planned use against urban populations as a violation of the church's teachings on human dignity and life. He also insisted that "segregation and the arms race . . . are very much connected," and "the vicious seeds of one help to promote the other."[10] In light of these realities, Philip concluded that the Josephite ideal of spiritual service to American blacks required a radical and substantial expansion into a fight against all those things that built upon antihuman values, starting with America's nuclear war preparations. Christianity had no choice, Berrigan declared. People of faith would either reassert their right to define the moral dimensions of right political action or the faith would pass into deserved decline.

Meanwhile, the Roman Catholic church advanced tentatively in opposition to the nuclear arms race. Pope Pius XII condemned "total war" in 1943; and he and his successor, John XXIII, became outspoken in their criticism of planned nuclear war. Both Berrigans invoked papal authority when speaking out on the issue. In addition, Philip and Daniel turned for support in their deepening opposition to the nuclear arms race and in support of working peace to the Catholic Worker movement and other Christian pacifists.[11]

Founded in 1933 by a sidewalk philosopher, Peter Maurin, a French Catholic immigrant, and Dorothy Day, a leftist Catholic convert, the Catholic Worker began as a radically activist but theologically orthodox alternative to capitalism and communism during the Great Depression. Committed to a "personalist" philosophy that the individual is responsible for promoting justice, the Catholic Worker advocated pacifism, which apparently resulted in loss of many of its supporters during the Spanish Civil War and the Second World War. But its first visible civil disobedience on behalf of pacifism came in the 1950s, when Ammon Hennacy, the self-proclaimed "one-man revolution," arrived for an extended stay at the Chrystie Street home of the New York Catholic Worker. By the mid-fifties, the Workers led the nation's first notable acts of opposition to government-mandated civil defense practices.[12] Thomas Berrigan's family subscribed to the cent-an-issue *Catholic Worker* paper, but the family evidently favored Day's views on labor issues rather than her uncompromising pacifism. By the early 1960s, however, Daniel and Philip "discovered" the Worker's pacifism. And, in the Catholic Worker spirit, they gradually began to act upon the radical nonviolent vision of this small, but durable group.

Generally, the first years of the Berrigans' involvement in the complex questions of war and morality in the nuclear age were marked with understandable caution and hesitancy. For one thing, they feared that an aggressive peace stand might provoke their religious orders into censuring them, an unbearable thought for two men still devoted so deeply to their religious vocations. In the second place, they knew how active citizen peace-seeking in Cold War America appeared in the eyes of many Americans as unconscionably disloyal and subversive. Daniel conceded regretfully that much of this tendency to see peace-seeking as unpatriotic and communistic was due to the immigrant Catholic ethos. American Catholics were "doubly patriotic because they were Catholic, and once had been commonly branded as somewhat less than American."[13] The large numbers of first and second generation Catholic ethnics who craved a sense of belonging and dreamt of upward mobility, coupled with the church's militant anticommunism in the Cold War years, forged a kind of American Catholic nationalism that inhibited the growth of peace sentiment within the institutional church in America until the Vietnam War era. In fact, the peace issue in the early 1960s seemed so inflammatory that Daniel, reluctant to risk disfavor with the Jesuits, published his early peace writings under a pseudonym.

Oddly, in spite of the larger anticommunist nationalism of the American Catholic church, the Berrigans did not become caught up in the 1950s politics of McCarthyism. The two men were viscerally opposed to tyranny and opposed the oppressive and militantly atheistic practices of the Soviet regime. Yet they declined for a number of reasons to lend their support to the American anticommunist crusade. The Berrigans did not agree with some conservative anticommunist partisans that social reform movements were politically suspect. But indeed, two of their older brothers did manage to link civil rights and labor concerns to a militant anticommunism. Instead, the priests' faith in religious over political or military means prevented them from adopting a rabidly anticommunist world view. Daniel's attraction to modern French theology, which sometimes attributed the decline of contemporary Christianity to a greater materialism of which communism was only one expression, moved him to reject the simple dualistic analysis of communism versus anticommunism. Thus he remained sensitive to the sinfulness and evil manifest in the western capitalist world as well. Finally, the Berrigans felt little enthusiasm for the politics of anticommunism because they believed that ardent anticommunists operated with the same kind of amoral methods that they condemned in communism. According to the Berrigans, the Christian faith did not exist to sanction the American Way in the cold war crusade. On the contrary, Christianity stood as an alternative to the excesses of American as well as communist secularism and materialism. Consequently, real anticommunism did not consist of uncritical support of U.S. governmental policies or of the conservative preachments of the defenders of the domestic and international status quo. More genuinely, said the Berrigans, it was in the spiritual tenacity of individual Christians and their reliance on God's goodness that there existed the most moral and effective means of countering communism and the greater problem of sinful materialism.

Experience leavened the brothers' attitudes and activities on the communism issue. Less of an idealist than his Jesuit brother, Philip shed his anticommunist impulses more slowly than Daniel. Nonetheless, Philip quickly found in the course of his civil rights work, as southern white racists attributed every attempt at change to foreign communist forces, that the national anticommunist obsession posed the latest form of anti-Christian nativist hatred. Daniel came to moderate his anticommunist inclinations in another way. More detached from the dominant anticommunism of Cold War American culture, he spent the years 1963–1964 in travels through Europe, where he had a chance to compare life on both sides of the iron curtain. In letters to his family, Daniel approvingly described the physical reconstruction of eastern Europe and estimated that the faith and courage of Christian dissenters there surpassed the superficial convictions of American believers. Ironically, he discovered that the militancy of atheistic communist regimes in eastern Europe nurtured a more courageous Christianity among the believers there than American Christians were demonstrating, for all their advantages of religious freedom.[14]

In 1964, encouraged by the earlier peace pronouncements of Pope John XXIII and the Second Vatican Council, the Berrigans joined other Catholic activists in forming the Catholic Peace Fellowship (CPF) as a new-style religious peace group affiliated with the fifty-year-old religious pacifist Fellowship of Reconciliation (FOR).[15] With Catholic Workers Martin Corbin, Thomas Cornell, and James Forest, the Berrigans formed the CPF in hopes of strengthening ties between peace-minded American Catholics and other Christian groups. Working with PAX, a Catholic peace group founded in 1962 to publicize peacemaking within the church, the CPF devoted itself to educating Catholics in the ethic and assumptions of nonviolence, and in providing such practical services as draft counseling and later a basis for attacking U.S. policy in Vietnam.

With the formation of the CPF, the Berrigans began to perceive the budding American Catholic peace movement as a new force in the church's effort at reintegrating prayer and social action into the mature Christian life. The two priests simply intended to help purify and renew Catholicism by calling upon individual Catholics to act upon their faith more aggressively and seriously. Militant in their Catholic spirituality, the Berrigans sought to combat the sins of materialism and secularism without slipping into a pious otherworldliness. And they insisted that other Christians live out their faith by addressing the principal social problems of this world. Indeed, they contended, prayer without good works amounted to hypocrisy, just as Christianity without active justice amounted to a sham. Therefore, wrote their friend Merton, insofar as worldliness meant selfishness, greed, and inhumanity, serious Catholics were obliged to plunge into "the world of everyday reality, of common duty, of work, of play, of sorrow and joy, the world in which man is called to work out his destiny as a son of God."[16] The Berrigans, as priests called by God to interpret Christianity for their society, felt doubly obligated to set an example of ideal Christian behavior. Their peace activism gave life to their determination after 1960 to combine prayer and social involvement.

The Berrigans began their commitment to peace activism convinced of the immorality of nuclear warfare.[17] They soon expanded their concern to other kinds of war and violence. The first years of their peace involvement brought them into familiar forms of liberal peace activism. They attended meetings, gave speeches, and joined massive protest marches similar to those organized earlier by civil rights activists. By 1965, however, the Berrigans showed an increasing interest in the practices of civil disobedience employed most recently by Martin Luther King, Jr., his followers, and the Catholic Workers. Inspired by the work of King and the determination of the Workers, the Berrigans increasingly turned to active nonviolence as the means of building a movement that would dramatize the evil of modern warfare, revitalize a moribund Christianity, and redeem American society from misguided national policies. After 1965, as the U.S. intervention in Vietnam escalated while the civil rights movement stagnated, the Berrigans began to think that the moral decay which they had long observed in American society was heading toward rapid putrification. Moved by the rising New Left and the emerging Black Power movement, the two priests concluded that traditional liberal reform methods acted within this new reality more as a palliative rather than a cure. They disavowed the radicals' talk of violent revolution. But they decided that, for themselves, the struggle for change had to pass beyond such efforts as public education, polite petitions, and meetings with public officials into the creative tension of civil disobedience.

Yet, long before the Berrigans traveled the full way toward non-violent civil disobedience, they succeeded in inspiring waves of controversy within the American Catholic church that resulted in disciplinary measures being taken against them. In 1963, Philip was transferred from New Orleans first to the Bronx and the next year to a teaching position in a Josephite seminary in Newburgh, New York, before protests by local conservatives against his views on the race issues and on the Vietnam War led to this dismissal. In spring 1965, in the middle of the school term, Philip was sent to a black parish in Baltimore, where he was expected to devote himself completely to traditional Josephite concerns. Undaunted, he sent squads of seminarians on fact-finding missions in the ghetto, organized blacks to challenge slum housing conditions and soon resumed his peace activities after a visit by Pope Paul VI to the United Nations late in 1965. Claiming to act on the implied authority of the Pope's statement for "war never again," Philip spoke out against the U.S. war in Vietnam, deliberately disobeying his Josephite superiors in their insistence that he quit antiwar activism and stand silent on the Vietnam issue.

Similarly, in these same months, Daniel's Jesuit superiors ordered him to undertake an extended trip to Latin America, in an apparent attempt to brake his increasing peace militancy, which climaxed when he preached a nonjudgmental funeral homily for a young Catholic who had burned himself to death in Buddhist fashion as a protest against the war. In response, liberal Catholics, angered by the church's failure to grant Daniel the right of conscience promised in the recently concluded Second Vatican Council, pressured the Jesuits into recalling the controversial priest from his travels after a few months.

American involvement in Vietnam meanwhile escalated dramatically, until, by 1967, nearly five hundred thousand Americans were in Vietnam and the war was costing the country about $2 billion per month.[18] A domestic antiwar opposition escalated in a parallel fashion, with several hundred thousand Americans involved in every form of public action, from letter-writing to mass marches. Increasingly, however, different antiwar critics concluded that their protests were going unheard in Washington. Philip Berrigan felt especially disturbed. In three years of antiwar activism, Philip had tried to voice and organize antiwar sentiment through lectures, letters, marches, and talks with government officials. Yet nothing seemed capable of slowing the administration's escalation of the war. With all signs pointing in precisely the opposite direction—toward America's deepening involvement in Southeast Asia—Philip turned to the prospect of serious civil disobedience. At first, he and a number of Baltimore-area clerical and lay supporters conducted some sit-ins on military property in Fort Myer, Virginia. Then he turned toward a more dramatic and risky form of protest. He turned toward resistance.[19]

At the start of 1967, after two years of military escalation and demonstrated political ineffectuality, the American antiwar movement spread itself over two major groupings: a far more numerous body of liberal dissidents and protestors, and an extremely small but highly vocal group of radical resisters. Philip felt himself drawn during the course of the year from the first to the second group for a number of reasons. In part, he decided that conventional protest tactics, ranging from letter-writing to mass demonstrations, were ineffectual and self-deceiving. Like his brother, he felt virtually no confidence in the utility of electoral action and little faith in continued attempts at conventional popular education efforts such as petitioning and vigiling. In fact, the Berrigans maintained that the American political structure was the very source of the war; it was not part of the war's solution. The movement was at hand to confront the government with its iniquity, not to pretend that it might be changed through reason and suasion.

Before 1967, resistance consisted mainly of a handful of individuals who chose publicly to burn their draft cards in symbolic but costly protest against the war. One of the first of these resisters was a Catholic Worker, David Miller, once a student of Daniel's at Le-Moyne, who deliberately violated a new federal law against draft-card burning by torching his card in a higly publicized rally in New York in October 1965. Draft resistance persisted at varying levels of intensity for the next several months until, late in 1966, a number of Students for a Democratic Society (SDS) activists at Cornell University, where Daniel later led a social service organization, proposed a mass draft-card burning at a scheduled antiwar rally in New York City if five hundred men would pledge to join in the resistance with them. On April 15, 1967, though only one hundred twenty young men signed the pledge, the mass burning took place in the Sheep Meadow in Central Park, with an estimated two hundred men involved in the civil disobedience. Later that year, as a sign that discontent against the war would not be easily silenced, hundreds burned their cards at the Pentagon in the largest mass torching of the war.[20]

In late October 1967, Philip Berrigan and three associates threw the resistance into a new phase of struggle—later termed "ultra-resistance"—when they conducted a planned raid upon an inner city draft board office in Baltimore. Quickly dubbed the Baltimore Four, the men entered the draft board office on the 27th of October, grabbed a number of records from file drawers, and poured containers of blood over the documents. While waiting for officials to come to arrest them, the Four told reporters that they had taken the action in order to challenge America's "idolatry of property" in paper records that led to "the pitiful waste of American and Vietnamese blood ten thousand miles away." Calling upon other antiwar critics to move with them from protest to resistance, the Four avowed their determination to stand with "this nation's Judeo-Christian tradition" and against the blasphemy of Vietnam and the larger threat of nuclear destruction.[21] In sum, the raid of the Baltimore Four was the first antiwar action so freighted with religious symbolism and significance, and fashioned in a sacrificial spirit in which the celebrants offered the gift of their blood in expiation for the guilt of their people and begged God's forgiveness. It marked a quantum leap in the antiwar movement, for it expanded draft resistance, permitting those ineligible for the draft to take effective action against the Selective Service mechanism and corporations profiting from war manufactures. This ultra-resistance also contributed to unmeasured confusion for the greater American public.

Privately, despite his brother's pleas for support, Daniel Berrigan at first expressed grave reservations over the tactics of the Baltimore Four. He worried that the escalation of nonviolent civil disobedience to the point of break-ins and property destruction might produce greater human violence. He also feared the consequences of his own involvement in further acts of resistance. Daniel had already been arrested and jailed during the October March on the Pentagon; and he agonized over the likelihood that more aggressive acts of resistance would only mean for him more imprisonment, expulsion from the Jesuit order, and estrangement from longtime friends who opposed the new tactics. At the same time, he was drawn toward becoming involved in planning and preparing for acts of ultra-resistance. He felt indescribable revulsion for the continuing war, and was animated by the need to do something dramatic and risky to shake the American people to their senses. He was also inspired by what he viewed as the heroism demonstrated by Cornell student draft resisters, who were gambling away their freedom and futures through open resistance, when they could have taken the quiet or easy way through various kinds of draft exemptions. Morally, he felt that he could not claim religious leadership among students unless he began to take some actions against the war that entailed risks to himself. Finally, after some lonely weeks of sober reflection and contemplation, he decided to join Philip and several others in preparing for the next action. They decided to attack a draft board in the Baltimore suburb of Catonsville.

In conceiving the Catonsville action, Philip invited about fifteen people to join in the planned destruction of draft records in a quasi-liturgical service of burglary, burning, and prayer. Nine agreed. Largely middle-class and well-educated, the conspirators were mostly Catholics with either extensive theological training or firsthand experience in trying to serve the needs of impoverished peoples in the third world. Harvard-educated David Darst was a teaching Christian Brother. John Hogan had been a Maryknoll religious brother. Tom Lewis was an artist-activist.[22] Thomas and Marjorie Melville had worked in Guatemala as Maryknoll missionaries before their marriage.[23] George Mische, married and father of a small child, was a one-time worker in the Alliance for Progress and the Association for International Development. Mary Moylan had worked as nurse-midwife in Uganda.

Late in the morning of May 17, 1968, five weeks after the assassination of Martin Luther King, Jr., and three weeks before the killing of Senator Robert Kennedy, a peace candidate for the presidency, the Nine entered the Catonsville draft board, which was, ironically, located in a building owned by the Knights of Columbus. After grappling briefly with office workers over the draft records, the raiders seized some 1-A files and escaped to an adjacent parking lot. Gathering before the cameras of news reporters who had been alerted earlier to the action, the nine conspirators piled the documents in the trash containers that they carried and poured over them a homemade napalm concoction of gasoline and soap flakes from a recipe in an Army Special Forces handbook. Ceremoniously, they tossed some matches onto the mix, stepped back as the flames shot out, and recited "The Lord's Prayer," while the reporters scribbled notes and police hurried in to arrest them.

The Catonsville Nine tried hard to communicate the complexity of their motives to a public unaccustomed to lawbreaking clergy. Declaring that they identified with "the victims of American oppression all over the world," the Nine announced that they had napalmed the draft records in order to contrast their crime with the everyday burning of innocents throughout Indochina. "It is better," Daniel explained simply, "to burn paper rather than children." In addition, they said that they had acted in order to disrupt the bureaucratic orderliness of the Selective Service System as it churned out young draftees to fight and die in needless foreign wars. In the third place, the Nine asserted that, on a moral plane, "some property" such as draft records "has no right to exist." They hoped that their action might catalyze America's "religious bureaucracy," clerics, and all believers to awaken to the crime being done in their name and emerge in sustained resistance to the U.S. war effort.[24] Lastly, the Catonsville conspirators insisted that their act of radical civil disobedience was in response to a higher law of conscience that upheld true human order, and that the government records they had destroyed were the actual representatives of lawlessness and disorder. The undeclared war in Vietnam, the deaths of untold numbers of civilians throughout Asia, and the unmet needs of impoverished Americans all pointed to an American order built upon naked violence and hypocrisy. In fact, they reasoned, the American ruling system was on the verge of moral and political bankruptcy; and the genuine law and order, founded on respect for all human life and on principles of social justice, would only arise as individuals of conscience presided over the liquidation of the existing order and its replacement with a democracy of love and selflessness.

In many ways, the Catonsville draft board raid marked a turning point in the lives of the Berrigan brothers. Gradually, young Jesuits and important members of the Jesuit community, including its superior general, Pedro Arrupe, came to Daniel's support. A few young Jesuits involved themselves in resistance. Arrupe stopped by Danbury prison to visit Daniel while conducting other Jesuit business in America. Others lent spiritual, emotional, and financial support. But Daniel was not accepted by some as a modern prophet in the Society of Jesus, one who followed the example of St. Ignatius himself and that of the Elizabethan Jesuit martyrs. Illustrating the relative unimportance of material wealth and success, Daniel emphasized the responsibility of peace-seekers to live fully a life of resistance. He refused to pay a telephone tax surcharge, which Congress originally passed to finance the Vietnam War. He took teaching jobs on a semester-by-semester basis, so that he could continue resistance and possible imprisonment without disrupting his classes, as well as insulate himself from the pressures of academic life that would tend to discourage activism. And he volunteered to work at a cancer hospital for the poor in order to underscore his belief that peacemakers must affirm human life and dignity in all ways possible.[25]

Catonsville meant something different to Philip. He grew increasingly estranged from the Josephites as a result of his radical antiwar deeds; and he began to doubt that he should remain a member of his religious order when his thinking no longer reflected their exclusive interest in serving black Americans. Philip's peace-leadership brought him into contact with many other activists; one of his acquaintances was a young religious sister who taught art history at Marymount College of Manhattan, Sister Elizabeth McAlister. In part they were brought together by their mutual peace interests, and in 1969 they secretly married, without having sought dispensation from their religious vows. Only after the Harrisburg conspiracy trial was their relationship publicly acknowledged; and they announced their formal wedding in 1973. For a time, much to their dismay, their private lives distracted the public from thinking about the political and moral questions they had raised about the Vietnam War.[26]

Although acts of ultra-resistance took place with increasing frequency, it remains difficult to measure their effects upon government policy and the public conscience during the Vietnam War years. A few people, such as Michael Cullen, an Irish immigrant who ran a Catholic Worker hospitality house in Milwaukee, were moved by the example of ultra-resistance into undertaking their own acts of resistance to the war.[27] The writings of Daniel Berrigan, especially his dramatization of the Catonsville trial, and the prison journals of Philip Berrigan all sold widely; and at least one American GI, after hearing of Daniel's peace activism, wrote to him for advice on filing for conscientious-objector status.[28] Their criminal notoriety likewise continued to make the Berrigans attractive figures on lecture tours of college campuses and church groups. For two priests, their fame was remarkably widespread. By 1971, a poll of American Catholics indicated that 38 percent were able to identify the Berrigan brothers, a figure that compared favorably with the customary number able to name the American vice president.[29] But that did not, of course, mean that those Catholics who could identify the Berrigans necessarily agreed with them and their politics.

If public reaction was ambiguous, the work of the ultra-resistance provoked sharp opposition within the larger peace movement, especially among pacifists normally allied with the Berrigans. The Catholic Worker leader Dorothy Day, already revered as the country's foremost American Catholic peacemaker, supported the Berrigans for their disobedient resistance to prevailing authority, but criticized their use of "violence" against property that they identified as immoral. As a pacifist who had long attacked right-wing Catholics for their willingness to destroy property in war and in defense of the status quo, Day refused to accept a double standard of judgment which allowed for the destruction of property in the name of peace together with protests against violence on all other grounds. Insistently, Day feared that property destruction might lead to accidental death.[30]

By contrast, the radical Catholic theologian Rosemary Ruether attacked the ultra-resistance on the grounds of its ineffectiveness. Unconvinced that high-risk operations changed either government policy or the popular conscience, Ruether condemned the raids for raising the level of domestic tensions and seeming to justify a sharper governmental crackdown on dissidents. Acting with the fanaticism of the ancient Zealots, according to Ruether, members of the ultra-resistance seemed more interested in saving their own souls than in helping to end the war.[31] Feminists raised still another issue. Catonsville defendant Mary Moylan and other women in the antiwar movement questioned the strength of male resisters' commitment to justice and equality. These women observed that machismo infected the movement and prevented women from making greater contributions to the antiwar effort. If male radicals could not treat female radicals as equals, then the aim of the antiwar resistance to free the world's oppressed citizens was both hypocritical and unattainable. Moylan announced in favor of separate women's projects.[32]

The Baltimore and Catonsville draft board actions raised the stakes in the conflict between the resistance and ruling authority to new heights of tension and costliness. And, as the Berrigans and their fellow conspirators went to trial for their crimes, a rash of similar actions spread across the country for the next several months. In Milwaukee fourteen people, mostly Catholics, broke into downtown draft board offices in September 1968 and removed ten thousand draft records for burning.[33] Others repeated similar actions throughout the country. In March 1969 the D.C. Nine destroyed files at the Dow Chemical Company, a corporation that manufactured the napalm that burned Vietnamese civilians. Anonymous persons, apparently including some Catholics, scored a brilliant success against the Federal Bureau of Investigation when they "liberated" and published papers from the Bureau's office in Media, Pennsylvania, in March 1971.

Charles Meconis, a radical Catholic writer and resister, claimed that altogether, some fifty-three "actions" took place in the five years between October 1967 and October 1972. These aimed at disrupting and discrediting the government's prosecution of the war through break-ins and property destruction, while avoiding any physical confrontation. Increasingly, too, the perpetrators sought to avoid arrest. Condemning the government as morally bankrupt, members of the ultra-resistance broke new ground in the tradition of civil disobedience when they refused to show up for prison and decided instead to go underground in America. They became political criminals in a system that they could neither tolerate nor change.[34]

Scheduled to report to federal authorities on April 9, 1970, Daniel and Philip and some other members of the Catonville Nine embarked on another form of resistance. In their minds, the war resulted not only from bad leadership but more fundamentally from a government and economy tied to profit instead of equality. They, therefore, refused to go peaceably into federal custody because they wished to disassociate themselves completely from the war crimes they believed the American government had committed in Vietnam. Philip and a companion from the Baltimore Four were picked up after twelve days underground. Daniel, however, eluded the F.B.I. for four months. On April 17, Daniel surfaced at a celebration on his behalf at Cornell University and spoke to a crowd of nearly ten thousand, including FBI agents. Escaping from the authorities in a gigantic costume from the Bread and Puppet Theater, Daniel embarrassed the government by popping up for two public lectures, granting interviews, and writing about his experiences. Finally, on Block Island, Rhode Island, federal agents, posing as birdwatchers, snared their prey while he visited with friends who risked legal jeopardy for harboring a fugitive. By choosing to go underground, the Berrigans hoped to publicize the continuation of the war and to radicalize friends. Here was a form of resistance that involved less severe legal penalties than the draft board raids, but encouraged greater personal sacrifice than that required by typically liberal dissent.[35]

Daniel Berrigan's underground activities no doubt proved to be especially embarrassing to the Federal Bureau of Investigation and its long-time director, J. Edgar Hoover. Shortly after the Berrigans were incarcerated, Hoover electrified the country with accusations against the Berrigans and other members of the ultra-resistance. Eventually, Philip Berrigan and seven others (not including Daniel) were named by the government as defendants in charges involving a conspiracy to bomb heating tunnels in Washington, D.C., and kidnap presidential adviser Henry Kissinger. The government's case at Harrisburg rested on evidence obtained from testimony by a prisoner paid by the government and letters between Philip and Elizabeth McAlister, which were smuggled in and out of prison by the prisoner-informer. Some members of the alleged conspiracy had indeed discussed the possibility of these acts but rejected them because of the likelihood of violent results. The prosecution's evidence and arguments resulted in a failure to convict on conspiracy charges. Instead, the jury found Philip and Elizabeth guilty of sending unauthorized letters, a conviction that was later appealed and reversed.[36] Hoover claimed to have broken the ultra-resistance, and acts of resistance did taper off after the trial in 1972. Yet the Berrigans and other resisters began to rebuild their movement. After the signing of the Paris Peace Accords in 1973, when American military forces quit Vietnam, the Berrigans widened their antiwar resistance to include challenging the ongoing military build-up in the United States.

In response to new imperatives, Elizabeth, Philip, and others planned a resistance community in Baltimore. Here, they could live as an extended family, sharing their peace concerns and supporting each other. Members of Jonah House shared their incomes and lived in voluntary poverty to show that they needed no part of America's prosperity, which, to them, seemed bound up in the production of military hardware. Connected to religious-based networks elsewhere, members of Jonah House undertook various acts of resistance and civil disobedience throughout the seventies. Seeking to stand in prophetic witness against the sinful state-corporate violence of their time, they gathered at different times to dig graves on the lawn of the White House (or, in their words, the "Blight House"), carve up a globe on Thanksgiving Day outside the home of Secretary of State Henry Kissinger, chain themselves to the doors of the Pentagon, and call out their opposition to the neutron bomb in the Baptist church where President Jimmy Carter sat in worship. In 1980, eight of them broke into the G.E. plant in King of Prussia. Three years later, Elizabeth and other resisters entered Griffiss Air Force Base near Rome, New York, and damaged some nuclear bomb-carrying equipment in a hangar before being detected by security police. Even the children of Jonah House have assumed roles within the war resistance movement. Frida Berrigan, age 10, and her nine-year-old brother Jerry were arrested at a peace protest outside the Reagan White House in October 1984.[37]

In practice the Berrigans' approach to peacemaking remained essentially the same since the 1968 Catonsville draft board raid. They hoped to shock the sensibilities of their fellow citizens so that the consciences and concerns of enough people might be alerted to the destructiveness that their government was doing in their name. Like the Nobel Peace Prize recipient, Mother Theresa of Calcutta, the Berrigans believed that Christians were not called to be successful in this world but to be faithful to God's eternal word. Out of this commitment, they tried through any number of means since the early sixties to break through encrusted public apathy and penetrate the country's larger sense of fatalism with a new spirit that might yet spark a popular outcry against imperial interventions abroad, the ceaseless production of weapons of mass destruction, and the disposition among ruling authorities to prepare for more and greater wars while ignoring pressing human needs. They originally sought to produce a groundswell of opposition against the war, pressuring the government to swiftly end its military engagement in Vietnam. But their first commitment was to live the moral witness which they believed coincided with lasting human values.

With a number of their comrades, the Berrigans began their adult lives as serious-minded young Christians who became nonviolent revolutionaries. They decided that they could not in conscience support a structure of state and corporate power whose preoccupation with material profit and physical security did violence to the dignity and bodies of peoples at home and abroad. They chose instead to resist. Yet the Berrigans did not consider themselves political revolutionaries or ideologues. They viewed themselves as moral witnesses in the ancient Judeo-Christian prophetic tradition. Rather than espousing any predictable political "line," Daniel variously criticized Israeli expansionism in the Middle East and Sandinista revolutionary violence in Nicaragua.[38] And, when they felt their words were insufficient, the brothers used their bodies to communicate their abhorrence of this world's obsession with acts of violence. Daniel once declared: "The only message I have to the world is: We are not allowed to kill innocent people. We are not allowed to be complicit in murder. . . . Our plight is very primitive from a Christian point of view. . . . Thou shalt not kill; we are not allowed to kill. Everything today comes down to that—everything."[39] Determined and disobedient, McAlister, the Berrigans, and their associates still animate a tiny antiwar American resistance that sees persisting social injustice and massive military coercion as the flawed bases of a false peace. And they aim yet to make a real one.

NOTES

1. The most complete story of the Plowshares Eight was compiled in *The Plowshares 8: The Crime, the Trial, the Issues* (New York: Plowshares Defense Committee, 1982?). Daniel Berrigan's "Self-Portrait" in his *Portraits: Of Those I Love* (New York: Crossroad, 1982), pp. 127–60 presents his view of the Plowshares action. See also the sections by Molly Rush and Daniel Berrigan in *Peacemakers: Christian Voices from the New Abolitionist Movement*, ed. Jim Wallis (San Francisco: Harper & Row, 1983), pp. 61–68 and 147–54.

2. Quoted by Daniel Berrigan in "My Father," *Prison Poems* (Greensboro, N.C.: Unicorn, 1973), p. 52. For additional material on family influences, see especially Daniel Berrigan, *No Bars to Manhood* (Garden City, N.Y.: Doubleday, 1970), pp. 11–27 and his *Portraits*, pp. 50–70 and 102–26. Another source for background material, which was researched from unpublished letters and talks as well as oral history interviews, is Anne Klejment, "In the Lions' Den: The Social Catholicism of Daniel and Philip Berrigan, 1955–65" (Ph.D. thesis, State University of New York at Binghamton, 1980), especially pp. 67–112.

3. Daniel Berrigan, *Portraits*, p. 107.

4. The significance of Ignatius Loyola's theology for Daniel Berrigan is explored at greater length in Klejment, "In the Lions' Den," pp. 113–59, which also assesses the influence of the worker-priest movement of France on Daniel's

understanding of priesthood. His views on contemporary Jesuit life can be found in George Riemer, ed., *The New Jesuits* (Boston: Little, Brown, 1971), pp. 38–64.

5. Changes in the Berrigans' approach to racial issues are best traced in their unpublished letters and talks from the late fifties and early sixties. For more thorough documentation of these shifts see Klejment, "In the Lions' Den," pp. 160–99 and a refinement of that work in " 'As in a Vast School without Walls': Race in the Social Thought of the Berrigans," *University of Notre Dame Working Paper Series* 10, Fall 1981. Philip's evolution from a civil rights to a peace activist can be traced in his lively book, *No More Strangers* (New York: Macmillan, 1965). Also see his other publications from the period 1961–65. These are listed in Anne Klejment, *The Berrigans: A Bibliography of Published Works by Daniel, Philip, and Elizabeth McAlister Berrigan* (New York: Garland, 1979), pp. 113–15.

6. Daniel's incarnational theology formed the heart of two of his early works, *The Bride: Essays in the Church* (New York: Macmillan, 1959) and *The Bow in the Clouds: Man's Covenant with God* (New York: Coward-McCann, 1961).

7. Philip discussed some of the works that influenced his thinking in an interview in James Finn, ed., *Protest: Pacifism & Politics* (New York: Vintage edn., 1967), p. 77.

8. Two of Daniel's pieces on Archbishop Roberts were published in the *Catholic Worker* under the pseudonyms "John Paulson" and "Jonas Winters." See "Archbishop Roberts: The Council and Peace," *CW* (October 1963): 2,7; and "Archbishop Roberts and the Peace Question," *CW* (November 1963): 2,6,7. He wrote on Gandhi for a student audience. See his series "Exploring Our Freedom" in *Today* 19, (January 1964):12–15; (April 1964):12–14; and (June 1964):18–20.

9. Philip Berrigan, *No More Strangers*, p. 106.

10. Ibid., p. 107.

11. The Catholic Worker's profound influence on American Catholic peacemaking since the 1930s cannot be overemphasized. An indispensable study of Catholic peacemaking with useful material on Dorothy Day and the Catholic Worker is Patricia McNeal, *The American Catholic Peace Movement, 1928–1972* (New York: Arno, 1978), especially pp. 58–80. Also insightful are William D. Miller, *A Harsh and Dreadful Love: Dorothy Day and the Catholic Worker Movement* (Garden City, N.Y.: Image edn., 1974), especially Chapter 10; Mel Piehl, *Breaking Bread: The Catholic Worker and the Origin of Catholic Radicalism in America* (Philadelphia: Temple University Press, 1982), pp. 189–239; and Nancy L. Roberts, *Dorothy Day and the 'Catholic Worker'* (Albany: State University of New York Press, 1984), 139–67. Sadly, the most detailed treatment of CW pacifism is unpublished, John Leo LeBrun's "The Role of the Catholic Worker Movement in American Pacifism, 1933–1972" (Ph.D. thesis, Case Western Reserve University, 1973). Anne Klejment and Alice Klejment have completed a lengthy guide to the writings of the CW movement, *Dorothy Day and the Catholic Worker: A Bibliography and Index* (New York: Garland, forthcoming 1986).

12. Dorothy Day and Ammon Hennacy wrote accounts of their civil defense resistance. See Day's "Picture of a Prophet," in *Loaves and Fishes* (New York: Harper & Row, 1963) and Hennacy's *The Book of Ammon* (n.p.: Hennacy, 1970), especially chapters 12–14.

13. Daniel Berrigan, *No Bars to Manhood*, p. 20. For a stimulating discussion of the issue of Catholics and nationalism, see Dorothy Dohen, *Nationalism*

and American Catholicism (New York: Oxford University Press, 1968) and Donald Crosby, S.J., *God, Church, and Flag: Senator Joseph R. McCarthy and the Catholic Church, 1950–1957* (Chapel Hill: University of North Carolina Press, 1978).

14. A more detailed account of the Berrigan's views on communism is available in Klejment, "In the Lions' Den," pp. 96–112, 236–77.

15. The history of the Catholic Peace Fellowship is reviewed in Thomas Cornell, "The First 10 Years of the Catholic Peace Fellowship," *Catholic Peace Fellowship Bulletin* (February 1975): 5–6, 12–14.

16. "Introduction" by Thomas Merton in *No More Strangers*, p. xix.

17. The best sources on the Berrigans' early views on nuclear weapons are Daniel Berrigan, "Total War Is a Total God," *Unity* (Montreal) (May 1965): 1–4, and Philip Berrigan, "Segregration and the Nuclear Arms Race," in *No More Strangers*, pp. 105–32.

18. Hugh Higgins, *Vietnam* (second edn.) (London: Heinemann, 1982), pp. 78–80, discusses American troop strength through 1967. Statistics for the period through 1972 have been compiled in Table 4-1 by Guenther Lewy, *America in Vietnam* (New York: Oxford University Press, 1978), p. 147. On the cost of the war, see the Committee for Economic Development, *The National Economy and the Vietnam War* (New York: CED, 1968), p. 9.

19. Philip's analysis of the roots of war and his evolution into a war resister is presented in his *A Punishment for Peace* (New York: Macmillan, 1969).

20. Michael Ferber and Staughton Lynd have studied the Vietnam antiwar resistance in *The Resistance* (Boston: Beacon Press, 1971). Much of the background material on this topic is based on their study.

21. Quoted in Philip Berrigan, *A Punishment for Peace*, pp. 146, 147.

22. Lewis contributed drawings and an introduction to Daniel Berrigan's *Trial Poems* (Boston: Beacon Press, 1970).

23. The Melvilles' story is eloquently told in their book *Whose Heaven, Whose Earth?* (New York: Alfred A. Knopf, 1971) and in two newspaper pieces they wrote, "The Catholic Resistance," *New York Times*, 26 April 1971, p. 22, and 27 April 1971, p. 41.

24. "The Statement of the Catonsville Nine" is reprinted in *A Punishment for Peace*, pp. 171–74.

25. For recent biographical material on Daniel Berrigan, see John Deedy's interesting but occasionally inaccurate *'Apologies, Good Friends . . .': An Interim Biography of Daniel Berrigan, S.J.* (Chicago: Fides/Claretian, 1981), pp. 121–39. Also valuable is Daniel's *Ten Commandments for the Long Haul* (Nashville: Abingdon, 1981), especially "Responsibilities: A Diary of Sorts," pp. 13–75.

26. Philip and Elizabeth's announcement of their marriage was published as "Text of the Berrigan-McAlister Statement," *National Catholic Reporter*, 8 June 1973, p. 21.

27. Cullen's evolution from immigrant seminarian to war resister is recounted in Michael Cullen and Don Ranly, *A Time to Dance: The Mike Cullen Story* (Celina, Ohio: Messenger, 1972).

28. See Daniel's "The G.I. Who Wouldn't Cry 'Kill,'" *National Catholic Reporter*, 23 November 1966, p. 6.

29. The poll, which was conducted by *Newsweek*, is cited in Charles A. Meconis, *With Clumsy Grace: The American Catholic Left, 1961–1975* (New York: Seabury Press, 1979), p. 170.

30. Some of Day's reservations about property destruction as civil disobedience are covered in her piece "The Berrigans and Property Rights," *Fellowship* 37 (May 1971): 25. Cf. Dwight Macdonald, "Revisiting Dorothy Day," *New York Review of Books*, 28 January 1971, p. 18. Thomas Merton, another prominent Catholic pacifist, who likewise worried about a tendency toward "violence" within the Catholic peace movement, wrote sympathetically of the Catonsville action in "Does Napalm Really Communicate?" *Ave Maria* 108 (7 September 1968): 9–10. Unfortunately, Merton's accidental death a few months later has robbed us of the possibility of a more sustained review of this new form of war resistance. One area of potential disagreement between Merton and the Berrigans was their refusal to go directly to jail in April 1970 for their Catonsville convictions. Merton had emphasized the need for nonviolent activists to accept prison as an integral part of their act of civil disobedience.

31. A series of writings on the Berrigans by Rosemary Ruether is listed in Klejment, *The Berrigans: A Bibliography*, p. 202. Perhaps Ruether's most provocative piece on the subject, and a good introduction to her views, is "Monks and Marxists: A Look at the Catholic Left," *Christianity and Crisis* 33 (30 April 1973); 75–79.

32. Moylan's reservations about machismo in the movement are explored in her piece, "Underground Woman," in Mitchell Goodman, ed., *The Movement Towards a New America* (Philadelphia: Pilgrim/Knopf, 1970), pp. 61–63. Her observations were documented by other members of the Catholic antiwar resistance. Especially valuable are interview fragments scattered throughout Charles A. Meconis, "Religion and Radicalism: The American Catholic Left as a Social Movement," (Ph.D. thesis, Columbia University, 1977). In his more recent study, *With Clumsy Grace*, he suggested that one reason for the decline of the Catholic Left in the early seventies was the existence of sexism in the movement. For a provocative analysis of this issue in the larger war resistance movement, see Barrie Thorne, "Women in the Draft Resistance Movement: A Case Study of Sex Roles and Social Movements," *Sex Roles* 1 (1975): 179–95.

33. The "Statement of the Milwaukee Fourteen" has been reprinted in Richard Zipfel, ed., *Delivered into Resistance* (New Haven: Advocate, 1969), pp. 71–74.

34. Charles Meconis's work presents the only substantial overview of the radical Catholic peace movement of the Vietnam era. *With Clumsy Grace* is less satisfactory than the more heavily documented "Religion and Radicalism."

35. The story of Daniel Berrigan's underground and resurfacings is fairly well documented. See Philip Nobile, "The Priest Who Stayed Out in the Cold," *New York Times Magazine*, 28 June 1970, pp. 8–9, 38, 40, 43–44, 50; and William Stringfellow and Anthony Towne, *Suspect Tenderness: The Ethics of the Berrigan Witness* (New York: Holt, Rinehart and Winston, 1971). Daniel's views can be explored in *The Geography of Faith: Conversations between Daniel Berrigan, When Underground, and Robert Coles* (Boston: Beacon Press, 1971) and *America Is Hard to Find* (Garden City, N.Y.: Doubleday, 1972), pp. 35–98.

36. The two standard accounts of the Harrisburg trial were published shortly after the trial ended, Jack Nelson and Ronald J. Ostrow, *The FBI and the Berrigans: The Making of a Conspiracy* (New York: Coward, McCann, Geoghegan, 1972); and William O'Rourke, *The Harrisburg 7 and the New Catholic Left* (New York: Thomas Y. Crowell, 1972). These should be supplemented by John C. Raines, ed., *Conspiracy: The Implications of the Harrisburg*

Trial for the Democratic Tradition (New York: Harper & Row, 1974); Elizabeth McAlister, "Review of 'Conspiracy: The Implications of the Harrisburg Trial,'" *Fellowship* 40 (November 1974): 20; and James Forest, "Harrisburg Conspiracy: The Berrigans and the Catholic Left," *WIN* 9 (15 March 1973): 4–31.

37. Elizabeth McAlister discusses resistance community life in "A Prison Letter: Raising Children, Resistance, Community," *Radix* 8 (May-June 1977): 3–7. For a brief chronology of Jonah House activities, see "A Chronicle of Hope, 1973–1977," in Philip Berrigan, *Of Beasts and Beastly Images: Essays under the Bomb* (Portland, Ore.: Sunburst, 1979), pp. 79–90.

38. Daniel's controversial speech on the Middle East, "Responses to Settler Regimes" was first published in *American Report*, 29 October 1973. For his views on Central America see "Berrigan to Cardenal: 'Guns Don't Work,'" *National Catholic Reporter*, 5 May 1978, pp. 12, 18; "Berrigan on Nicaragua: 'Why no public outcry?'" *National Catholic Reporter*, 14 September 1984, p. 16; and in the same issue, "'One thing we could do: go to Nicaragua. . . . El Salvador with our shame, concern,'" pp. 16–17. Philip, however, chose to point out similarities between his position on violence as a last resort and Ernesto Cardenal's. See "Violence and Nonviolence: A Dialogue Between Ernesto Cardenal and Philip Berrigan," *River Valley Voice* (Mass.) 4 (September 1984): 36.

39. Quoted in Wallis, ed., *Peacemakers*, p. 154.

FURTHER READING

A number of works, written both by the Berrigans and others provide valuable guides to their thought and action. Philip's *No More Strangers* (New York: Macmillan, 1965) details his shift from civil rights to antiwar activism. Daniel's *Night Flight to Hanoi* (New York: Macmillan, 1968) recounts his impressions of a trip to North Vietnam in early 1968, shortly before he decided to join in the Catonsville raid. Especially helpful in tracing the personal histories and motivation of antiwar resisters is Daniel's dramatic rendition of testimony in *The Trial of the Catonsville Nine* (Boston: Beacon, 1970), which Hollywood star Gregory Peck used in producing a critically acclaimed film version of the play in 1972. A solid but brief introduction to Elizabeth McAlister's conversion to peace activism can be found in her piece "A Member of a Resistance Community," in *Peacemakers: Christian Voices from the New Abolitionist Movement*, ed. Jim Wallis (San Francisco: Harper & Row, 1983), pp. 125–28.

For an introduction to the Berrigans' antinuclear concerns, see Philip's *Of Beasts and Beastly Images* (Portland, Ore.: Sunburst, 1978) and Daniel's *Ten Commandments for the Long Haul* (Nashville: Abingdon, 1981). The Plowshares Defense Committee published an anthology called *The Plowshares Eight: The Crime, the Trial, the Issues* (New York: Plowshares Defense Committee, 1982?). Filmmaker Emile de Antonio produced a stirring quasi-documentary of the court proceedings, "In the King of Prussia," which featured the Plowshares defendants playing themselves in a reenactment of the trial.

As yet no complete biography of the Berrigans has been published, but Francine du Plessix Gray, *Divine Disobedience: Profiles in Catholic Radicalism*

(New York: Alfred A. Knopf, 1970), is lively, if dated and somewhat unreliable. William Van Etten Casey, S.J. and Philip Nobile, eds., *The Berrigans* (New York: Avon Books, 1971) offers some penetrating reflections on the activities of these dissident priests. The best analyses of the Harrisburg trial have been collected in John C. Raines, ed., *Conspiracy: The Implications of the Harrisburg Trial for the Democratic Tradition* (New York: Harper & Row, 1974). Charles A. Meconis, *With Clumsy Grace: The American Catholic Left* (New York: Seabury, 1979), examines the rise and fall of the Berrigan-influenced Catholic resistance. Anne Klejment, *The Berrigans: A Bibliography of Published Writings by Daniel, Philip, and Elizabeth McAlister Berrigan* (New York: Garland, 1979), lists all known publications by the Berrigans through 1977, as well as major works about them.

An Afterword

Peace Leaders and
the American Heroic Tradition

Many factors and circumstances played a part in the emergence in twentieth-century America of a few men and women whose challenge to war and violence helped establish them in the minds of many people as a new kind of public figure—as peace heroes and heroines. In many ways, the very notion of peace heroism in the American experience seems incongruous. War established national independence and kept the Union from breaking up. Pacifism could not lay claim to a single hero associated with these great events. When Americans were reminded that Benjamin Franklin had said "there never had been, nor ever will be, any such thing as a GOOD war, or a BAD peace,"[1] the words fell on unmindful ears. Moreover, even apart from war, violence had marked much of American history. Violence was used to displace the native Indians and to seize Africans for bondage in America. It was the means of controlling labor during industrial disputes, and of challenging and maintaining order in urban slums.

Other experiences and traditions, however, left a legacy more conducive to identifying heroic qualities among advocates of peace. Dissent has played a crucial role in shaping America. In religion, the marketplace, education, race relations, law, and government, dissent was an important means of achieving social changes, including steps toward a greater measure of justice and well-being. Even more to the point, the outbreak of every war in American history has provoked sharp internal division. The typical way of expressing this dissent was through organized groups of varying size, held together by a common purpose. These groups sometimes broke up in disagreement over tactics, but many of them persevered with a doggedness that carried their concerns into peacetime and made them the very sinews of an ongoing American peace movement. In sum, the all but universal acceptance of the legitimacy of organized dissent at least opened the door to heroic achievement on the part of outstanding opponents of war and architects of peace.

Twentieth-century America also inherited feelings and ideas that lent certain definition to heroism, a notion whose meaning changed from the time that ancient Greeks first designated its nature and role.[2] In a most general way, Americans early in this century understood heroism to include a number of characteristics, some from the model of ancient Greece, some from the remnants of feudal European Christianity, and some from nineteenth-century Romanticism. From all these traditions, early twentieth-century Americans saw the hero as brave and resolute, unselfish to the point of self-sacrifice, possessing a vision for his people, and prepared to struggle for order and justice in a world weary of evil and disarray. The classical Greek Homeric hero achieved a godlike stature from his success in overcoming every imaginable danger. In a related way, the tragic hero of Greek mythology met doom because of his or her defiance of the king and community in conscientious objection to the prevailing ways of living and dying by the laws of the gods. To these attributes, the Christian hero and heroine of medieval Europe added the mystical dimension that sustained the believer in the search for greater sanctity and the redemption of self and community. At the utmost, the hero-saint heralded and hastened the millennium and Christ's own victorious return.

Then, with the feudal age, nobility of character and untainted loyalty took high rank. In combination with the Christian hero-figure, the crusading knight-errant came to epitomize the redemptive function of heroism. Finally, nineteenth-century Romantic heroes synthesized most of these attributes, and linked the heroic role to the consolidation and expansion of the nation-state through battle and through mobilization of the masses and radically expanded warfare. Perhaps the American Romantic Ralph Waldo Emerson best summed up this attitude in seeing Napoleon as a leader possessed of an "iron will" that swept multitudes before it and reshaped civilizations. An overweening ambition flawed Napoleon's character, however; and, as in the case of the tragic Greek heroes, it brought him downfall and doom.[3]

Distinctively American experiences put a unique stamp on the models of heroism that were encouraged in the schoolhouse stories, prose and poetry, and folk traditions of an evolving national history. The most critical common experience was the frontier. In the reality and lore of the frontier experience, expansion and survival in the wilderness demanded down-to-earth skills in clearing forests and building settlements. Frontier life required hardihood, ambition, a willingness to persevere, and a capacity for solitariness, all of which Americans hailed in the name of individualism. The requirements of frontier heroism did little to encourage great esteem for thinkers, writers, artists, saints, or even entrepreneurial frontiersmen. Rather, the heroic figure defined in the American frontier tradition was an idealized masculine type, rich in patience, brawn, and self-confidence.

He also possessed considerable capacity for violence. From The Deer-slayer to George Custer, the white expansion into Indian homelands gave us illustrious models whose exploits and reputations rested on the ample use of rifles and bowie knives rather than diplomacy and conciliation. Jonathan Chapman was one nineteenth-century excep-tion. Better known as Johnny Appleseed, Chapman walked unarmed among Indians and roughneck whites in the western wilderness, sowing appleseeds for the benefit of future generations. Chapman quite literally embodied themes of peace and love on the frontier. But he never enjoyed anything like the fame of such Indian fighters as Daniel Boone or Andrew Jackson. Indeed, he was either dismissed as a kindly crackpot, or mythologized as a fantastical figure like Paul Bunyan.[4]

The nineteenth-century conflict over slavery and its abolition also bred heroes and heroines in a uniquely American tradition. In the face of danger, sacrifice, and death, both black and white, male and female abolitionists struggled for their beliefs, becoming heroic examples for their minority of sympathetic followers. The great majority of their contemporaries treated them as cranks and troublemakers. Yet they fought with the weapons of the powerless—reason and moral right-ness—for a cause in which they believed. Painfully, they also believed in the reason and rightness of Christian peacemaking. Desperate for emancipation and peace, they had to work their way through one of the worst dilemmas in American history as the Civil War, the greatest military slaughterhouse in the nineteenth-century western world, wound on and toward the realization of their long-held dream of slavery's destruction.[5]

Another formative influence on the American notion of heroism derived from the middle-class glorification of material success. From Benjamin Franklin to Richard Nixon, Americans traditionally es-teemed men who succeeded in gaining wealth through diligent uphill struggle in the face of confounding challenges. Indeed, the Horatio Alger figure of late nineteenth-century popular literature, embodying the virtues of pluck, luck, and honest hard work, was a quintessen-tially American contribution to the notion of the hero. At the same time, Americans also treated lost causes- most notably, the failed Southern rebellion of the Civil War-as objects of sentimental interest yielding their own failed yet unvanquished heroes. Walt Whitman, the archetypical democratic American poet, expressed the familiar idea that a hero's success was made up of the failures and defeats that led up to it: "Vivas to those who have fail'd!. . . . and the numberless unknown heroes, equal to the greatest heroes known."[6] Ralph Waldo Emerson in his lecture "Success" echoed the same sentiment.[7]

America's advancing industrialization simultaneously sped and profited from radical changes in science, technology, and the organization of production; and these, in turn, had a notable impact on the making and conceiving of heroes. On the one hand, industrialization proved a deglamorizing force, flattening out individual personalities in its profit-minded drive toward standardization and efficiency. Thus, the mythical figure of John Henry, the steel-driving man, became displaced in reality if not legend by mechanical and electrical power; and the storied Mountain Men of the West gave way to the presence of corporate-controlled mining and lumbering operations. At the same time, by means of a combination of technological advances, public relations was born. First through the penny press and then through radio, motion pictures, and television, shrewd entrepreneurs succeeded in fashioning a new highly systematized means of communication and a new way of manufacturing public heroes. Drawn from the expanding new world of mass consumer advertising, the enterprise of public relations was in some part the brainchild of a New York publicist named Ivy Lee, whose skill in manipulating media coverage and public perceptions succeeded within twenty years in changing the image of John D. Rockefeller from an industrial pirate into a greathearted public benefactor. Equipped with increasingly sophisticated opinion polls for measuring the public pulse and developing new strategies for reaching the public psyche, this self-styled "science" of public relations promised a whole new way of inventing heroes for an industrializing America that had passed beyond the frontier experience.

Curiously, however, even with the sophisticated devices of modern public relations, industrial America succeeded in producing few great heroes. On the national stage, even the most startling innovations in science and technology failed to create long-term heroes. In fact, heroes seemed to be less needed now that science had given human hands and minds the power to shape events and, in some eyes, destiny itself. Such a notion was expressed by the poet Bertolt Brecht when he wrote: "God help the society with no heroes, and God help the society that needs them."[8] In addition, like so much else in the twentieth century, stunning technological triumphs did not result from the lonely struggle of the irrepressible individual hero of American folklore, but from the colossal investment of public resources and the cooperation of many people with varied skills. Thus, Neil Armstrong, who in 1969 was the first human to set foot on the moon, did not achieve heroic stature for his accomplishment in the way that Charles Lindbergh did when he completed the first solo nonstop transatlantic flight in 1927. And even Lindbergh was an ambivalently heroic figure to his contemporaries. After all, anyone with the slightest knowledge of internal combustion engines and navigational skills knew that "Lucky Lindy" was not simply courageous but also the beneficiary of the work of many different people and organizations. Popularly, he was the "Lone Eagle." But, in reality, most understood him to be the venturesome executor of the world's industrial inheritance.

Modern industrialism even made war, the time-honored ground for the harvest of heroes, into a highly coordinated and mechanized operation that militated against the identification of individual heroism. Thanks to his incredible self-promotional skills, Theodore Roosevelt made himself the hero of the Spanish-American war through report of a fictitious charge up San Juan Hill in Cuba. But few warrior-heroes emerged from American wars in the years 1914–75 with the kind of remarkable individuality that would make their names familiar to later generations of schoolchildren. Ironically, the warrior-heroes most familiar to Americans in the age of industrialism lay in Arlington Memorial Cemetery in the templelike Tomb of the Unknown Soldier. As unidentified dead chosen to represent the larger loss sustained in every major twentieth century American war, the tombs of the unknown dead symbolized all too powerfully the anonymity of mechanized warriors in the industrial era.

In the first years of this century, there did emerge a new view of peacetime heroism that lionized those who showed daring courage, self-sacrifice, and persistence in rescuing endangered persons, overcoming serious handicaps, and achieving technological triumphs over formidable obstacles. Convinced that war in the industrial age was madness and eager to establish, in the words of the philosopher William James, some "moral equivalent for war," the philanthropist Andrew Carnegie gave $27 million to the formation in 1904 of the Carnegie Hero Fund Commission for the purpose of issuing cash awards and recognition to men and women who showed extraordinary courage in coming to the aid of physically endangered people. In addition, at the same time as new groups like the Boy Scouts were coming into being for the purpose of instilling some stronger character into American youth, sharp new attention was given to people who persisted in overcoming serious handicaps and in working significant new technological or medical achievements. While the Swedish philanthropist Alfred Nobel gave money to recognize the work of peacemakers and scientists, Americans lavished attention and honors upon people like the indominatable Helen Keller, the Brooklyn Bridgebuilder George Washington Roebling, the Panama Canal-builder George Goethals, and the tropical disease fighter Walter Reed and his associates. A stream of new books, with titles like *Heroes of Peace* (1930), disseminated the idea of this new kind of heroism. Interestingly, however, the only person remembered during this heightened concern for peacetime heroism for his work in the actual nonviolent resolution of major conflict was William Penn, the founder of the Quaker colony of Pennsylvania. He was the only hero identified with the ongoing work of making peace among peoples.[9]

Other events and circumstances in the twentieth century contributed to developing a climate that increasingly allowed those who worked for peace and against war to be conceived of as heroes. America had to some degree inherited a notion of itself as peacekeeper. According to the traditional American sense of mission, Americans had a redemptive responsibility to save the world from tyranny, oppression, and the destructiveness of war; and, within this context, citizen peacemakers possessed a special calling and a certain claim to respectability and even emulation. The possibility of conceiving of citizen peace-seekers as heroes grew larger in the atmosphere of disillusionment that followed in the wake of the First World War and in the midst of similar skepticism about the wisdom of government war policy during the Korean and Vietnam wars.

However, the most important factor that worked to fashion an ongoing tradition of citizen-heroism through the pursuit of peace was the work of the changing but continuing American peace movement. A phenomenon made up of many parts, the twentieth-century American peace movement knew some successes and more failures in the course of its search for a world order based on peace and justice. But one of its main accomplishments, effected through the work of thousands of rank-and-file activists, was the achievement of general public recognition for existence of such a thing as citizen peace-heroism.

Many opinions exist as to what constitutes citizen peace-heroism, and what experiences lead people to live as peace leaders and perhaps as peace heroes. In reflecting on the American peace tradition, it is worth noting that many of its leading activists effected their greatest achievements as the result of a sudden psychological breakthrough. Quite unexpectedly, various peace activists have found a sudden capacity to stretch their vision and strength beyond ordinary limits by seizing what William James once called "the receptive moment." A. J. Muste, for instance, made such a breakthrough when he succeeded during the bitter Lawrence (Massachusetts) textile strike of 1919 in persuading workers to resist armed harrassment without firing their own weapons. Albert Einstein, who had contained his antiwar sentiments during the fight against the Nazis, suddenly felt compelled to seize the "receptive moment" and reinvigorate his war resistance when he learned of the atomic destruction at Hiroshima. Similarly, Norman Cousins felt such a shock of awareness upon hearing of Hiroshima that he concluded that humankind could only survive in this world as it re-conceived some notion of true global community and built an international organization able to enforce decisions taken in common toward the resolution of major conflict. Martin Luther King, Jr. felt compelled to act against systematized racial injustice, by nonviolent resistance, because of the spark set by a woman who refused to change her seat on a segregated Montgomery bus.

In considering the common features that distinguished the peace leaders profiled in this book, it is impossible, moreover, to escape the significance of their largely middle-class origins and aspirations. Jane Addams was the daughter of a doting and well-to-do central Illinois lawyer, and dutifully went off to an elite women's college in preparation for a proper female life in Victorian America. Even Gene Debs, who came from the working class, shared some of the middle-class values with which his wife was identified; while A. J. Muste spent his early years in a Dutch Reformed home, where his parents, although ordinary working folk, encouraged his studies at Hope College and his ministerial aspirations. Norman Thomas grew up in Marion, Ohio, as the latest in a long line of Protestant ministers, and graduated from Princeton and Union Theological Seminary with plans for the clerical life. Norman Cousins prepared for a career in education, once his dreams of becoming a professional baseball player vanished, by attending Columbia University's Teachers College. Martin Luther King, Jr. was born to an influential Atlanta family; and the Berrigan brothers, whose father was a railroad worker and labor organizer, grew up in a combative world of ideas that carried them through seminary training and into bourgeois respectability as Catholic priests.

Now, in America, middle-class status not only provided a sense of security and belonging. It also stood for the adherence to certain distinctive values, including rational discussion, individualism, belief in mutually beneficial cooperation and in the efficacy of moral power. In addition, traditional American middle-class values included a commitment to gradual social change in the name of progress, although this commitment was not to be pursued to the point of undue risk, let alone the deliberate defiance of law and order. It is therefore all the more remarkable that, within this context, the people profiled in this book chose to pursue their peace concerns so determinedly as to force them to break away from so many middle-class values. Some defied almost every middle-class standard of right behavior. Muste, King, and the Berrigans, for example, challenged the middle-class respect for propriety, order, and property when they organized mass demonstrations or undertook nonviolent attacks on property (as did the Berrigans in their draft board raids) on the grounds that "some property has no right to exist."[10] Most, furthermore, at one time or another chose to engage in deliberate breaking of what they deemed to be unjust laws, a practice which had been limited before the 1950s to a very small number of people inspired by the Christian anarchism of the Russian writer Leo Tolstoy or the experiences of Mohandas Gandhi. The drive toward massive civil disobedience proved even more unsettling to middle-class America when it blended early in the 1960s with a larger cultural crisis that often centered, oddly enough, on comparatively petty matters of appearance. As beards, long hair, and miniskirts became more common in street demonstrations, peace leaders tugged and hauled over questions of whether or not to establish dress codes for demonstrations in order not to alienate middle-class Americans. Sometimes Norman Cousins and Norman Thomas declined to support huge antiwar demonstrations, partly because they had little control over the politics of the mass actions and partly because they feared that the appearance of unkempt street demonstrators only drove middle-class Americans away from their cause. Martin Luther King, Jr., similarly tried to provide for the proper appearance and behavior of the marchers that he organized and led in the drive toward black civil rights. For he knew that, in the middle-class scheme of values, the deportment and appearance of the petitioners was as important as the merits of their cause.

Another characteristic common to almost every one of these peace leaders is that of being deeply motivated by a religious or humanitarian commitment in general and by the Social Gospel in particular. Addams was steeped in the nineteenth-century Protestant religious reform spirit; and Muste felt the indwelling of the Inner Light even before he decided to call himself a Quaker. Debs responded to and exemplified an ethical humanism that owed a good deal to Hebraic-Christian teachings, and Norman Thomas was, alongside Muste and Reinhold Niebuhr, one of the country's leading practitioners of the early twentieth-century Social Gospel. Like Einstein, Norman Cousins charted his own way toward a philosophy of ethical humanism. King and the Berrigans never lived far from a sense of God's directing presence.

Yet a religious or humanitarian commitment was not in itself sufficient to catapult these people into active peace leadership. After all, millions of their contemporaries professed serious religious faith without committing themselves to determined peace activism. Another common denominator among these leading peace figures, however, was their concern not only with peace activism but with other social reforms as well. Addams was best known and most loved in Progressive America for her settlement-house work with impoverished immigrants. Indeed, her opposition to American intervention in World War I, her support of conscientious objectors, and her subsequent leadership of the Women's International League for Peace and Freedom—all the things that won her a Nobel Peace Prize—effectively cost her the elevated status, even sainthood, that her reform efforts had won her prior to the Great War. Debs in a similar way identified himself principally as a socialist, who supported the class struggle toward the inevitable downfall of capitalism in the expectation that these developments would bring about the end of exploitation, imperialism, and war. Norman Cousins fostered several reforms through the widely read *Saturday Review,* while Muste was a labor educator and organizer and the Berrigan brothers immersed themselves in struggles against racial injustice and in defense of the poor.

There is no way of assessing the relative importance of genetics, upbringing, peer relationships, religious experiences, and education in making these people so unusually sensitive to social wrongdoing and so unusually intolerant of war and determined to search aggressively for other ways of settling disputes. But they were so sensitive; and they were so determined. All grew up in loving families, where they knew encouragement and stability. These were hardly people who were unbalanced, either socially or emotionally. They evidenced no overt frustration over their social status, unless King's resentment with racial humiliation is considered of some clinical significance.[11] They were not in Oedipal rebellion in ways that can be documented. What disturbed them was injustice and war. And what distinguished them was their determination to do something about these evils.

These activists also share an unusual capacity for leadership. Whatever its sources, this capacity entailed an unqualified conviction of the rightness of the cause and a willingness to make great personal sacrifices for it. Leadership meant an ability to live with tensions and through crises. It meant an ability to share a vision with the larger public, to stir people to action in quest of their vision, and to discount any failure as a temporary setback in the ongoing cause whose victory would be a triumph for humanity itself. It meant, above all, the ability to work both as a persuasive master and dedicated servant, leading and following in the realization of the new way.

The ways in which these peace leaders met suffering and sacrifice tested a crucial ingredient of their heroism. Every one of them, to a greater or lesser extent, endured harassment and hounding, governmental surveillance, anonymous hate mail, telephone threats, physical attacks upon themselves and their loved ones, charges of treason and disloyalty, separation from family, jail and imprisonment. They took risks for peace; and they paid the price exacted of peace heroes.

After years of public adulation, Jane Addams was shunned and condemned for her commitment to peace and neutrality during World War I. Unlike many of her associates, she did not have to meet the test of prison. But she did have to endure what she called "the long loneliness" of standing apart from the crowd, being showered with the contempt of her former friends and associates. Former President Theodore Roosevelt, a man whom she had supported for reelection in 1912, decided in 1917 that she was "the most dangerous woman in America;" and the great bulk of the nation's editorial writers agreed. Accepting her role as a social "outlaw," Addams learned "to take rebuffs without a sense of grievance," although she failed to find ways of stilling the pain altogether. Often, in reflecting upon her convictions, she wondered whether her defiance of the mass judgment and the consequent isolation from friends and intimates were not actually indicative of arrogance and self-righteousness on her part. Sometimes she even questioned her very sanity. In the end, she threw herself into the work of trying to feed those left hungry in a broken world; and she rose from the self-pity and self-doubt while fulfilling what she believed was a special gift of her sex—the nurture of those in need and want.[12]

Debs paid for his principles with imprisonment. Facing the jury at his 1918 federal trial on charges of sedition for his public antiwar criticisms, he declared that "I would not, if I could, escape the result of an adverse verdict. I would not retract a word I have uttered."[13] Sentenced to a ten-year term, Debs never, by his account, indulged in self-pity or doubt. He knew that, in the eyes of the capitalist courts, he was a man guilty of sedition; and, as such, he neither asked for nor received favors. He rather found support from his fellow inmates and lent them in turn strength and cheer. In reflecting on his prison experience, Debs found new reason to condemn the capitalist disorder, and detailed the mental torture, degradation, and brutality of prison life. He tried to make his experience socially constructive and to show how, even in prison, a person of conscience is free.[14]

As a German Jew who had opposed the Kaiser's war in 1914 and who stood thereafter for war resistance and then opposition to Hitlerism, Albert Einstein knew the torture of excruciating dilemmatic choice. This was particularly true after he decided to urge the United States to develop an atomic bomb as a means of beating the Nazis and maintaining some hope for a peaceful world.[15] He lived uneasily with the bomb and his conscience ever after. Like Einstein, A. J. Muste had opposed World War I as an absolute pacifist. Driven from his church for his stand, he forsook his Christianity during the 1920s in favor of Trotskyism, only to abandon the Marxist path toward revolution in 1936 and return to the Christian pacifism of the Fellowship of Reconciliation. During and after World War II, however, he moved on toward nonviolent Christian revolutionism, urging young men to burn their draft cards and suffering arrest for trespassing into U.S. military installations and draft boards during the 1950s and 1960s. With his fellow Union Theological Seminary graduate, Norman Thomas, Muste believed that "the blood of martyrs has been the fruitful seed of the progress and freedom of mankind."[15] Yet these men were not playing at the politics of martyrology. They intended, through their sacrifices, to bring about a better world. Suffering and sacrifice, Muste maintained, cut the way toward human betterment. "The capacity to suffer unto death on behalf of our fellows," he once wrote, "is the real power that makes human life possible, and creates and maintains human society."[16]

For his work on behalf of racial and class justice and against war, Martin Luther King, Jr., endured countless indignities and attacks. His house and church were bombed; he suffered frequent arrest, often on ridiculous charges; he survived extended terms in jails and prisons normally known as deathhouses for defiant Southern blacks; and he received numerous threats against his life and the lives of his family. One threat became real. In addition, King's policies and actions often provoked opposition among civil rights activists or black leaders, resulting in frequent intramural squabbles and recriminations, much to King's grief and dismay. When he began to criticize U.S. intervention in Vietnam in early 1967, many of his associates in the civil rights movement condemned his attacks on the ground that they distracted attention from the first needs of his people. He lost even more black and white support when he decided, toward the end of his life, that the American and international power structures must undergo nonviolent revolution before the interests of the poor and oppressed might be met. Outwardly calm and self-possessed, King lived with constant self-doubt and fear of failure. Yet he persisted in believing that, through his efforts and those of others, the lives of the poor and the weak might yet be redeemed. He persisted in believing in the face of incredible odds that truth and justice might yet win out, that people of good faith and deeds might yet overcome. Here he was accepting the redemptive, even millenial note in American cultural traditions.

Leading American opponents of the U.S. Vietnamese War often operated in a manner most contrary to established middle-class norms of propriety. Yet few either worked with the audacity or experienced the degree of official opposition as did the brother-priests, Daniel and

Philip Berrigan. Undaunted by the disapproval of their ecclesiastical superiors (including, for Daniel, an episode in *de facto* exile to Latin America), the two men and their associates conducted intentionally symbolic protests of ritual purification in which they smeared draft board records with blood and incinerated another set of records with homemade napalm while praying, singing, and waiting for arrest. Predictably, the Berrigans' attacks upon government property antagonized large numbers of middle-class Catholics and other domestic defenders of the prevailing structure of law and order. Confronted by disapproval, the Berrigans only carried their acts of resistance further. In 1971 the two men refused to stand before another court on charges of breaking the law; and, in defiance of customary practices of pacifist civil disobedience, they went underground. Finally captured after extended FBI searches, the two brothers were sent to different federal prisons. While in the maximum security federal penitentiary in Lewisburg, Pennsylvania, Philip Berrigan was charged along with six others for plotting to infiltrate a steam tunnel system in Washington, D.C., in order to capture and hold for political ransom national security advisor Henry Kissinger. Based on the testimony of one of Philip Berrigan's fellow prison inmates, the case against Philip and his associates was dismissed by a Harrisburg, Pennsylvania, federal jury. But the bizarre story of the Harrisburg 7 intensified suspicions among many that the work of the Berrigans was egotistical and masochistic, not to say counterproductive. The Berrigans, however, saw things differently. In their eyes, nonviolent revolutionary action was necessary in order to disrupt and bring finally under control an American ruling system corrupted by the consistent abuse of power. The Nixon regime represented in their minds a government unworthy of respect, let alone obedience.

Historically, heroes are those whose vision, courage, leadership, and sacrifices lead them to great actions, deemed significant in themselves, and resulting in concrete, memorable, almost miraculous solutions to public woes. In many ways, the peace leaders examined in this book effected such significant actions. They did not, however, bring about in their lifetime any transforming solutions to long-standing problems. But then who in this century has? Self-sacrificing, courageous, and possessed of the driving vision that people might yet know living peace, these leaders certainly did not win heroic stature among the great body of their contemporaries, most of whom dismissed them as troublemakers and subversives. Yet, in the long span required for serious historical judgment, it is possible that sustained reflection upon their methods and objectives might move those who come after us to consider these figures as pioneers of heroic significance. Indeed, even at this moment, these peace leaders can be viewed with other crusaders in the recorded story of causes yet-to-be-won (like the eighteenth-century American abolitionist John Woolman), as representative of the untiring men and women who bore forward a wondrous vision whose time of realization for many reasons had not quite come.

For now at least we know this: our national reputation, in fact our recent national history would be significantly reduced and diminished were it not for the character, hopes, and efforts of these great human beings. As this century nears its end we can speculate that their compelling voices may still set off other "receptive moments" of dissent and inspire still greater citizen-heroism in the current struggle to prevent nuclear war and global extinction. Until then, we should realize that these figures were not simply American heroes, but heroes to humankind as well.

NOTES

1. This often quoted sentence appeared in a letter from Franklin to Josiah Quincy, Sept. 11, 1783, *The Writings of Benjamin Franklin*, ed. Albert Henry Smyth, 10 vols. (New York: The Macmillan Co., 1906), 9, p. 96.

2. The following discussion is especially indebted to Sidney Hook, *The Hero in History. A Study in Limitations and Possibilities* (New York: The Humanities Press, 1943); Eric Bentley, *A Century of Hero Worship: A Study of the Idea of Heroism in Carlyle and Nietzsche, with notes on Wagner, Spengler, Stephen George, and D. H. Lawrence* (Boston: Beacon Press, 1944, 1957); and the articles on Heroism in The *Dictionary of the History of Ideas*, ed. Philip Wiener (New York: Charles Scribner's Sons, 1968, 1973, 5 vols.)

3. *The Complete Works of Ralph Waldo Emerson*, Centenary ed., 12 vols. (Boston and New York: Houghton Mifflin Co., 1903), 4, p. 253.

4. I am indebted in this discussion of American heroism to Marshall Fishwick, *The Hero, American Style* (New York: David McKay, Inc., 1969), Mark Gurzon, *A Choice of Heroes: The Changing Faces of American Manhood* (Boston and New York: Houghton Mifflin, 1982); Orrin E. Klapp, *Heroes, and Villains, and Fools: The Changing American Character* (Englewood Cliffs: Prentice-Hall, 1962); and, especially, Dixon Wecter, *The Hero in America: A Chronicle of Hero Worship* (New York: Scribner's Sons, 1941, 1972).

5. Philip T. Drotning, *Black Heroes in Our Nation's History* (New York: Cowles Book Co., Inc. 1969), p. 209 ff.

6. Walt Whitman, *Leaves of Grass* (Philadelphia: David McKay, Publisher, 1900). See also "To a Foil'd European Revolutionaire," pp. 326–27.

7. Ralph Waldo Emerson, "Success," in *Society and Solitude* (Boston and New York: Houghton Mifflin and Co., 1904), pp. 283–312.

8. Stephen Halpert and Tom Murray, eds., *Witness the Berrigans* (Garden City, N.Y.: Doubleday, 1972), pp. 187–88.

9. Archer Wallace, *Heroes of Peace* (New York: Richard R. Smith, 1930) is one of over thirty similar collections in the Swarthmore College Peace Library.

10. "A Statement from Maryland," Catholic Peace Fellowship *Bulletin* (June 1968):2

11. Perhaps, as Allen F. Davis has argued in *American Heroine: The Life and Legend of Jane Addams* (New York: Oxford University Press, 1973), Jane Addams in some sense found compensations in her dedication to social reform.

12. Jane Addams, *Peace and Bread in Time of War* (New York: The Macmillan Co., 1922), pp. 74, 130 ff.

13. *Writings and Speeches of Eugene V. Debs,* with an Introduction by Arthur M. Schlesinger, Jr., (New York: Hermitage Press, 1948), pp. 433–34.

14. Debs, *Walls and Bars* (Chicago: Socialist Party, 1927)

15. Norman Thomas, "Is Violence the Way?", *The World Tomorrow* 2 (May 1919):119.

16. *The Essays of A. J. Muste,* ed. Nat Hentoff (Indianapolis: The Bobbs Merrill Co., Inc., 1963), p. 294.

INDEX

Editor: Lee Weiskopf
Book designer: Matt Williamson
Jacket designer: Matt Williamson
Production coordinator: Tarry Curry
Typeface: Garamond and Helvetica Light
Typesetter: Coghill Book Typesetting
Printer: Murray Printing Co.
Binder: Murray Printing Co.

CHARLES DEBENEDETTI is Professor
of History at the University of Toledo and
author of *The Origins of the Modern
American Movement, 1915–1929,* and
The Peace Reform in American History.